GUNS ON THE CHESAPEAKE

The Winning of
AMERICA'S INDEPENDENCE

Gene Williamson

HERITAGE BOOKS
2007

HERITAGE BOOKS
AN IMPRINT OF HERITAGE BOOKS, INC.

Books, CDs, and more—Worldwide

For our listing of thousands of titles see our website
at
www.HeritageBooks.com

Published 2007 by
HERITAGE BOOKS, INC.
Publishing Division
65 East Main Street
Westminster, Maryland 21157-5026

Front cover based on design by Avenue C Productions

Copyright © 1998 Gene Williamson

Other Books by The Author:
Of the Sea and Skies: Historic Hampton, Virginia and Its Times
Chesapeake Conflict: The Troublesome Early Days of Maryland

All rights reserved. No part of this book may be reproduced or transmitted in any form or by any means, electronic or mechanical, including photocopying, recording or by any information storage and retrieval system without written permission from the author, except for the inclusion of brief quotations in a review.

Library of Congress Catalog Card Number: 97-072928

International Standard Book Number: 978-0-7884-0962-X

- Dedication -

For Kara and Eliza

- Contents -

Acknowledgments vii

Introduction. Chesapeake Bay: Avenue of War ix

Map xxix

1. Preliminaries 1763-1769 1

2. Riots, Resolutions, Revolts 1770-1774 23

3. Inevitable War 1775 47

4. Military Buildup 1775 65

5. A City Aflame 1775 105

6. Independence 1776 123

7. Blockade 1777-1779 157

8. Seat of War 1780-1781 183

9. Battle of the Capes 1781 223

10. Surrender 1781 241

11. Peace 1782-1783 267

Bibliography 277

Index 285

- Acknowledgments -

I wish to thank the individuals and institutions which have given me encouragement and valuable assistance in the preparation of this book, especially my family and my Heritage Books editor Roxanne Carlson.

- Introduction -

Chesapeake Bay: Avenue of War

The small Virginia port town lay exposed to the hostile warships patrolling the lower Chesapeake. The townspeople had sunk several small vessels in the channel of their shallow river to block an attack from the bay. On the morning of October 24, 1775, cannons signaled the approach of a heavily armed British schooner, a sloop, and three tenders carrying marines. Under orders from Lord Dunmore, Virginia's royal governor, the British commander threatened to burn the town. That threat was prologue to the first naval engagement of the Revolutionary War.

Unlike the episode above, so many tales about America's Revolution are told with a New England accent that it often comes across as a regional event. Perhaps the reason was cited by Thomas A. Bailey: "New Englanders wrote most of the early chronicles."

A larger look shows that the Revolutionary War was fought up and down the eastern seaboard of the newly declared United States, from Georgia's Savannah River to Kennebec Bridge in Maine, and as far west as the Mississippi Valley. Thirteen states contributed to the making of the new nation, and none more than the two situated on Chesapeake Bay.

Chesapeake warriors fought on the seas off the West Indies and as far away as the British Isles. They experienced early victory at Saratoga, served with George Washington's Continentals in defense of Boston, in the fight for Long Island and the battles at White Plains, Brandywine, Germantown,

GUNS ON THE CHESAPEAKE

Trenton, Princeton, and Monmouth, the bayonet charge at the Cowpens and the siege at Savannah, the struggles at Hobkirk Hill and Eutaw Springs, the fall of Charleston and the battle that forced the British surrender at Yorktown. Bay families were honored by the spirit and valor of the Maryland Line, a famous regiment of Continental troops easily recognized by their blue jackets faced with red, and by the number of proud Virginia regiments, some in plain uniforms of green or black, others rigged out in blue coats cuffed and faced with yellow.

The historic Chesapeake region embraces the geography of two states: the Virginia peninsulas located between the James and York rivers, between the York and Rappahannock, and the Northern Neck between the Rappahannock and Potomac Rivers; the Eastern Shore of Virginia and Maryland; lower Maryland; and the Maryland counties along the upper Chesapeake bordering on Delaware and Pennsylvania. The great rivers that flowed into the bay from points west, well beyond the rapids of the upstream fall line, dominated the culture of the region during the revolutionary period.

Chesapeake Bay, with a shoreline of some thirty-six hundred miles, is a submerged valley of the Susquehanna River. It has been called the American Mediterranean. Seagoing vessels can sail its length, running north for two hundred miles from the two Virginia capes (Charles and Henry) to the mouth of the Susquehanna which spills into the bay from Pennsylvania. Algonquin Indians named it Great Salt Water (K'che-sepiack), but only the lower bay is salty; the waters are brackish further up, and fresh at the head of the bay.

Forty-eight principal creeks and rivers empty into the bay, some of which are navigable up to one hundred miles. The major tributaries are the James, York, Rappahannock, Potomac, and the Susquehanna. Key Virginia ports are Norfolk and Portsmouth, both of which were destroyed during the Revolutionary War. Maryland's chief port of Baltimore is

CHESAPEAKE BAY: AVENUE OF WAR

situated at the head of the Patapsco River, but because of shallow waters most of its commerce during the war was transacted at Fells Point, the narrow strip of land extending into the Patapsco south of the city. At the time of the war, there was a navigable inlet between the narrow beaches which now enclose the Chincoteague lagoon, permitting the transport of supplies into the region when the bay entrance was blockaded by the British Navy.

Virginia was the most populous American colony at the time of the Revolution. Its population in 1770 was 447,000, of which forty percent were slaves. Next in population size was Pennsylvania with 327,300; slaves accounting for two percent. The Maryland population in 1770 was 202,600, of which thirty-one percent were slaves.

Most of Maryland's population prior to the Revolution was concentrated in that area along the Potomac at about the midway point of the bay. The expanse of water from there to the Susquehanna and Elk Rivers in upper Chesapeake separated the two Maryland shores, geographically, culturally, and politically.

In Virginia, that slender land mass separating the James and York Rivers is known simply as The Peninsula. The proximity of Hampton, Newport News, Jamestown, and Yorktown to the Chesapeake and its entrance to the Atlantic made this peninsula the center of colonial Virginia's political and social life, and also the first port-of-call (Old Point Comfort) for vessels en route to Maryland as well as Virginia. Located on this peninsula was the colonial capital of Williamsburg and later the state capital of Richmond. At its southern tip, America's oldest stone fortress guarded the lower bay and the natural harbor of Hampton Roads, large enough to hold the navies of the world. The peninsula's strategic position made it a hub of military activity in every war in which the United States has been involved.

GUNS ON THE CHESAPEAKE

The first white man to settle in Maryland was a Virginian, William Claiborne, who discovered and named Kent Island where he established a Chesapeake trading post in 1631. Claiborne lost his claim when Maryland was created a proprietary colony in the 1632 charter granted to Sir George Calvert, first Lord Baltimore. Sir George died before the charter could be honored and the grant was transferred to his son Cecil Calvert, second Lord Baltimore. The Maryland charter recognized Calvert and his heirs as rulers of the vast province carved out of territory which had been included in Virginia's original charter. As proprietor, each of the Lords Baltimore owned all the land (and half the bay), enjoyed all the revenues from it, and controlled the appointment and dismissal of all Maryland officials. Initially, Maryland was to be a sanctuary for England's oppressed Catholics, but in 1649 the General Assembly passed the Toleration Act which officially tolerated the religious views of all but the Unitarians, Jews and other non-Christians.

England's permanent colonization of America was motivated as much by the need to make money as by the challenge from Spain and other nations for global expansion. After failed attempts by Sir Walter Raleigh in the 1580s, a group of 120 English settlers arrived in lower Chesapeake Bay in 1607 and established the first permanent colony at Jamestown. They were employees of a joint stock enterprise called the Virginia Company; their objective was to locate precious metals and develop trade with the Indians.

Most original settlers soon died of starvation or disease. Those who followed were sons of aristocracy and dregs of London's poor, farmers and tradesmen, convicts and craftsmen, clergymen and malcontents, servants and slaves, soldiers to man the forts and surveyors to map the country. They were a cross-section of European society transported across treacherous seas aboard tiny vessels in which they

CHESAPEAKE BAY: AVENUE OF WAR

shared cramped quarters with swine, cattle, horses, and baggage. The majority were unprepared by training or temperament to deal with the wilderness. As legendary Captain John Smith declared at the outset: "In Virginia, a plaine Souldier that can use a pick-axe and spade is better than five Knights." Those who survived did so by robbing the Indians of their crops and land. Soon, dreams of gold and silver disappeared along with the ancient Algonquin tribes which had populated southeastern Virginia.

But English America would remain true to its mercantile roots: During the Revolutionary War, when Washington's troops went unpaid for months, American businessmen were making so much money that the Continental Congress threatened to pass an excess profits tax. Some patriots, however, depleted their resources with large loans to the Continental Army that were never repaid by Congress.

Prior to the Revolution, the colonies were far from unified. Cultural and religious differences, jealousies and suspicions separated the population clusters that made up colonial America. New England Puritans admonished the plantation aristocracies of Virginia and Maryland, and these two neighbors were often at war over Chesapeake Bay fishing rights. New York and Vermont quarreled over claims to the New Hampshire area. Connecticut disputed lands possessed by Pennsylvania. Frontiersmen wanted nothing to do with the "civilized" easterners and their squabbles with Parliament. The thinking in some colonies was too *laissez faire,* in others it was too reckless. Feelings of distrust and animosity which prevailed among the colonials in 1765 inspired the observation from abroad that "America would be a mere shambles of blood and confusion" if allowed to rule itself.

Leadership in the colonies was concentrated in the educated, wealthy landowners, merchants, and professionals who dominated America's political and social affairs. These men of privilege were largely a traditional, pragmatic elite, slow to anger and loyal to their monarch, and were usually prepared to accommodate demands of the British government to advance their own interests. This was particularly so of the Scottish merchants who were fierce in their opposition to American independence. It was not so with the rabble-rousers who nurtured the seeds of rebellion. Among these radicals—skilled in politics and propaganda—were Patrick Henry of Virginia and Sam Adams of Massachusetts. Others included Charles Thompson of Pennsylvania, Christopher Gadsden of South Carolina, John Hancock of Massachusetts, Rezin Hammond of Maryland. Radicals rallied the cry for revolution, more moderate men (George Washington and Thomas Jefferson, Virginia; John Adams, Massachusetts; Charles Carroll and Samuel Chase, Maryland; John Jay, New York; Benjamin Franklin and Robert Morris, Pennsylvania) supplied the energy and resolve that kept the Revolution going to a successful conclusion.

Except for the poor who were virtually invisible in a social order dominated by property and position, a belief in liberty was inherent in the makeup of most eighteenth-century Americans. They had been accustomed to some form of self-government from almost the beginning of colonization. In 1638, for example, when freemen in newly established Maryland were told to ratify the laws which the proprietor Lord Baltimore had framed for his province, thirty-seven freemen advised their fellow Marylanders to reject the proposal. Under the leadership of Thomas Cornwallis, they created a set of their own laws granting the same rights and privileges as enjoyed by all native Englishmen under the British Constitution. Actually, constitutional reform in America can be dated back to 1614 when Sir Edwin Sandys, liberal leader of the Virginia Company, gave a speech in Parliament which maintained that Parliament cannot give liberty to the king to make laws; [that] the origin of every monarch lay in election; [that] the people gave its consent to the king's authority upon the express understanding that there were certain reciprocal conditions which neither king nor people might violate with immunity; and that a king who pretended to rule by any other title, such as that of conquest, might be dethroned, whenever there was force sufficient to overthrow him.

It is little wonder that James I (champion of the divine right of kings) said "Choose the Devil if you will but not Sir Edwin Sandys" when his faction in the Virginia Company called for an election in June 1620 to select a new leader. The king's candidate lost to the third Earl of Southampton, Henry Wriothesley, who was close friend and political ally of Sandys. Under the progressive leadership of Sandys and Southampton, a charter provision was made in 1618 to establish representative government in Virginia. Andrew Brown, in *English Politics in Early Virginia History* (1901), called it "the first example of a domestic parliament to regulate the internal concerns of this country, which was afterwards cherished throughout America as the dearest birthright of freemen." The Sandys alliance risked imprisonment in the Tower of London to create in America a free form of government they could not establish at home. The love of freedom, sustained in generations of Americans, would manifest itself in political independence.

Sandys' principle of popular government was inspired by his teacher, Richard Hooker, whose concepts of the natural law of equality, pursuit of happiness, and government by consent would one day influence the men who sparked America's separation from Great Britain. Hooker endorsed an *aristodemocratic* form of government in which power is vested in the nobility and the common people. In Jefferson, an elitist who sometimes remembered he was a populist, it became "the aristocracy of virtue and talent, which nature has wisely provided for the direction of the interests of society."

Love of freedom was transported to America. In 1917 Charles Mills Gayley wrote:

> The liberty we enjoy today is what it is, primarily because Southampton, Sandys and the Ferrars, Selden, Brooke, Coke, Sackville, Cavendish and other patriots were Englishmen; because Gates, De La Warr, and Strachey, Dale, and Wyatt, the Bradfords, Brewsters, and Dudleys, willing to venture, were Englishmen; because in the decades when England was awakening to the perils of arbitrary rule at home, these contemporaries of Hooker and Shakespeare established in the New World an advance guard of English rights. From Shakespeare's England in an age when such civil and political rights were, with the possible exception of the United Netherlands, elsewhere unrealized, proceeded our common law, our trial by jury, our system of representative government, our free institutions. It is to Shakespeare's England that the Americans of the colonies owed—that Americans today, of whatever stock they be, owe—the historic privileges that have made the New World a refuge for the oppressed and a hope for humanity. The sapling of civil liberty had drawn vigor from deep roots of Anglo-Saxon, Anglo-Norman consciousness, and for centuries had strained steadily upward. In the seventeenth century it towered as an oak, and sheltered with its far-spread arms the Britons at Home and Britons in America.
>
> The thoughts that were common to Hooker and Shakespeare and Shakespeare's friends, the

dream of the well-ordered state where merit shall govern, and not the favoritism of kings or their fabled divinity—the ideals of individual worth, duty, and patriotism, were common to our English forefathers, the planters of Virginia, the pilgrims of the Mayflower and Plymouth, the puritans of Massachusetts Bay.... The political freedom that, between 1609 and 1640, our English ancestors of Virginia and New England put into form and practice is the political freedom for which our grand-uncles of old England fought from 1642 to 1649, nay, to 1689. Brewster, Harvard and Thomas Hooker, of New England, Alexander Whitaker, Clayborne, Bennett, and Nathaniel Bacon, of Virginia, belong to the history of English ideals no less than to that of America.

Gayley's views were echoed in a lecture by English scholar Sir Adolphu Ward before the British Academy in 1919. Ward asserted that the "incorporation of the English conception of law into colonial thought and practice constitutes one of the most fundamental of all influences of England upon America."

Sandys was right to call America "an advance guard of English rights." Despite the strictures imposed on American society by the power elite, there was a degree of social mobility in the colonies that was not present in England, with its rigid adherence to class distinctions. Benjamin Franklin, for example, used his talents to rise from the son of a soapmaker to Founding Father. Patrick Henry started as a clerk in a country store.

Colonial hostilities against British rule did not begin with the American Revolution. Bacon's Rebellion in 1676, attempting to shape a new social order in Virginia, had ridiculed the colony's power elite as "sponges [which] have suckt up the Publique Treasure."

Virginia Governor William Berkeley, royalist to the bone, had no sympathy for representative government. Thomas J. Wertenbaker summed up the governor's views: "The King alone should rule; the people's duty was to obey." Nathaniel Bacon charged Berkeley with overthrow of the legislature, harsh trade restrictions, political corruption, a spoils system that favored the privileged, and excessive taxes on the poor. Conditions were right for insurrection; and the failed rebellion has been called a harbinger of the American Revolution. Yet it solved nothing; the ruling class survived. Or as Bernard Bailyn wrote, "there was an acceptance of the fact that certain families were distinguished from others in riches, dignity, and in access to political authority." It was the establishment of these elite families that marked the rise of aristocracy in the bay colonies. And even they were subservient to the will of Parliament.

In 1696, when individual colonies passed laws asserting Magna Charta principles of national liberty to support the rights vested in their legislatures, Parliament restated its authority over the colonies, declaring "that all laws, bye laws, usages, and customs, which shall be in practice in any of the plantations, repugnant to any law made or to be made in this kingdom relative to the said plantations, shall be void and of no effect."

Long before the Revolution, the Chesapeake Bay region had discarded its reputation as "an unhealthy place, a nest of Rogues, whores, dissolute and rooking persons; a place of intolerable labour, bad usage and hard Diet." The two bay colonies now rivaled England in the ostentation of the plantation culture which had sprung up on the banks of their major rivers. Virginia's gentry had accumulated wealth and rank through land acquisition, tobacco, and slavery. Many of its members had evolved from their wilderness background as fashionable men of enlightened political vision—a group described by one historian as "a remarkable cadre of articulate and energetic leaders." They enjoyed, compared to most of the world's societies, an enviable degree of economic, political, and personal liberty. Yet a visitor noted that Virginians, "jealous of their liberties," looked upon "the colonies as independent states not connected with Great Britain, otherwise than by having the same common king, and being bound to her with natural affection."

Maryland's capital city and cultural center was Annapolis, of which a London official observed in 1769: "There are few towns of the same size in any part of the British dominion that can boast a more polished society." Oxford, first port of entry on Maryland's Eastern Shore, was an international shipping center prior to the Revolution, surrounded by wealthy tobacco plantations. The Maryland economy, compared to Virginia's, was not as dependent on tobacco. Described by James Chalmers as "the most fertile and delectable wheat country in America," Maryland was increasingly sustained by grain and revenues generated from cargo vessels sailing in and out of its busy port at Baltimore.

What would become a fight for nationhood began as resistance to taxes and regulations Parliament imposed on America to replenish Britain's treasury following a costly war with the French. Before the French and Indian War, Britain's colonists were virtually free to do as they pleased. After the war, they complained of exploitation when the British government, driven by mercantile interests to fortify the nation's economy, expected them to share in the cost of their protection. Colonial actions seemed to reflect no sense of obligation to the British government for driving the French from American soil.

GUNS ON THE CHESAPEAKE

Though the governing elite of the bay colonies was loyal to the crown, its members were among the first colonials to oppose Parliament's interference in what they considered their "internal" concerns. They were offended not so much by new taxes but by the *idea* of the taxes. Parliament's taxes were modest when compared to the taxes Americans levied on themselves through elected representatives. What the Chesapeake elite resented was the arrogance of a distant body that forced Americans to accede to laws of which they had nothing to say and which they felt imperiled their liberties. In time this sense of indignation was shared by men of power and influence throughout America, as colonial speakers clamored for more control over colonial affairs. A decade before the Declaration of Independence, progressive Americans were demanding *home rule*, with or without the blessings of the British government.

Yet, even among the gentry who protested the loudest when the new taxes and trade regulations were proposed, there were those who criticized talk of separation from the mother country. They were conservatives who supported the cause of peace because it was true to their traditional values and also good for business. They wanted "as little change as possible," wrote James Truslow Adams. But the less fortunate Americans "clamored for any change that would better their condition." Frontiersmen simply wanted to be left alone.

Such radicals as Sam Adams and Patrick Henry were feared and distrusted at first, but ultimately their impassioned actions and words began to unify the factions—once it was apparent to rich as well as poor that their special interests could best be served by independence. The disenfranchised heard hope in the declarations of Sam Adams that "the natural liberty of man is to be free from any superior power on earth." But the gentlemen planters and many of the businessmen continued to

CHESAPEAKE BAY: AVENUE OF WAR

worry that accelerated demands by discontented mobs for new rights and more representation would disrupt the government and retard economic development. They were not, with rare exception, friends of the common man. As Staughton Lynd observed: "The ambiguity of the Revolution's philosophy lay in affirming personal liberty while at the same time linking it to private property and economic self-interest."

By the middle 1770s, of course, it was a series of British blunders which joined radicals and conservatives in defiance of policies that threatened personal liberty regardless of class restrictions on America's economy through laws which not only regulated prices and denied profitable trade outside the British empire but also limited opportunities for colonial manufacturing endeavors and prohibited speculation in western lands. Though there was some talk of revolution, it was not as yet a popular cause on either side of the ocean. Many in England, Wales, and Scotland felt uncomfortable in waging war on their kinsmen, and most merchants and traders feared losing a market that accounted for one-fifth of all British exports.

In America, independence was supported by only thirty percent of the people, but that minority had the political clout to stifle the large but disorganized loyalist opposition.

The British war strategy was to isolate New England, then capture American naval bases in Rhode Island and New York so as to control the eastern seaboard with their superior fleet. The plan was to be executed by Major General William Howe, who would hold the line at the Hudson River and Lake Champlain, in belief that the British could separate New England (the center of the rebellion) from the other colonies. After securing a base in New York, Howe was to push north to Massachusetts. But the British government weakened his hand, diverting part of his New York force to Canada to repel an expected American invasion there. The divided command saved New England and proved to be one in a series of mistakes that would hamper British movements in America.

When the strategy failed to yield significant success in the early stages, the British decided to camp in New York and carry on a war of endurance. They would outwait America's money supply and will to fight. Perhaps one day Richard Oswald, military adviser to the British ministry, would regret the following advice:

> One thing however is past doubt...it will require very little Generalship to conduct the Military part in opposition to American troops; any Lieutenant Colonel of common Sense in the Army I suppose is equal to the task.

That the colonials were an impulsive people with no strength of character had been decided during the French and Indian War by British hero General James Wolfe who wrote:

> Americans are in general the dirtiest, the most contemptible, cowardly dogs you can conceive. There is no depending on 'em in action. They fall down dead in their own dirt and desert by battalions, officers and all.

Phase two of the British strategy was to maintain the strong position in New York to seal off New England and, at the same time, invade the Carolinas with the expectation that southern loyalists would rise in large numbers to join the British forces. Once the Carolinas and Georgia were conquered, the British would be able to apply pressure on the middle colonies from both north and south.

But the plan did not take into account poor communications, split command, and disagreements. Britain's strategy would disintegrate into poorly managed and frustrated field operations for the rest of the war.

Great Britain's first mistake was in designating New England the center of American resistance. Future events would demonstrate that ultimate victory would require control of Chesapeake Bay, a reality that British General Cornwallis would fail to grasp in the summer of 1781.

Distance contributed to Great Britain's failure. The king's judgment that the colonials could not withstand the overwhelming supremacy of the Royal Army and Navy ignored one factor favoring the colonies: an ocean that took two months to cross. Such distance would make it too costly and difficult to put down an insurrection, especially when Britain was already at war with France and Spain and expecting hostilities with the Dutch.

Disarray was another cause of Britain's failure. Royal Army officers, the product of social position or political influence, were frequently at odds over tactics, and often were too cautious to act or too ambitious to follow the orders of their superiors.

At its peak the British Army numbered fifty thousand men, and a large segment of that fighting force was mercenaries, including thousands of German soldiers purchased from the principality of Hesse (hence, *Hessians*, a term applied to all mercenaries). These hired warriors lacked the dependability and the loyalty of British regulars, and many deserted. In addition, the British were allied with American loyalists (Tories), runaway or captured slaves, and Indian tribes, notably Six Nations and Cherokee—an alliance which inflamed the anti-British passions of American patriots.

Despite experience and numbers, the British were never strong enough to overwhelm the Americans; there was neither the manpower nor the arms to occupy every colony. Even by

GUNS ON THE CHESAPEAKE

January 1781, British troops in America had gained no more territory than they held five years earlier.

The management of America's military actions during the Revolution supports the argument that wars are not necessarily decided by the number of battles won or lost. Most encounters between American and British forces resulted in standoffs or American setbacks. In major engagements, there were two decisive American victories: Saratoga in 1777 and Yorktown in 1781. The first influenced France to enter the war as an American ally and the second, with French support, in effect ended the war and won American independence.

Washington fought mainly a defensive war. His tactic of dodging and retreating only to surprise the enemy with a counterpunch earned him the "Old Fox" nickname and perplexed many a commentator. Forest McDonald was almost right when he wrote: "Washington's army never lost a major engagement, but it never won one either." Samuel A. Johnson thought it "amazing that Washington could lose so many battles and still win the war." But as Marvin Kitman explained, his policy seemed to be to lose all of the battles except the last one. The French were perhaps generous in their praise of Washington as "the liberator of America." On the other hand, Tom Paine probably underrated Washington's influence on the war: "Mr. Washington had the nominal rank of Commander in Chief, but he was not so in fact." It was rank alone, wrote Paine, that made Washington "appear as the soul and center of all military operations in America."

Though discipline in the Continental Army was a continuing problem (understandably) among men who were poorly fed, poorly trained, poorly supplied, and frequently unpaid, the factors in favor of the American soldier were his familiarity with firearms and the fighting terrain, and generally his desire to win, fearing the consequences of defeat. Influenced by years

CHESAPEAKE BAY: AVENUE OF WAR

of Indian warfare, Americans were less predictable than the British, more flexible, more elusive, and more adaptable to the wilderness.

American fighting forces consisted of minutemen, ready to act at a minute's notice, state militia companies, and volunteers in the Continental Army. Virginia and Maryland supplied about eighty thousand troops (including multiple enlistments), more than half of whom were Continentals. Washington's peak strength in the field at any one time was about seventeen thousand regulars and militia; and it was often much less than that. Whatever strength he had came at the expense of state militia.

Maryland and Virginia militia companies, even a year after the war had begun, were undermanned at all levels—including too few officers. Most of the best fighting men had been recruited into the Continental Army. There was some improvement in enlistments when suffrage was expanded to everyone regardless of rank; Jefferson and others had argued that any man willing to fight deserved the right to vote without the usual education or property qualification. Then when wartime needs created a shortage of gentlemen officers, the two states were forced to elevate men who in the past would have been denied the opportunity by economic and social background. For the first time, Maryland and Virginia men outside the gentry class would move up the social ladder to rank and privilege.

The genius of Washington was not revealed in the battles he fought or won but in the ability to hold together his underpaid, undisciplined troops and the early realization that his army's best chance was to avoid battles it could not win. This meant taking the fight to the British only when the odds appeared to be even; it was a tactic which Washington and the young French volunteer, the Marquis de Lafayette, would develop to an artistic level of frustration for British generals. The strategy worked. It let the Americans pursue the war until they got help. Britain's likelihood of victory would vanish the day the French fleet entered the Virginia Capes.

The philosophy or purpose of the Revolutionary War, as articulated by Jefferson and Adams and other Founders who largely represented the colonial hierarchy, was little known or understood by many, if not most, of the colonials who fought the battles. Instinctively, these men were fighting either out of love of freedom that was the legacy of their forebears or to acquire the liberties they assumed would come with America's independence. What was never explained to them was that the Revolution was more a struggle for personal power than it was for universal freedom. The Constitution was written by the privileged few for the benefit of the privileged few. As to the idea that a revolution is based on principles, McDonald wrote:

> The first function of the founders of nations, after the founding itself, is to devise a set of true falsehoods about origins—a mythology—that will make it desirable for nationals to continue to live under common authority, and, indeed, make it impossible for them to entertain contrary thoughts.

The real struggle for America would begin after nationhood was secured. It would require generations of Americans gradually coming together to forge out of the mythology of revolution the principles revered today (but not yet universally practiced). Washington saw the Constitution as an imperfect document made more perfect by the right of future Americans to amend it, adding: "I do not think we are more inspired, have more wisdom, or possess more virtue, than those who will come after us."

CHESAPEAKE BAY: AVENUE OF WAR

The focus of this book is the Chesapeake region and its role in the American Revolution. No other part of America endured more hardship or suffering. The region was crisscrossed with rivers and streams and their uncountable tributaries. Most Marylanders and Virginians lived near these waterways, depending on them for their livelihoods and their chief mode of transportation. Richard Oswald underscored the commercial value of the Chesapeake area when he declared that the means of carrying on trade was "no where, in all America, so abundant as round the whole Coasts of that Bay, there not being perhaps a more plentiful district of Country upon Earth."

By the time the colonies announced their independence in 1776, Chesapeake Bay, "a colonial avenue of trade, had become an avenue of war," wrote Jean B. Lee.

That avenue led to a new nation.

GUNS ON THE CHESAPEAKE

The Chesapeake Bay Region

(Keys to the Map)

1. Chesapeake Bay
2. Cape Charles
3. Cape Henry
4. Norfolk
5. Portsmouth
6. Elizabeth River
7. Hampton Roads
8. Hampton
9. Old Point Comfort
10. James River
11. Newport News
12. Jamestown
13. Petersburg
14. Yorktown
15. York River
16. Williamsburg
17. Charles City
18. Richmond
19. Pamunkey River
20. Mattaponi River
21. Rappahannock River
22. Fredericksburg
23. Potomac River
24. St. Mary's
25. Port Tobacco
26. Mt. Vernon
27. Alexandria
28. Patuxent River
29. Annapolis
30. Petapsco River
31. Baltimore
32. Susquehanna River
33. Head of Elk
34. Brandywine
35. Philadelphia
36. Oxford
37. Choptank River
38. Pocomoke River
39. Eastern Shore
40. Onancock
41. Delaware Bay
42. Atlantic Ocean

CHESAPEAKE BAY: AVENUE OF WAR

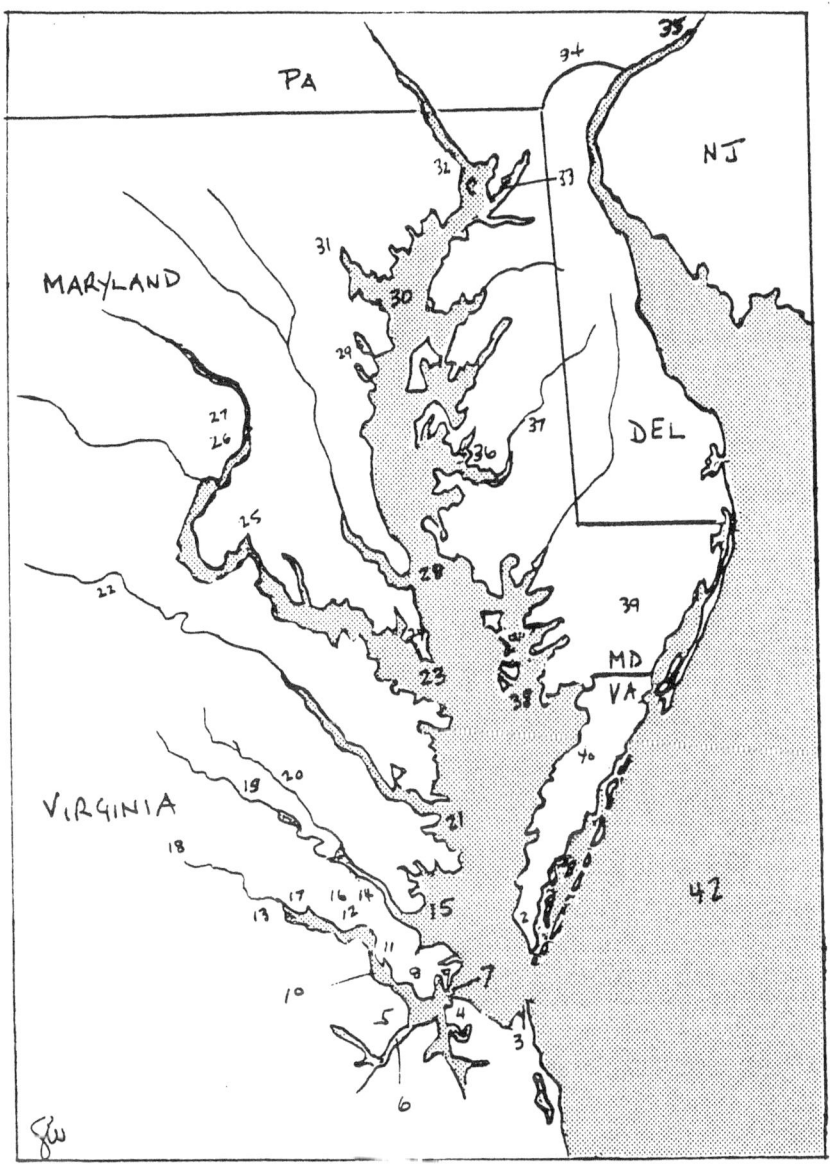

- 1 -

Preliminaries

1763-1769

It was thirteen years before Thomas Jefferson's document declared that government derived its power from the consent of the governed, and that whenever government abused that power, it was "the Right of the People...to institute new Government." It was the year the British won Canada from France and Florida from Spain but wound up with a staggering debt which had to be paid by taxing America. It was the year that Great Britain ended the French and Indian War and began the American Revolution. It was 1763.

One year later Parliament passed the Sugar Tax. It was the first time a tax had been imposed *directly* on Americans specifically to raise money for the British crown.

As far back as 1676, Virginia had disputed Parliament's right to impose a direct tax on goods manufactured and traded within the colonies. Charles II, in response, declared that such taxes should not be levied "but by the common consent of the general assembly."

The 1764 tax on sugar and other commodities applied to both imports and exports and was justified by Parliament as necessary "for improving the revenue of this Kingdom, and for extending and securing the navigation and commerce between Great Britain and your Majesty's dominions in America, which, by the peace, have been so happily enlarged: and whereas it is just and necessary, that a revenue be raised, in your Majesty's said dominions in America, for defraying the expences of defending, protection, and securing the same." This implied that the tax would offset the cost of posting British troops in America to protect the colonies against invasion. But the colonists were suspicious of the troops. Virginia's Patrick Henry said: "They are meant for us; they can be meant for no other. They are sent over to bind and rivet upon us those chains, which the British ministry have been so long forging."

In the upper bay region, Marylanders were not particularly concerned about the Sugar Tax. They believed that such an oppressive act would not be sustained because their proprietary charter protected them against taxes not enacted by their own legislature. Charles I had stipulated that neither he nor his successors would "impose, or make, or cause to be imposed, any impositions, customs, or other taxations, quotas, or contributions whatsoever, in or upon the residents or inhabitants of the province." Of course, succeeding monarchs made it a practice to ignore colonial charters.

Taxation was only half the problem. The other half was Great Britain's protectionist policy. America's role was to supply raw materials to Britain, serve as a market for Britain's manufactured goods, agree to trade conditions which favored Britain; i.e., the transporting of designated commodities, such as tobacco and sugar, only to Britain, only in British vessels, and at a price set by British merchants. A series of navigation acts had been in effect since 1645, forbidding importation of certain products into the colonies except in British or colonial vessels, and limiting or prohibiting trade in some commodities. To enforce the restrictions, Parliament had recently authorized the use of British naval vessels stationed in lower Chesapeake Bay at Hampton Roads harbor. The navy was instructed to stop the Americans from smuggling goods into the colonies in order to evade the new import duties.

But smuggling was impossible to stop. For example, smugglers accounted for eighty-two percent of all molasses brought into New England in 1763. And some Americans during the French and Indian War (including Boston shipowner John Hancock) built large fortunes on illicit trade with France.

Many prominent colonists, suffering a critical cash flow, worried about financial ruin when the Currency Act passed in 1764, aggravating the new tax and trade regulations with heavy penalties for issuing legal-tender currency. Increasingly, Parliament was taking a hard line on Americans in response to complaints at home that the British people paid higher taxes than any Europeans and received no financial support from the colonies. Now, the Currency Act deprived Americans of the use of their own paper money in dealings with British merchants, who insisted upon being paid in coins. The new law threatened to deplete America's supply of hard currency which had been acquired in its trade with nations other than Great Britain. Parliament compounded the crisis by declaring America's "cheap money" illegal and prohibiting British merchants from sending gold or silver coins to the colonies.

The shortage of hard currency was most acute in Virginia where tobacco planters were on the verge of bankruptcy. Because of heavy credit, these planters were described by Jefferson as "a species of property, annexed to certain mercantile houses in London." And his friend James Madison said it was impossible to find proof "of a man's getting out of debt who was once in the hands of a tobacco merchant." Even a small tax increase would be a burden, and trade regulations would further reduce the markets for a tobacco crop already in surplus—despite the fact that Virginia planters had destroyed much of their crop in order to improve tobacco prices. Emory G. Evans, in his account of planter indebtedness in the *William and Mary Quarterly* (vol. 19, 1962), showed that the book debt to British merchants on the eve of revolution was almost $10,000,000. Planters had to look to the House of Burgesses to express their rage at Parliament's repeated interference in their internal affairs, arguing that the credit impact would be felt not only among large landowners but also among shopkeepers, craftsmen, mechanics, and others whose livelihood was tied to the vagaries of Virginia's tobacco economy.

America's lack of sympathy for Britain's need for revenue was to be expected. First, because the planters and merchants were so deeply in debt to British creditors. Second, because the British government, which claimed absolute rule over the colonies, had all but abdicated that control through years of indifference. The term *American* was synonymous with *Indian*, not with the English colonist who had been left to survive the wilderness almost entirely on his own. Thus, wrote Robert M. Adams, "After years of what one could call either freedom or neglect, both tempered by vague threats, the Americans had become a truculent and quarrelsome breed."

The Treaty of Paris concluding the French and Indian War also ended France's territorial claims in British America. Americans saw this as an opportunity to migrate beyond western boundaries—until the Proclamation of 1763 restricted them to the territories already established, easing Great Britain's cost of policing ever-expanding borders. The western frontier was declared off limits, and the vast region between the Appalachian Mountains and Mississippi River was designated as an Indian Reservation. A ban was placed on trading ventures as well as land acquisitions, but the march to the west continued, particularly among the poor families excluded from the opportunities of the east. The decree was also grating to George Washington and other prominent Virginians who had already staked western claims and dreamed of extending their holdings all the way to the Pacific. They would be incensed again when Parliament passed the Quebec Act, permitting the Canadian province of Quebec to annex lands west of the Appalachians and north of the Ohio River.

Thus colonial grievances against the British government after the French and Indian War included resentments of:

a) New direct taxes and trade regulations imposed to pay the expenses incurred by the war and the cost of stationing redcoats in the colonies for protection against potential invasions;

b) Large indebtedness to British creditors, especially among southern planters;
c) Ban on use of colonial money in transactions with British merchants;
d) Prohibitions on manufacturing among commercial interests in the middle colonies;
e) Restrictions on western expansion, mainly among frontier colonies which had been speculating in western lands and seeking to expand trade with the Indians.

America's aristocracy felt oppressed by Parliament and betrayed by a king indifferent to their special concerns. Unrepresented in the House of Commons, these men of money and connections refused to acknowledge Parliament's power to regulate their lives and claimed they owed allegiance only to the throne. At first, wrote Norman Gelb, it was only this "privileged American elite which bore the brunt of British transgressions." But as economic pressures began to lessen and members of the moneyed class relaxed their attacks on Parliament, anti-British zealots turned to the poor for support. Highly charged propaganda transformed the "most gracious sovereign" into a cruel tyrant the majority of Americans could learn to hate.

And by the time that British Prime Minister George Grenville introduced the Stamp Act in the House of Commons on February 7, 1765, American opposition had begun to swing from conservative to radical. The new act, which would affect everyone, provided that "a stamp duty of three pence" be paid

> for every skin or piece of vellum or parchment, or sheet or piece of paper, on which shall be engrossed, written or printed, any declaration, plea, replication, rejoinder, demurrer, or other pleading, or any copy thereof, in any court or law within the British colonies and plantations in America.

The act passed by a vote of 5 to 1 in the House of Commons, met no opposition in the House of Lords, and was signed by George III on March 22. It would place a tax on every document circulated in the colonies—from almanacs, newspapers, and pamphlets to legal documents, insurance policies, and licenses.

On the heels of the Stamp Act, Parliament passed the first of the Quartering Acts in April 1765, requiring the colonies to "billet and quarter the officers and soldiers in his Majesty's service," and ordering civil authorities in the colonies to supply barracks and provisions for the British troops. If not enough barracks were available, the colonists were to provide quarters in inns, stables, ale-houses, and, if necessary, uninhabited houses and barns. The government decreed again that since it was necessary to maintain a standing army in the colonies as protection against an uprising by the western Indians or an invasion by the French Canadians, the colonies should help pay the cost. The colonies used the creation of their own militia, and the military experience they had gained in the French and Indian War, as rationale for no longer requiring the presence of British troops. Americans had become self-reliant and believed they were now capable of taking care of themselves. Of course, Patrick Henry had warned earlier that the royal troops were there not to protect but to enslave the colonies. But at the moment his greater concern was the Stamp Act.

On May 30 Patrick Henry urged the Virginia House of Burgesses to defy the crown and reject the tax. Even shouts of treason could not restrain Henry's oratory. "Tarquin and Caesar each had his Brutus, Charles the First his Cromwell; and George the Third may profit by their example," he said. "If *this* be Treason, make the most of it!" Henry offered the following resolutions:

> *Resolved*, That the first adventurers and settlers of this his majesty's colony and dominion of Virginia,

brought with them, and transmitted to their posterity, and all others his majesty's subjects since inhabiting in this his majesty's colony, all the privileges and immunities that have at any time been held, enjoyed and possessed by the people of Great Britain.

Resolved, That by two royal charters granted by King James I, the colonies aforesaid are declared entitled to all the privileges of denizens, and natural born subjects, to all intents and purposes as if they had been abiding and born within the realm of England.

Resolved, That the taxation of the people by themselves, or by persons chosen by themselves, to represent them, who can only know what taxes the people are able to bear, and the easiest mode of raising them, and are equally affected by such taxes themselves, is the distinguished characteristic of British freedom, and without which the ancient constitution cannot subsist.

Resolved, That his majesty's liege people of this most ancient colony have uninterruptedly enjoyed the right of being thus governed by their own assembly in the article of their taxes and internal police, and that the same hath never been forfeited nor any other way yielded up, but hath been constantly recognized by the King and people of Great Britain.

Resolved, Therefore, that the general assembly of this colony have the sole power to lay taxes and impositions upon the inhabitants of this colony; and that every attempt to vest such a power in any person or persons whatsoever, other than the general assembly aforesaid, has a manifest tendency to destroy British as well as American freedom.

A clique of moderate-to-conservative jurists in the House attempted to defeat the resolutions. Although they had expressed opposition to the Stamp Act—and were torn between the need to override Parliament's restrictive tax and trade regulations and the need to maintain economic stability—they now preferred to lobby for its repeal through petition or some other constitutional means. The group included Jefferson's enlightened friend and law teacher George Wythe and his cousin Richard Bland, both of whom identified legal grounds on which to base resistance to Britain's tax policy. Wythe wrote that Americans could not be taxed by a government body in which they were not seated. Said Jefferson: George Wythe "took the stand on the solid ground that the only link of political union between us and Great Britain" was the king and that "Parliament had no more authority over us than we over them." To Bland the rights of *all* British subjects were so secured by law that they could not "be deprived of the least part of their property but by their own consent." Ironically, Richard Bland's reasoned pamphlet, *An Inquiry into the Rights of the British Colonies*, would be used to support Patrick Henry's more radical positions.

All resolutions passed, with the fourth amended as follows:

> *Resolved*, that his majesty's liege people of this his most ancient and *loyal colony* have, *without interruption*, enjoyed the *inestimable* right of being governed *by such laws respecting their internal polity and taxation as are derived from their own consent, with the approbation of their sovereign or his substitute*, and that the same hath never been forfeited or yielded up, but hath been constantly recognized by the king and people of Great Britain.

Henry's protest was shared by progressives George Mason and Richard Henry Lee, who joined with him to draft a plan that would enable certain Virginians (landlords and debtors) to circumvent the use of stamped paper and avoid payment of the taxes required by the act. Mason announced that another such law "would produce a general revolt in America." This possibility alarmed the conservatives who were unprepared to go beyond protests to resolve their grievances, but the warning of mob violence was echoed by agitators throughout the colonies.

Massachusetts called for a Stamp Act Congress in June 1765 to meet in New York to draft a declaration of rights and grievances of all colonists. Delegates from nine of the thirteen colonies attended. Maryland, which declared the Stamp Act illegal, sent three delegates—Matthew Tilghman of Oxford in Queen Anne's County, William Murdock of Prince George's, and Thomas Ringgold of Kent County. The following declaration, similar in spirit to Virginia's resolutions, was adopted:

> That his Majesty's liege subjects in these colonies, are entitled to all the inherent rights and liberties of his natural born subjects, within the kingdom of Great Britain.
>
> That it is inseparably essential to the freedom of a people, and the undoubted right of Englishmen, that no Taxes be imposed on them but with their own consent, given personally, or by their representatives.

A notable absentee was Benjamin Franklin, who had initially supported the Stamp Act—until a Philadelphia mob threatened to burn down his house. The Pennsylvania peacemaker advocated that Great Britain "possessed the best constitution and the best king [that] any nation was ever blessed with." Later, when the British ministry tried to bribe him into arranging a reconciliation with the colonies, Franklin joined the revolutionaries.

A Virginia planter wrote: "If Parliament indeed have a right to impose taxes on the colonies, we are as absolute slaves as any in Asia, and consequently in a state of rebellion." A Marylander, Charles Carroll of Carrollton (said to be the wealthiest man in America) agreed: "Should the Stamp Act be enforced by tyrannical soldiery, our property, our liberty, our very existence, is at an end. And you may be persuaded that nothing but an armed force can execute the worst of laws." Carroll was right.

A group of Maryland freemen gathered at the Eastern Shore and talked of "takeing up arms." They resolved to "risk their lives and fortunes," wrote Charles Albro Barker, in order "to preserve the rights which the Stamp Act threatened to destroy."

The Stamp Act had hit Maryland at a time of great depression, brought on by denial of credit by London merchants, cheap prices, trade restrictions, and lack of currency. "Our trade is ruined," lamented Council member Benedict Calvert. He said that "upon every road you ride you meet people going from different parts of the province to get out of the way of their creditors." Later Calvert reported that there was "not enough [money] in Maryland to pay one year's tax." Nor enough jails to hold the debtors.

Thus it was a dark day in Annapolis when the *Maryland Gazette* appeared with a black border and announced that it would no longer publish if forced to print on stamped paper. By the end of the year Maryland's ports as well as its courts and government offices would close rather than use the duty stamps.

Political scientist Samuel A. Johnson maintained that "revolution normally starts with protests of moderate groups against the curtailment or threatened curtailment of their liberties. A radical group then appears that demands very extreme changes and usually resorts to mob violence." One such group was the *Sons of Liberty*, a secret organization that started in New York in the summer of 1765 and took its name from a House of Commons speech which labeled the colonists "these sons of liberty." The movement rapidly spread to other colonial towns, instigating nonimportation protests and forcing stamp agents to resign.

Charles Campbell described the experience of George Mercer, distributor of stamps for Virginia, who was "rudely treated" on landing at Hampton in October 1765. Later, in Williamsburg, as Mercer was "on his way to the governor's palace, he was required by several gentlemen from different counties, the general court being in session, to say whether he intended to enter on the duties of his office." The pressure from impatient crowds continued. Finally, Mercer promised that he would "not undertake the execution of the stamp act until he received further orders from England, nor then, without the assent of the assembly of Virginia." He was escorted "out the capitol gate, amid loud exclamations, and carried to the coffee-house, where an elegant entertainment was prepared for him, and was welcomed there by renewed acclamations, drum beating, and French-horns and other musical instruments. At night the bells were set a-ringing, and the town was illuminated." Five years later George Mercer would be the lieutenant-governor of North Carolina.

Annapolis merchant Zachariah Hood was named stamp agent for Maryland while in London on business. When the news reached Talbot County on the Eastern Shore, a twenty-foot tall gallows was built, from which the agent's effigy would hang as a warning until the Stamp Act was repealed. Effigies of Hood were burned in Annapolis by a Sons of Liberty mob reacting to an inflammatory letter printed in the *Maryland Gazette* and written by a young politician named Samuel Chase. The violence of the Sons of Liberty was opposed by some prominent Marylanders as the product of "ignorance, prejudice, and passion," although the mob leaders included Matthias Hammond and his brother Rezin Hammond, two of the richest citizens of Anne Arundel County. The Hammonds were known for their skills in using street demonstrations to apply political pressure. They destroyed Hood's warehouse and prevented his ship from docking at Annapolis.

The Sons of Liberty movement was duplicated in Baltimore under the name, *Society for the Maintenance of Order and the*

Protection of American Liberty, and succeeded in getting the city clerk to transact business without using stamped documents. Hood was forced to leave his native Maryland for New York, where he remained until his stamp commission was relinquished.

As he had threatened, Jonas Green published "the last edition" of his newspaper under an altered masthead:

> THE MARYLAND GAZETTE Expiring:
> In uncertain Hopes of a Resurrection to Life again.

Green would resume publication of the *Maryland Gazette* at the end of 1765 on unstamped paper.

Many Marylanders were unhappy when their Assembly voted to reimburse Zachariah Hood for his warehouse. Two months later an effigy of Hood showed up at a mock funeral in Frederick County. His effigy was the lone mourner at a coffin bearing the inscription: "The Stamp Act, expired on a mortal slab received from the genius of liberty in Frederick County Court, 23d November 1765." County magistrates had urged the people to ignore the tax and continue to conduct business as usual.

British apologists argued that taxes and trade regulations were justified not only on the basis of the costly military protection provided to the colonies but also because of the exclusive English markets granted to a variety of American commodities. They called the process a "reciprocity" of mutual interests. Yet the effect of Britain's economic policies was "to keep the American colonies in a subordinate relationship with the Empire," wrote Lewis M. Hacker in *Triumph of American Capitalism* (1940). Opposition was dominated by the two groups which had the most at stake: northern merchants and southern planters.

An active pamphleteer against the Stamp Act was Daniel Dulany of Annapolis. In October 1765 he published

Considerations on the Propriety of Imposing Taxes in the British Colonies for the Purpose of Raising a Revenue by Act of Parliament. The powerful pamphlet argued that Americans, as British subjects, should not be taxed without their consent, and that consent could not be given because the colonies were not represented in Parliament. Dulany asserted: "The colonies have a complete and adequate legislative authority, and are not only represented in their assemblies, but in *no other manner.*" His pamphlet was praised in Parliament by William Pitt and influenced the repeal of the Stamp Act.

Dulany had responded to a pamphlet published by Soame Jenyns, *The Objections to the Taxation of Our American Colonies by the Legislature of Great Britain, Briefly Considr'd.* In defense of Parliament's right to tax the colonies, Jenyns had written that liberty was not "an exemption from taxes imposed by the authority of the Parliament of Great Britain." To those Americans who cried no taxation without representation, he replied that "not one in twenty" of the British people was represented in Parliament, and that many of the nation's "richest and most flourishing trading towns send no members to Parliament." No more than four percent of the nation's total population had the right to vote. Every citizen was taxed on the principle that "whether he has a right to vote for a representative or not, [he] is still represented in the British Parliament." Therefore, asked Jenyns:

> Why does not this imaginary representation extend to America as well as over the whole island of Great Britain? If it can travel three hundred miles, why not three thousand? If it can jump over rivers and mountains, why cannot it sail over the ocean? If the towns of Manchester and Birmingham, sending no representatives to Parliament, are notwithstanding there represented, why are not the cities of Albany and Boston equally represented in that Assembly? Are they not alike British subjects? Are they not Englishmen? or are they only Englishmen when they solicit for protection, but not

Englishmen when taxes are required to enable this country to protect them?

Dulany's concern about the taxation issue was economic not political. No advocate of American independence, he would declare himself a loyalist when the colonies separated from Great Britain and see his Maryland property confiscated. Thomas Whately, one of the secretaries to the British prime minister, also wrote in support of the constitutional principle that "Inhabitants of the Colonies are represented in Parliament." This was accepted as fact even though the colonials "do not indeed chuse the Members of that Assembly; [but] neither are Nine Tenths of the People of *Britain* Electors; for the Right of Election is annexed to certain Species of Property, to peculiar Franchises, and to Inhabitancy in some particular Places; but these Descriptions comprehend only a very small Part of the Land, the Property, and the People of this Island."

The phrase *Taxation without representation is tyranny*, which became the first important slogan of the American Revolution, has been traced back to 1637, when it was used by Squire John Hampden of Buckingham in a legal argument against Charles I. Hampden lost the argument.

Of course the cry "no taxation without representation" was a shameless slogan to be brandishing in America, where most colonists were unrepresented in their own legislatures. In America, as in the British Isles, government was in the hands of a ruling class. Only those who owned property could hold public office or vote in general elections. In Virginia, for example, only six per cent of all white adult males owned enough property to qualify to vote; in Philadelphia, it was only two per cent. The talk of change did not change this reality. Those who talked the talk were the elite who wanted to free themselves from the chains of Parliament regulation and preserve or enlarge their positions of power and influence in the colonies—usually at the expense of the poor or disenfranchised who somehow hoped that any change would be a change for the better.

The nonimportation agreement among the colonies was an effective weapon against the Stamp Act. British imports valued at nearly 2,500,000 pounds in 1764 had declined by 300,000 pounds by the end of 1765—despite the fact that the colonies accused each other of secretly breaking the ban and profiting on smuggled British goods. But it was nonimportation as much as mobs or constitutional arguments that put an end to the Stamp Act. When Britain's influential mercantile community complained that the tax was bad for business, the Stamp Act was repealed (on March 18, 1766) and the colonies discarded the nonimportation pact.

Philip Freneau, called the Poet of the American Revolution, was inspired by George III to write *An Ancient Prophecy*, which included the following lines:

> When a certain great king, whose initial is G.
> Shall force stamps upon paper, and folks to drink tea;
> When these folks burn his tea and stampt paper, like stubble,
> You may guess that this king is then coming to trouble....
>
> The face of the lion shall then become pale,
> He shall yield fifteen teeth, and be sheared of his tail.
> O king, my dear king, you shall be very sore;
> The Stars and the Lily shall run you on shore,
> And your Lion shall growl—but never bite more.

As soon as news of the repeal reached bay region residents, the taverns were scenes of victory celebrations. Maryland's House of Delegates voted money to erect a statue of America's friend in Parliament, William Pitt, but the appropriation was rejected by the governor's Council as unconstitutional. This former prime minister and House of Lords member would soon ask the House of Commons: "How can America trust you, with the bayonet at her breast?"

Sans statues, the Stamp Act Victory would have to stand as its own monument—except that Parliament was unwilling to admit defeat. It immediately passed the Declaratory Act, reserving the right to pass any law affecting the "subordinate" and "dependent" Americans, declaring that it had "the power to bind the colonies in all cases whatsoever."

Conservatives in America shrugged off the Declaratory Act and looked ahead to stability and a new prosperity, and viewed any new attacks on Parliament as dangerous to their economic interests. But discontent continued to smolder among radical agitators seeking to win support for a new slate of political freedoms. Men like Sam Adams in Massachusetts and Patrick Henry in Virginia would succeed in generating *popular* support. History notes that Adams, a former brewer and legislative clerk, failed at just about everything he tried but revolution. H.J. Eckenrode called the emergence of Henry "a momentous event in American history, for it marked the spread of revolt from the [legislative] assembly to the body of the people, and the rise of the Democratic Party." It was Patrick Henry who inspired the political philosophy which Jefferson and James Madison would expand beyond Virginia boundaries to the nation at large.

In Virginia, following the Stamp Act repeal, wrote Eckenrode, "there were two more or less clearly defined parties—the conservatives headed by the old leaders, and the democrats, or more properly, the progressives." On occasion there was some cooperation. And some inconsistencies. The old order conservatives, for example, while hesitant to endorse any move that would separate the colonies from the crown would ultimately join the progressives in attempts to control or exile Virginians who remained loyal to the king.

In proprietary Maryland there also were two political factions prior to the Revolution: the *Court Party* headed by the governor and his Council (or Court), all of whom owed their positions of power and influence to a proprietor (Lord Baltimore) who lived in London; and the *Country Party*, a loosely defined and unstructured faction, with no titular head, which looked to progressive members of the House of Delegates to support broader participation in government. The Court Party would die in 1774 when Maryland ceased to be a proprietary colony and its authority was appropriated in the name of the people by the crown. But the inequality growing out of the vast differences in wealth, position, and opportunity would still dominate the political and social system. The privilige of government would remain with Maryland's elite, and their general fear of "the infection of discontent" would discourage the radical talk of political equality.

Bay region conservatives, moderates, and progressives did attempt to work together, but rarely without friction over the tactics employed by the more radical elements to compel rather than convert supporters to a progressive agenda. Conflicting viewpoints were expressed in the streets and pamphlets, and later in heated arguments exchanged in the Maryland and Virginia Conventions which supplanted the legally elected legislative assemblies.

As soon as the Stamp Act was no longer a matter of concern, the Maryland General Assembly returned to traditional conflicts over such divisive issues as proprietary abuse. In the House of Delegates, noisy complaints were directed at the Upper House and Council over the practice of reimbursing the governor for the cost of the seals used on his proclamations. House members argued that not only were many of the governor's pronouncements unnecessary, but that Marylanders "perfectly well knew of the contents of laws without being reminded by proclamation."

Into this quarrelsome atmosphere in May 1766 walked a visitor from Virginia, the twenty-three-year-old Thomas Jefferson, on his way to New York. Jefferson described the proceedings in a letter to his friend John Page:

I went into the lower [house], sitting in an old courthouse, which, judging from it's form and appearance, was built in the year one. I was surprised on approaching it to hear as great a noise and hubbub as you will usually observe at a publick meeting of the planters in Virginia. The first object which struck me after my entrance was the figure of a little old man dressed but indifferently, with a yellow queue wig on, and mounted in the judge's chair. This the gentleman who walked with me informed me was the speaker, a man of a very fair character, but who by the bye has very little the air of a speaker. At one end of the justices' bench stood a man whom in another place I should from his dress and phis have taken for Goodall the lawyer in Williamsburgh, reading a bill then before the house with a schoolboy tone and an abrupt pause at every half dozen words. This I found to be the clerk of the assembly. The mob (for such was their appearance) sat covered on the justices' and lawyers' benches, and were divided into little clubs amusing themselves in the common chit chat way.

I was surprised to see them address the speaker without rising from their seats, and three, four, and five at a time without being checked. When [a motion was] made, the speaker instead of putting the question in the usual form only asked the gentlemen whether they chose that such or such a thing should be done, and was answered by a yes sir or no sir: and tho' the voices appeared frequently to be divided, they never would go to the trouble of dividing the house, but the clerk entered the resolutions, I supposed, as he thought proper. In short every thing seems to be carried without the house in general's knowing what was proposed.

Jefferson was impressed with Annapolis, a place he considered "extremely beautiful, and very commodious for trade having a most secure port capable of receiving the largest vessels." He concluded his letter to Page: "I would give you an account of the rejoicings here on the repeal of the stamp act but this you will probably see in print before my letter can reach you."

When Charles Townshend, Chancellor of the Exchequer, persuaded the parliament in 1767 to enact new duties on glass, lead, paint, tea, paper, and other goods entering the colonies, the nonimportation agreement was renewed. The Townshend Act tightened Great Britain's control by authorizing search and seizure procedures, establishing new vice-admiralty courts with jurisdiction over trade, providing that colonial governors and judges be chosen and paid by the crown, and compelling colonial governments to be supported by a standing army subsidized by the taxes imposed on the colonies. In addition, British warships were dispatched to Boston to put down hostilities anticipated between the people and the king's officers. Resistance to the Townshend Act was less intense than the response inspired by the Stamp Act. In Maryland and Virginia, for example, many of the merchants were Scots who would side with the British government in the Revolutionary War. This made the embargoes on British imports difficult to enforce—until the Sons of Liberty groups threatened to publish rosters of the uncooperative merchants as "Enemies of the liberty of the American people."

The Massachusetts Circular Letter was another response to the latest attempt by Parliament to enforce its legislative authority over the American colonies. Drawn up by Sam Adams and approved by the Massachusetts House of Representatives, its aim was to inform the other colonial assemblies of steps being taken by Massachusetts to denounce the parliamentary actions as "infringements of natural and constitutional rights" and to urge them to follow suit. Though the royal governor of Massachusetts urged the other governors to prevent their legislatures from taking a similar action, Virginia drafted its own Circular Letter in support of Massachusetts.

On October 1, 1768, troops arrived. Two regiments of British infantry, supported by artillery, landed in Boston on the pretense of an imminent war with France. Merchants in Boston and New York agreed to adopt a more stringent boycott of British goods until the Townshend Act was rescinded. By the following year, the agreement was endorsed by all the colonies but New Hampshire.

On May 16, 1769, nonimportation resolutions composed by the Virginia Association were introduced to the House of Burgesses by George Washington. These resolutions, framed by George Mason, not only censured the British ministry for attacks on the Massachusetts and Virginia Circular Letters but also condemned the proposal by Parliament that American malcontents be transported to England for trial. Next day Governor Botetourt dissolved the House of Burgesses and the burgesses met informally in Williamsburg's Raleigh Tavern to adopt the Virginia Association resolutions. One of the men who signed the nonimportation agreement was Thomas Claiborne, a burgess from King William County and a fifth-generation descendant of the Virginia/Maryland pioneer William Claiborne.

A similar association was created in Maryland in July 1769, when merchants, traders, and other Annapolis inhabitants drafted a nonimportation agreement in harmony with those agreements supported in other colonies. Association members pledged not to import any articles taxed under the Townshend Act, plus 125 other commodities, as long as the Townshend duties were in effect. They also refused to do business with anyone who violated the embargo. Because most of the men who signed the agreement were members of the House of Delegates, the Maryland Association wore an official face (as was the case in Virginia). Imported goods, when they reached

Baltimore docks or river landings in the counties of Charles, St. Mary's, Talbot, Anne Arundel, and Prince George's, were put in storage or sent back to the British Isles.

The result of renewed nonimportation efforts in the colonies was to reduce again the value of British imports, from more than 2,150,000 pounds in 1768 to 1,330,000 pounds by the end of 1769.

In addition to drafting resolutions against Parliament actions and boycotting British trade, residents of the Bay colonies found other ways to resist the British government in 1769. At a time that Daniel Boone defied the royal decree against western expansion by settling a group of North Carolinians in the Virginia country that would become Kentucky, Virginians also moved beyond their western border to settle near the Watauga River on land that would become Tennessee, and Marylanders forced their proprietary governor to resign and return to England.

Though the British government had once been described by the Virginia House of Burgesses as "our greatest happiness and only security," the first bloodshed of revolution was just months away.

- 2 -

Riots, Resolutions, Revolts

1770-1774

By 1770 American colonists had survived a forbidding wilderness for more than 160 years. Population had grown to more than two million. A select few of the colonists were men of wealth and position. Many more were descendants of misfits and outcasts who had been shipped to the colonies as laborers or indentured servants. There were the slaves who now outnumbered whites by two to one in some southern colonies. There was the steady flow of immigrants who had begun to modify America's original English character with increasing numbers of Scotch and Irish, French and Germans, Swedes and Poles. America remained a haven for victims of religious and social oppression, whether Puritan, Catholic, Quaker, or Jew. There were the homeless, the unwanted, the prostitutes and felons. And mixed in with the newcomers, many of whom were uneducated or illiterate, were a few scholars and men of rank. There were the seekers of treasure and adventure, and the disenfranchised poor seeking land and a better life on the western frontier. Thus, 1770 America was populated by individuals, whether native born or newly arrived, who increasingly had little or nothing in common with the England most of them had never seen. Though some were proud to be British and never voiced a desire to be otherwise, the majority thought of themselves not so much as British subjects but as Pennsylvanians or Rhode Islanders or Marylanders. It was Jefferson who said, "Virginia, Sir, is my country."

Soon the majority would call themselves Americans and believe that the policy of the British government was to deprive the colonists of their liberties. It was a belief more perceived than real, inspired by propaganda schemes which encouraged separation from the mother country.

America's move toward independence, initially a conservative but focused protest by the political elite against Parliament control of colonial commerce, would evolve into the popular anger that served the cause of liberty for all discontented Americans. As a *people's cause* it would be as much an attack on *American* politics as it was on ill-conceived actions taken by Great Britain. There remained therefore a very real concern within America's ruling class that a greater popular voice in colonial affairs would oust not only traditional values but also the men who traditionally held the power by virtue of their wealth and social rank. Already, many of the "discontented" were rioting in the streets and refusing to pay taxes until they had a voice in their local governments.

In early 1770 that popular discontent erupted into the first bloodshed between American colonists and British troops, resulting from actions taken to prevent the soldiers from posting broadsides. This New York incident, overblown as the Battle of Golden Hill, was a British reaction to colonial broadsides posted in late 1769 by Alexander McDougall of the Sons of Liberty. McDougall had attacked the New York Assembly for appropriating funds to supply the British troops quartered in the colony. He was imprisoned for contempt.

There was more bloodshed on the night of March 5, 1770, when a small group of rowdy Bostonians threw snowballs at a British sentry in front of the customs house. By the time the main guard of twenty redcoats was summoned to the scene, the group had grown to a mob of several hundred men and boys now beating the British with clubs and stones. In the confusion, a soldier fired into the crowd. Suddenly, the screams and taunts of the frenzied mob mixed with the sharp crack of gunfire from other soldiers. Three Bostonians were killed and two were wounded. Later it was observed that this riot—which history records as the Boston Massacre—was a propaganda ploy inspired by the radical Sam Adams and his Sons of Liberty in order to persuade the governor of Massachusetts to withdraw the British troops from Boston to an island in the harbor. To Thomas A. Bailey, in his study of American *Slogans, Sayings, and Songs*, the massacre was more of a "Boston Brawl."

The propagandists aroused cries for independence and stirred up sympathy for Boston in most colonies. In Annapolis, however, the antagonism toward the British had relaxed and the Boston Massacre was ignored in the *Maryland Gazette*. But not by Maryland's Matthew Tilghman who said he admired "the spirit of the northern people" and was "ashamed to think that the southern colonies do not keep pace with 'em."

British soldiers involved in the Boston Massacre were tried in Massachusetts but escaped severe punishment, perhaps because they were defended by the instigator's cousin, John Adams. In defense, the more reserved Adams informed the jury that the incident was provoked by colonists who could not be described as proud patriots resisting attack by arrogant redcoats. He called them "a motley rabble of saucy boys, Negroes and mulattoes, Irish teagues and outlandish jack tars." Then continued: "And why should we scruple to call such a set of people a mob? I cannot conceive." Adams felt the name was "too respectable for them."

In May 1771 Matthew Tilghman's criticism of southern inaction would find exception in North Carolina. There, two thousand armed insurgents protested the absence of political representation for frontier communities and charged the colony's eastern political establishment with oppression. A militia company, led by the royal governor, put down the rebels in a battle at Alamance Creek near Hillsboro. Insurgents not found guilty of treason and executed had to take an oath of allegiance to the North Carolina government.

That spring the brig *Good Intent* sailed into Annapolis with Townshend-dutied goods consigned to Maryland merchants. The cargo was returned to England by a private nonimportation organization which threatened violators again with the "pain of being branded enemies of the liberties of America."

When the Townshend Duties were rescinded, only the tax on tea was exempt. Though this put a temporary end to the nonimportation agreement, American merchants still refused to purchase British tea which was being imported into England at the rate of ten million pounds per year. Consequently, the tea accumulated in warehouses of Britain's East India Company until the government had to come to the company's aid with a pricing policy that would spark another of Sam Adams's violent propaganda schemes. But that was two years off.

Meanwhile, in March 1772, Rhode Island patriots burned the British cutter *Gaspee*, which had run aground while searching for smugglers in Narragansett Bay. A royal commission investigated the incident and threatened to ship the Rhode Islanders to London for trial. This inflamed Virginia's House of Burgesses. Under pressure from Thomas Jefferson, Patrick Henry, and Richard Henry Lee, the House adopted a resolution accusing the commission of endangering the legal rights of American colonists.

The Committee of Correspondence was a radical idea originated in 1772 by Sam Adams in order to communicate Boston's concern about British abuse to other Massachusetts towns and to other colonies, requesting their support. The concept was copied in most of the colonies and evolved into a central committee within each colony linked to committees at the local level. It provided a means of disseminating propaganda and coordinating revolutionary activities through continuing correspondence between the various committees.

In March 1773 the Virginia House of Burgesses appointed a "standing committee of correspondence and inquiry...whose business it shall be to obtain the most early and authentic intelligence of all such acts and resolutions of the British parliament, or proceedings of administration, as may relate to, or affect the British colonies in America; and to keep up and maintain a correspondence and communication with our sister-colonies...."

In Maryland, too, the House of Delegates created a standing Committee of Correspondence and Enquiry

> whose Business it should be to obtain the most early and authentick Intelligence of all such Acts and Resolutions of the British Parliament or Proceedings of Administration as may relate to, or affect, the British Colonies in America, and to keep up and maintain a Correspondence and Communication with our Sister Colonies respecting these important Considerations, and the Result of such their Proceedings from Time to Time to lay before the House.

The establishment by Congress of an eleven-man intercolonial committee included Virginia's Patrick Henry, Thomas Jefferson, and Richard Henry Lee among its members.

At that time Henry was asked if he thought that an infant nation, "without discipline, arms, ammunition, ships of war, or money to procure them, [would be able] to oppose successfully the fleets and armies of Great Britain." His reply prophesied things to come: "I will be candid with you. I doubt whether we shall be able, alone, to cope with so powerful a nation. But where is France? Where is Spain? Where is Holland? the natural enemies of Great Britain. Where will they be all this while? Do you suppose they will stand by, idle and indifferent spectators to the contest? Will Louis XVI be asleep all this time? Believe me, no! When Louis XVI shall be satisfied by our serious opposition, and our *Declaration of Independence*, that all prospect of a reconciliation is gone, then, and not till then, will he furnish us with arms, ammunition, and clothing; and not with these only, but he will send his fleets and armies to fight our battles for us...against our unnatural mother. Spain and Holland will join the confederation! Our independence will be established! and we shall take our stand among the nations of the earth!" In view of the fact that the essence of this speech was not communicated to William Wirt (Patrick Henry's early biographer) until 1805, Henry's amazing prophesy in 1773 may be less predictive than retrospective. Nevertheless, Wirt wrote that Virginia legislators were startled at the word *independence*, "for they had never heard anything of the kind before even suggested." Or of *union*.

Until now the purpose of the American protests was to force the British government to change or modify its policies toward the colonies. But suddenly in June 1773 the idea of union received an impassioned endorsement in Rhode Island's *Providence Gazette*:

> The united Americans may bid Defiance to all their open as well as secret Foes; therefore let it be the study of all to make the Union of the Colonies firm and perpetual, as it will be the great Basis for liberty, and every public Blessing in America. In this Union every Colony will feel the Strength of the Whole; for if one is invaded, all will unite their wisdom and Power in her Defence. In this Way the weakest will become strong, and America will soon be the Glory of the World, and the Terror of wicked Oppressors among the Nations.

Most of the Founding Fathers, especially the men of commerce and property who dominated the more conservative faction, were not yet ready for such fiery rhetoric. Virginia's Washington and Jefferson and other reluctant revolutionaries shared views not dissimilar to the concerns of Maryland's Charles Carroll, who warned that unless radical schemes were "vigorously counteracted by all honest men," anarchy would follow. This would engage Maryland, said Carroll, "in all the horrors of an ungovernable and revengeful Democracy...dyed with the blood of its best citizens." What America's "hierarchical society" wanted was political and economic independence without a turbulent social revolution. They desired, wrote John C. Chalberg, all "the 'rights of Englishmen'...the right to a jury trial, the right to be free of unreasonable searches, the right to be secure in one's property, and the right to be free of unwarranted taxes." In short, they wanted limited government that would not interfere with class barriers and traditional privileges. And even the less privileged commoners, who thought first of common needs rather than private interests, resisted talk of independence—not because they were satisfied with British rule but because they were wary of the quality of treatment they would get "at the hands of an independent American government."

William Eddis, who had recently migrated to Maryland to become surveyor of customs in Annapolis, said that revolutionaries, "under the pretence of supporting the sacred claims of freedom and of justice, [were] fomenting jealousy and discontent [that would] involve this now happy country in complicated misery."

Taxes on tobacco in Maryland had been replaced by inspection fees which proved to be a negative influence on tobacco prices although deemed necessary by the Maryland governor and his council if the proprietary government were to survive. When the fees continued beyond their scheduled expiration date on October 20, 1773, some members in the House of Delegates linked the tobacco inspection law to Parliament's control of production and competition as ongoing threats to Maryland self-government. House members were ignored by Council members who unanimously supported the fee principle, not only in establishing the tobacco inspection law but also in setting the generous fees paid to Lord Baltimore's government officials.

Of course, the House of Delegates, as "representatives of the freemen," claimed the sole right to establish taxes or fees. Most delegates favored an embargo on tobacco exports *if* Virginia and North Carolina agreed to do likewise. And it must have occurred to the more radical faction that a break with Great Britain would also bring independence from the proprietary government which had bled the province for nearly 150 years. Indeed, the days of proprietary privilege were numbered. Judge Alexander Contee Hanson, in *Laws of Maryland* published in 1787, would look back on the spring of 1774 and write:

> Here ends the laws under the Proprietary Government.... From this period, notwithstanding the mere forms of the ancient governments were permitted a little longer to subsist, there was not real authority, except that derived immediately from the people.

Lord Frederick North, the British Prime Minister under George III, pursued arrogant and often incompetent policies toward the American colonies. His indifference to colonial reaction to the Stamp Act and other revenue measures led him to encourage Parliament to pass the 1773 Tea Act. The purpose of the act was to grant relief to the nearly bankrupt East India Company whose stockholders included the king and most members of Parliament. By permitting the company to ship its tea to America free of export duty and with only a modest import duty, the act would allow East India to sell the tea through its own agents at a much more competitive price and thereby reduce its enormous inventory. North hoped to put a stop to trade between the colonies and Holland and give the East India Company absolute control of American markets.

The Tea Act was a serious threat to American merchants who had ignored the boycott by smuggling tea into the colonies; some, with the aid of Sam Adams, raised mobs to oppose the landing of British tea in colonial ports. John Hancock, who would accumulate some five hundred indictments for smuggling, persuaded fellow merchants that the act was another parliamentary attempt to exhort revenue and regulate American trade. By ignoring the interests of America's mercantile community the British government continued to alienate its most logical ally against colonial radicalism. Called Britain's "colossal blunder" by James Truslow Adams, the decision to give the East India Company a virtual monopoly for selling tea in America would unite wealthy merchants and planters with the poor farmers and others in the struggling lower class who considered themselves patriots—despite the fact that the colonists would be able to buy East India tea for less than they were paying for smuggled tea. Whether it added taxes or reduced prices, the British government was destined to lose in its relations with the colonies. Propagandists would succeed in turning an "unjust" tea duty into a constitutional argument that looked beyond the preservation of commercial interests to embrace the rights and liberties of *all* Americans.

Ships carrying East India tea were denied permission to dock in Philadelphia and Charleston, and had to return home with their cargoes. Broadsides in New York warned pilots against guiding any tea ship into harbor. At Greenwich, New Jersey, a shipment of tea was destroyed by fire. In Boston ships could dock but not unload. Bay region use of tea was generally abandoned, and the following sentiment was published by "a Young Woman of Virginia":

> Begone, pernicious, baneful tea,
> With all Pandora's ills possessed!

Then, on the evening of December 16, 1773, under instructions from Sam Adams, 342 chests of tea were dumped into Boston harbor by a group of men (including Paul Revere) disguised as Mohawk Indians. Adams and his army were following the orders of Hancock and other merchants hoping to protect their profitable smuggling operations.

Some historians have found it hard to understand the American reaction to the Tea Act, although it should be apparent that the Boston Tea Party was inspired by American merchants who saw the act as supporting cheap prices that would place their smuggled tea at a market disadvantage. Still, early opposition to the Tea Act was not unanimous. After a group in Plymouth, Massachusetts, resolved to defy the act, other residents, fearing British reprisal, tried to distance themselves from the resolution with this announcement published in the *Massachusetts Gazette* in December 1773:

> We who are inhabitants of the town of Plymouth neither captivated by sounds and declamations, nor deceived by the cunning stratagems of men who under the specious masque of patriotism have attempted to delude an innocent and Loyal people; But firmly and steadily fix'd and determin'd to defend our rights and privileges, and to endeavor to hand to our posterity the blessings of peace and good government which were procured by our fathers and transmitted to Us,— Having taken into serious consideration the dangerous and fatal consequences which may arise from the late resolves pass'd at a meeting of this town on the seventh day of this instant December; Fearing that they may bring upon us the Vengeance of an affronted Majesty and his insulted authority, We cannot answer it to our God and our consciences unless we protest against the proceedings of said meetings, and publish to the world that we were not instrumental in procuring those mischiefs which may naturally be expected from such conduct.—And we do by these presents solemnly protest against the whole of said resolves being repugnant to our ideas of Liberty, law and reason.

On March 32, 1774, in retaliation for "dangerous commotions and insurrections...by divers ill-affected persons" involved in the Boston Tea Party, Parliament passed the Boston Port Bill. It was the first of Parliament's Coercive Acts (known in the colonies as the Intolerable Acts). The bill banned the loading and unloading of ships in Boston harbor until the East India Company was reimbursed and there was evidence that new customs duties could be collected.

To reduce Massachusetts to submission, the Assembly was dissolved, troops were posted in Boston to enforce British authority, and the port was blockaded by British warships.

The Boston action was seen as a threat of war in London where George III told his prime minister: "The die is cast. The colonies must either submit or triumph."

There were few signs of submission. Indeed, tea duties imposed after the Boston incident increased colonial protest. When a ship attempted to land a secret cargo of tea at New York, the cargo was spilled into the harbor by the Sons of Liberty (again disguised as Indians).

By May 1774 anti-Britain attitudes had spread throughout the colonies, motivated by the Coercive Acts which not only closed the Boston port and outlawed Massachusetts town meetings but also moved trials for murder to England and announced a new policy for housing British soldiers in private homes. When radical groups made it an issue of *natural rights* and attempted to incite rebellion, British General Thomas Gage arrived in Massachusetts to assume the duties of royal governor and tighten military control.

Meanwhile, in Fairfax County, Virginia, a committee of planters was taking steps to improve their colony's military defenses. Committee members (led by George Washington and George Mason) resolved that "a well regulated militia is the natural strength and only stable security of a free government." The resolution repeated a familiar theme: that the militia, in relieving Great Britain of the further expense of defending the colony, would "obviate the pretence of a necessity of taxing us on that account, and render it unnecessary to keep standing armies among us."

Robert Eden, Maryland's proprietary governor, accused the colony's "infernal independents" of being "in League with the Bostonians." That Chesapeake Bay residents were alarmed at the British blockade of Boston was evident in the words of one Marylander who said they "were determined to dispute the matter with the sword." While the citizens of Maryland's New Towne (today's Chestertown) dumped tea from the brigantine *Geddes* into the Chester River, another vessel was burned on landing its tea at Annapolis. In Annapolis a group of citizens resolved that "no lawyer within the province should bring suit for the recovery of any debt due from a Marylander to any inhabitant of Great Britain until the [Boston] Port Act should be repealed."

Virginia, which from the beginning had joined with Massachusetts in opposition to the new parliamentary actions, refused to allow the British merchant vessel *Mary and John* to unload its cargo of nine chests of tea at Norfolk, and a crowd from Williamsburg boarded a British ship on the York River and destroyed its cargo.

On May 25, 1774, in support of the Boston action, citizens of Annapolis passed a resolution that called for a colonial system to ban all exports to Britain and to refuse trade with any colony that failed to join the effort. When this new nonimportation agreement was adopted, it was vigorously enforced even though it severely restricted commercial life on the Chesapeake. Maryland prices on wheat, corn, and tobacco would drop by nearly fifty percent; and Virginia's trade with Britain, which far surpassed that of any other colony, would show similar declines. As Robert W. Coakley showed in his 1949 dissertation on "Virginia Commerce During the American Revolution," the British Isles accounted for forty-seven percent of Virginia's export and forty-four percent of its import tonnage. Annual exports to Britain from Virginia and Maryland combined were valued at one million pounds sterling, and the value of British imports to the two Chesapeake colonies was nearly eight hundred thousand pounds.

The problem for American trade was defined by Samuel Seaburg of New York: "We have no trade but under the protection of Great Britain. We can trade nowhere but where she pleases. We have no influence abroad, no ambassadors, no consuls, no fleet to protect our ships in passing the seas, nor our merchants and people in foreign countries. Should our mad schemes take place, our sailors, our ship-carpenters, carmen, sail-makers, riggers, miners, smelters, forge-men, and workers in bar-iron, etc. would be immediately out of employ; and we should have twenty mobs and riots in our country, before one would happen in Britain." A merchant of Piscataway, Maryland, expressed a similar concern to his Scottish employer on October 31, 1774. He felt that should restrictions of "imports & exports be strictly adhered to, the poor people and all those who would not lay in more Goods than would answer their present Necessitys will be in the Utmost Distress, and will I am afraid be exceeding riotous against the better sort of people who have fully supplyed themselves for a Length of time."

While it was true that nonimportation would do more economic harm to America than to Great Britain (which was not as limited in its markets), the threat of "mobs and riots" was avoided and the agreement was able to unite the colonies. Politically, however, the recession did endanger the bay region's "traditional leadership," wrote David C. Skaggs, and furthered the rise of radical movements intent on "a more drastic alteration of society." Thus, as British authorities continued to ignore grievances in America, the spirit of resistance gradually encompassed the general populace. William Eddis described "the impending storm" around him in Annapolis and observed: "All America is aflame!"

Judge Hanson declared that America's revolution had "taken place contrary to all reasonable calculation."

The British government was obviously shortsighted in not localizing the dispute at Boston, against whom the Coercive Acts were mainly directed. In using military might instead of diplomacy Britain had encouraged other colonies to make the cause of Boston their own. John Upshaw of Essex County, Virginia, informed the Overseers of the Poor of the Town of Boston that a thousand bushels of corn had been shipped "for the use of our suffering brethren in your Town." Bostonians were assured that Virginians were "warmly disposed to assist them, and hope for their steady and prudent perseverance in the common cause of our country...." Another Virginia sympathizer wrote: "'Tis with pity, mixed with indignation, that we have beheld the cruel and unmanly attacks made by the British Parliament on the loyal and patriotic Town of Boston." Virginia's Richard Henry Lee emerged as a champion of the cause when told by his brother that the intention of the Boston Port Bill was "to totally annihilate the town of Boston."

The Duke of Richmond protested the Coercive Acts in the House of Lords: "I wish from the bottom of my heart that the Americans may resist, and get the better of the forces sent against them." William Pitt announced to the House of Commons that "the Americans were upholding those eternal principles of political justice which should be to all Englishmen most dear [and that] a victory over the colonies would be of ill omen for English liberty." Edmund Burke, in his plea for Parliament's conciliation with the colonies, said: "An Englishman is the unfittest person on earth to argue another Englishman into slavery."

Still the king's ministers persisted in attacking the rights assumed by the colonies. If the colonial position on "no taxation without representation" were granted, they argued, it would become necessary to agree to the principles of parliamentary reform and advance the power of the liberals in

England. The king's ministers were right: American independence would result in administrative reform in England.

The Boston Port Bill was condemned as a "hostile invasion" by the Virginia House of Burgesses, which set aside a day of fasting and prayer and implored divine intervention to safeguard America's "civil Rights and [avert] the evils of civil War." On May 26 the actions resulted in dissolution of the House by Virginia's royal governor, John Murray, Lord Dunmore. In his message to the Speaker and "gentlemen in the house of burgesses," he said:

> I have in my hand a paper published by order of your house conceived in such terms as reflect highly upon his majesty and the parliament of Great Britain, which makes it necessary to dissolve you, and you are dissolved accordingly.

On May 27 the members of the House again found it necessary to assemble at Raleigh Tavern in Williamsburg, where Speaker Peyton Randolph called for election of delegates from each county to a Virginia Convention. They took the stand "that an attack on one of our sister-colonies, to compel submission to arbitrary taxes, is an attack made on all British America, and threatens ruin to the rights of all." Randolph recommended that a new Committee of Correspondence be organized to communicate with the other colonies about appointing delegates to meet annually in a general congress "for the purpose of uniting and guiding the councils, and directing the efforts, of North America."

Lord Dunmore, displaying the hauteur of a man descended from kings, refused to grasp the seriousness of the Virginia resolutions creating a central Committee of Correspondence for intercolonial communication. He described the resolutions as "a little ill humour in the House of Burgesses." Then the governor announced: "I thought them so insignificant that I took no matter of notice of them."

On June 2 the Maryland Convention assembled at Annapolis to voice resentment over the "unjust taxation" imposed by Parliament and the stationing of troops in the colonies to exact payment. Resolutions were passed authorizing the collection of funds for relief of the "depressed inhabitants of Boston." (Baltimore residents had already sent bread and rye whiskey.) Convention delegates were named to "a general Congress of Deputies from the Colonies." The purpose of this congress was to develop a plan of conduct to be followed in preserving American liberties. Delegates included the Convention Chairman William Tilghman, from one of the richest, most powerful families on Maryland's Eastern Shore; Frederick County's Thomas Johnson, Jr., future governor; William Paca and Samuel Chase of Annapolis; Robert Goldsborough of Dorchester County; and Charles Carroll of Carrollton. The Convention would assemble from time to time and replace the House of Delegates as Maryland's legislative body until a state constitution was written and ratified.

As early as 1756 the Maryland House of Delegates had refused to support British troops on Maryland soil, leading officials to declare that the colony's action tended to subvert all government. As Barker wrote: "A summary view of Maryland as a member of the old colonial system shows a minimum of administrative connection with the mother country, and a minimum of conscious interest in the military and other affairs common to the British colonial world." Under rule of the Lords Baltimore the Maryland House had always assumed the constitutional power to accept, refuse, or frustrate proprietary proposals for expenditures. Now, on the eve of the Revolutionary War—Maryland's proprietary government had virtually disintegrated under pressure of independence-minded House members. Its collapse would end the flow of revenues which had permitted generations of Lords Baltimore to live luxuriously in England.

In the summer of 1774 the moderate tones of Virginia's two great statesmen were taking on a militant ring. George Washington wrote to a friend: "I think the Parliament of Great Britain hath no more right to put their hands in my pocket, without my consent, than I have to put my hands in yours for money." Though he was not yet an advocate of American independence, Washington announced: "I'll raise a thousand men, subsist them at my own expence, and march at the head for the relief of Boston." Thomas Jefferson published his pamphlet, *A Summary View of the rights of British America*, stating that the colonists' natural rights were preeminent to their duties to Britain. Jefferson urged that colonists "immediately cease to import all commodities from every part of the world, which are subjected by the British Parliament to the payment of duties in America."

In August the brig *Mary and Jane*, from London, appeared in the Potomac River with chests of tea bound for Port Tobacco in Charles County, Maryland. County officials ordered the ship to return to England without unloading its cargo.

The Virginia Convention assembled in August and resolved to stop all exports to Great Britain unless American grievances were addressed by the tenth of the month. The Convention also elected Washington, Jefferson, Lee, Henry, Randolph, Bland, and Edmund Pendleton to represent Virginia at the Continental Congress called by Massachusetts after closure of the Boston port.

The First Continental Congress met in Philadelphia on September 5, 1774. In attendance were fifty-six delegates from all the colonies but Georgia. Virginia's Peyton Randolph was elected president. John Adams said that he urged the election of Virginians to positions of leadership in order to gain support for independence and "to take British military pressure off New England." There was concern in the north that the lower colonies would resent New Englanders and minimize the

British threat. But Pennsylvania's lieutenant governor put that fear to rest. "The Delegates from Virginia were the most violent of any," he said. "Those of Maryland and some of the Carolinians were little less so." He concluded: "These Southern Gentlemen exceeded even the New England Delegates."

Adams called Congress "a school of political prophets...a nursery of American statesmen." Its purpose was expressed in instructions given to the Virginia delegation: "to secure British America from the ravage and ruin of arbitrary taxes, and as speedily as possible to procure the return of that harmony and union so beneficial to the whole Empire and so ardently desired by all British America." The delegates were jurists and lawyers, church leaders and educators, merchants and planters, physicians and scientists. Some were radicals or progressives seeking a new government, but the majority were quiet men who still regarded themselves as loyal subjects of a monarch whom they believed had been given dangerous advice by his self-serving ministers. Talk of reconciliation persisted in the hope that colonial rights, under the British constitution, would be restored. It was an uneasy hope. So when the British government failed to offer any sign of accommodation to American appeals, a consensus among conservative, moderate, and radical factions led to adoption of the Continental Association. Under a pledge of secrecy, with Maryland taking the lead, delegates from each colony agreed to muster a standing militia and impose economic sanctions against Great Britain until all grievances were redressed by the crown. They agreed to discontinue the slave trade, but not slavery. Yet even in their stubborn resolve to resist all tyranny, they assured the king of their judgment that "there was yet much virtue, much justice, and much public spirit in the English nation."

Among the delegates who sought compromise with Great Britain was Joseph Galloway, a wealthy Pennsylvania lawyer who proposed a "Plan of Union between Britain and the Colonies." Galloway urged that the various colonial assemblies share legislative power with Parliament. He wrote: "I have been particularly attentive to the rights of both; and I am confident that no American, who wishes to continue a subject of the British state, which is what we all uniformly profess, can offer any reasonable objection against it." In opposition, Patrick Henry feared the plan would usurp the power of the colonial assemblies. Samuel Chase warned that peace overtures would only weaken America's cause. Even Benjamin Franklin said it would "corrupt or poison us."

That the plan was only narrowly defeated in Congress was of no consequence in England, where just a few of America's supporters were willing to welcome any attempt at conciliation. William Pitt addressed the House of Commons:

> How can America trust you, with the bayonet at her breast? ...I contend not for indulgence, but for justice.... What is our right to persist in such cruel and vindictive acts against a loyal, respectable people! They say you have no right to tax them without their consent. They say truly. Representation and taxation must go together. They are inseparable.

In reply the House of Commons stopped all commerce with the colonies. George III proclaimed that a general rebellion existed and swore to bring the traitors to the blade.

If the goals of the American Revolution were not as apparent to "the people" as they were to the revolutionary leaders, most of the people nevertheless put their trust in the leaders. They expressed this confidence in September 1774 to Benjamin Harrison as he left his James River plantation to represent Virginia at the First Continental Congress: "You assert there is a fixed intention to invade our rights and privileges; we own that we do not see this clearly, but since you assure us that it is so, we believe the fact."

Declarations and Resolves adopted by the Congress pronounced the Coercive Acts and the recently passed Quebec

Act (extending the boundaries of Quebec to the Ohio River, dismissing territorial claims of Virginia, Connecticut, and Massachusetts) as unconstitutional. The delegates were critical of parliamentary revenue bills, the dissolution of colonial assemblies, and the posting of a standing army in peacetime. Resolutions reaffirmed colonial rights to "life, liberty, and property" and retained the exclusive power of colonial assemblies to make laws in "cases of taxation and internal policy."

The *County* Committees of Correspondence were established in 1774 in Chesapeake country. For the remainder of the revolutionary period, these local committees would regulate lives and control opinion in Virginia and Maryland as they did in other colonies. In the name of patriotism (two years before the Declaration of Independence was adopted) the committees crushed dissent to the point that Americans accused of being British sympathizers were driven into submission or exile. Eddis condemned the "petty tyrannies" established in the various colonial committees, "of which a few despots lord it over the calm and moderate, inflame the passions of the mob, and pronounce those to be enemies to the general good who may pressure any way to dissent from the creed they have thought proper to impose." Loyalists, or Tories, who argued that the committees denied them their civil rights, would account for one-third of the colonial population at the time independence was declared, and many would fight for the British in the Revolutionary War. *Tory*, according to the Oxford English Dictionary, was the term derived from an Irish word meaning *pursuer*, and in the seventeenth century was applied to Irish outlaws who "subsisted by plundering and killing the English settlers and soldiers." It was first used to describe an American colonist loyal to the crown in 1774. Though the Tories would prove to be troublesome foes to the American cause, many were less loyal to the king than to their own economic interests.

Originally, County Committees of Correspondence were organized to administer and police the boycott of British commodities which had been designated by the Continental Congress for the purpose of pressuring the British government to repeal the new taxes and trade restrictions. Committee members were chosen in each county in the way that Virginia burgesses or Maryland delegates were elected. These members were typically planters or other men of property and influence who could be trusted to enforce the boycott. The intent changed when the committees began to investigate and punish not only those who resisted the nonimportation agreement but also those who criticized the Revolution. As H.J. Eckenrode wrote, "revolution by its very nature cannot tolerate differences of opinion."

In the passion that governed Virginia in the months prior to the Revolutionary War, there was little evidence of the freedom of speech that would be written into the Bill of Rights by these same Virginians. It was a crime to drink a cup of tea. Private mail was seized and read. The names of boycott violators or "non-patriots" who failed "to show proper contrition" were published in the press as "inimical to the liberties of America." It was a penalty which ruined many a merchant unable to escape the scrutiny of committee inspectors. It was patriotism at any price. The committees had unlimited and unsupervised authority within their jurisdictions, and they were backed by the armed force of volunteer companies raised in the various counties.

Absolute rule by county committees would continue in Virginia until July 1775, when the Convention established the Committee of Safety which operated out of Williamsburg as the colony's central authority until the end of the war. This Committee would be responsible for directing the county committees, and under its control the county committees would become even more severe in suppressing disaffection.

The Massachusetts House of Representatives assembled in defiance of British General Thomas Gage and named John

Hancock to head a Committee of Safety empowered to call out the militia. The House established militia companies which were trained "to act on a minute's notice." Hence, minutemen.

In October 1774, in protest of British taxes and trade limits, Maryland staged its own Annapolis Tea Party when the *Peggy Stewart* arrived from London with two thousand pounds of tea consigned to Annapolis merchants, Joseph and James Williams. It was reported in the *Maryland Gazette* that a mob refused to allow the ship to dock, despite the fact there were fifty-three passengers aboard who were sick and exhausted from the long voyage. Under mob pressure, the ship's owner Anthony Stewart boarded the vessel "with her sails and colours flying, and voluntarily set fire to the tea, and in a few hours, the whole [cargo], together with the vessel, was consumed in the presence of a great number of spectators."

Perhaps no act was more influential in shaping Maryland attitudes toward the conflict with Parliament than the burning of the *Peggy Stewart*, wrote Chesapeake historian Ernest McNeill Eller. But those attitudes did not always endorse mob actions. A man who was described as a "Gentleman of Bladensburg" declared: "Since the burning of the ship at Annapolis, the common sort seem to think they may now commit any outrage they please." When he learned that a Georgetown merchant had been forced to lower his prices because they were deemed excessive, the Gentleman asked: "What do you think of this land of Liberty, when a man's property is at the mercy of any one that will lead a mob!"

The real architects of Maryland's revolutionary movement were the same men who had used the power of their wealth and political skills to remove Lord Baltimore's proprietary government. They were of course the planters, merchants, lawyers, and other professionals who now became active leaders in the series of Conventions which supplanted Maryland's General Assembly and assumed the central role of governing the colony's affairs.

The delegates at the second Convention, on November 21, 1774, endorsed the non-trading pact passed by the Continental Congress and also voted to discontinue fancy balls "during the present time of public calamity." The third Convention, on December 8, 1774, responded to the Continental Congress's recommendation to organize militia companies for the protection of their properties as well as their liberties. They proposed "a well regulated militia [as] the natural strength and only stable security of a free government." Marylanders echoed their Virginia neighbors in stating that "such militia will relieve our mother country from any expence in our protection and defence [and] will obviate the pretence of a necessity for taxing us on that account, and render it unnecessary to keep any standing army (ever dangerous to liberty) in this province." The Convention also passed a resolution that made every Maryland inhabitant duty bound to execute the nonimportation agreement with other colonies and to know that opposition to British attempts "to enslave America will be strengthened by a union of all ranks of men in this province," regardless of religion or politics, or "private animosities and quarrels." Finally, Maryland's Committees of Safety were formed to represent the will of the patriots in local communities only.

Historians have suggested that America's government by committee represented "no organized terror" and did not plunge the colonies into the kind of bloodbath that marked the French Revolution and the Bolshevik upheaval in Russia. Yet, once that war was at hand, Americans would have less freedom than they had under British rule.

- 3 -

Inevitable War

1775

In the bay colonies the latest nonimportation pact was working, according to trade figures reported by Ronald Hoffman in his study of economics, politics, and revolution in Maryland. The value of Virginia and Maryland exports to England had nearly doubled between 1766 and 1775, but the value of imports from England into the two colonies had plunged from 372,548 pounds to a mere 1,921, a decline of 99.5 percent.

Parliament's reaction was to tighten the trading reins on America, prohibiting commerce with anyone but Great Britain and the British West Indies. This was one of the governmental actions that caused Maryland to follow Virginia's lead in forming militia companies—"with great diligence and alacrity," boasted officials in Charles County. A visitor from England wrote that he "saw a Company of about 60 Gentlemen learning the military Exercise" in a field at Port Tobacco, just off the Potomac. Further up the river a militia company claimed to be the first that "Steppd out in the Glorious cause of Liberty."

Later, when Washington learned that a company of the Port Tobacco militiamen refused to bear arms, he wrote: "I cannot say but I am curious to learn the reasons why men, who had subscribed & bound themselves to each other & their Country to stand forth in defence of it, should lay down their arms the first moment they were called upon."

One reason was money, a problem that would plague American military forces throughout the revolutionary period. With Maryland lacking funds to support its militia units, a group of citizens in Anne Arundel County announced in January 1775 that anyone refusing to aid "the purchase of arms and ammunition [for the cause] is and ought to be esteemed *an enemy of America.*" Names of noncontributors would be published in the *Maryland Gazette.*

The man who would become known as *financier of the American Revolution* was Robert Morris, a prominent Pennsylvania merchant and son of the Maryland patriot of the same name. Morris had created a network of far-flung business connections and would be pressured by George Washington to use his influence in Europe to generate "coin" for the American cause.

Despite the gradual military build-up, some feeling of reconciliation persisted in most of the colonial legislative bodies. The Maryland Convention, for example, continued to express hope for "a happy settlement and lasting amity." Only a few Americans openly complained of British tyranny, and for many the talk of separation from the crown was frightening. For some, it was inconceivable. This was particularly true of that large group of Americans whose loyalty to George III was beyond dispute. So vocal were the Williamsburg loyalists in their outcry against anti-British colonial policies—notably the nonimportation agreements—that in February 1775 they were forced by Virginia's Sons of Liberty, under threat of tar and feathers, to sign an oath supporting the boycott of British goods.

America did not win a friend in English lexicographer Samuel Johnson, who denounced colonial attempts "to infect the people of England with the contagion of disloyalty." Dr. Johnson admitted: "I am willing to love all mankind, *except an American.*" In his 1775 pamphlet, *Taxation No Tyranny*, Johnson asked: "How is it that we hear the loudest yelps for liberty among the drivers of negroes?"

On February 1, even as many patriots and loyalists alike were trying to negotiate peace with Parliament, a second Massachusetts Provincial Congress was meeting at Cambridge to frame measures that would prepare the colony in event of war. About two weeks later, redcoats destroyed a patriot ordnance facility at Salem. In March, General William Howe relieved General Gage in Boston. Though his immediate focus was the military build-up in Massachusetts, it should have been apparent that the real danger of rebellion was being provoked considerably south of New England borders.

The rallying call for American independence was sounded in a speech by Patrick Henry on March 23, before the second Virginia Convention which had assembled at St. John's Church in Richmond. There is no written transcript of the speech, but it was on this occasion that Henry lashed out at the tyranny of George III in his proposal to equip the Virginia militia to do battle with the British Army. His resolution that the colony "be immediately put into a posture of defence" was supported by George Mason, Richard Henry Lee, Thomas Jefferson, and George Washington, but was strenuously resisted by conservatives Richard Bland and Benjamin Harrison and the moderates Edmund Pendleton, Robert C. Nicholas, and George Wythe—patriots who held that such a step was premature until the king's response to the last petition was known. An angry Patrick Henry asked: "What has there been in the conduct of the British ministry for the last ten years to justify hope?" He argued that war was the only course of action: "I repeat it, sir, we must fight! An appeal to arms and to the God of hosts is all that is left to us!" And again he cried: "The war is inevitable—and let it come! I repeat it, sir, let it come!" Henry's summation rang throughout America: "I know not what course others may take; but as for me, give me liberty, or give me death!" The resolution passed and a committee was chosen to prepare a plan of defense.

The "give me liberty" speech first appeared in William Wirt's 1817 biography of Patrick Henry. Since there was no text of the speech, Wirt reconstructed it from the recollections of men who heard the speech forty years earlier. A question that bothers some historians is how much of the speech is Patrick Henry and how much Wirt? A later biographer, Richard Beeman, observed that Henry was "notoriously careless" about preserving personal papers. And while Jay B. Hubbell has decided that "most of the phrasing was probably Wirt's," Bernard Mayo believes the *spirit* of the speech was "that of the fiery orator."

Wirt admitted that none of Henry's "speeches lives in print, writing or memory." All that is known is "that on such and such an occasion, he made a distinguished speech." Yet that did not hinder Wirt in his dramatic reconstruction, which reached its crescendo in these historic words:

> *Gentlemen may cry peace, peace—but there is not peace. The war is actually begun! The next gale that sweeps from the north will bring to our ears the clash of resounding arms. Our brethren are already in the field! Why stand we here idle? What is it that gentlemen wish? What would they have? Is life so dear, or peace so sweet, as to be purchased at the price of chains and slavery? Forbid it, Almighty God! I know not what course others may take; but as for me, give me liberty, or give me death!*

Wirt wrote that Henry ended the speech "with both arms extended aloft, his brows knit, every feature marked with the resolute purpose of his soul, and his voice swelled to its boldest note of exclamation." When Henry sat down, wrote Wirt, not a "murmur of applause was heard. The effect was too deep. After the trance of a moment, several members started from their seats. The cry, 'To arms!' seemed to quiver on every lip, and gleam from every eye."

INEVITABLE WAR: 1775

Regardless of how faithful the Wirt reconstruction, Henry's speech was a stirring call to action, one which "blazed so as to warm the coldest heart," recalled Edmund Randolph. Another convention delegate, Thomas Marshall (father of the future Chief Justice John Marshall), called it "one of the most bold, vehement, and animated pieces of eloquence that had ever been delivered." To Richard Henry Lee (also known for his oratory) it was unparalleled in its power to bind "a band of patriots together to hurl defiance at the tyranny of so formidable a nation as Great Britain." Silas Deane of Connecticut, who described Henry as "a lawyer and the completest speaker I ever heard," also wrote: "I can give you no idea of the music of his voice, or the highwrought, yet natural, elegance of his style and manner." Though Jefferson too viewed Henry as "the greatest orator who ever lived," he had to inquire after one of the great orator's speeches: "What the devil did he say?"

In 1823 the English poet Lord Byron would praise Patrick Henry as *the forest-born Demosthenes, whose thunder shook...the seas.*

The Henry speech was responsible for one of the Revolution's most popular slogans: Virginia militia carried a yellow standard proclaiming LIBERTY OR DEATH.

The first day of the Revolutionary War is now generally accepted as April 19, 1775, date of the Battles of Lexington and Concord which resulted from the decision by Massachusetts Governor-General Thomas Gage to take possession of the colony's military stores.

On the night before, Paul Revere mounted his horse to carry news of the planned redcoat assault to the countryside. This was Longfellow's famous midnight ride, but history shows that Revere was one of three men who made that legendary ride, and that he rode only a short distance before his capture by the British. William Dawes, the second rider, escaped capture but had to turn back. The ride was finished by Samuel Prescott, who would be captured three weeks later in the Battle of Ticonderoga and die in prison.

One historian said it was a poor comment on the teaching of American history that Paul Revere was listed second to Betsy Ross when a group of *college* students were asked to list all the people they could think of in the American Revolution. George Hornby, in *The Great American Scrap Book*, felt that Paul Revere must have used John Hancock's press agent.

It also has been suggested that the resistance at Concord was "stage-managed" by Hancock and Sam Adams to force the British to fire the first shot, the so-called "shot heard round the world." After a party of one thousand redcoats, en route to Concord to take the colonial stores, were confronted by a larger force of minutemen at Lexington, they asked to be reinforced. Although they were still outnumbered at Concord by disorganized militia, the British managed a retreat to Boston after heavy casualties. Of the four thousand colonials who saw action that day, less than a hundred were killed, wounded, or missing.

Redcoats, supported by the Royal Navy, occupied Boston, and Massachusetts' Provincial Congress authorized the raising of more than thirteen thousand troops. Massachusetts then asked the other colonies for aid. Boston would be under siege for eleven months.

Some of the earliest hostilities of the Revolution occurred in the bay region, in a series of military engagements engineered by Lord Dunmore. The infamous and multi-titled John Murray—fourth Earl of Dunmore, Viscount Fincastle, Baron of Blair, Baron of Moulin, and Baron of Tillymont—was a descendant of the royal Stuarts and, like James I, saw himself as a defender of "the divine right of kings." After a brief term as New York governor, Dunmore was transferred to Williamsburg on September 25, 1771, to succeed the popular Norborne Berkeley, the Baron de Botetourt, as governor of Virginia.

INEVITABLE WAR: 1775 53

Soon after arriving in Virginia, Dunmore violated Britain's policy on crown-owned western lands by granting the territory to himself and to veterans of the French and Indian War. This led to a battle between Virginia and the Shawnee nation, which had never ceded its rights to the land. When Chief Cornstalk was ultimately defeated at the junction of the Great Kanawha and Ohio Rivers, the Shawnee ceded their claims to this Kentucky land to Virginia.

Dunmore's tyranny had started when the governor dismissed the Virginia House of Burgesses after it had expressed sympathy for the shutdown of the Boston Port, whereupon the burgesses assembled at Raleigh Tavern and called for a convention to elect delegates to a Second Continental Congress in Philadelphia on May 10. Dissolution of the House backfired on Dunmore and would eventually remove the royal governor from Virginia's political affairs, as the convention assumed both administrative and legislative functions. Dunmore had responded on April 21 by ordering marines from the British schooner *Magdalen* to slip into Williamsburg before dawn and seize fifteen half-barrels of gunpowder from the city's magazine. The powder was stored aboard the *Magdalen* at Burwell's Ferry on the James. Later it was moved to the *Fowey*, a British warship anchored at Yorktown.

Dunmore had acted on a crown directive that governors should confiscate all colonial munitions. The Williamsburg incident led to immediate threats of mob violence; and so enraged were the Virginia burgesses that the quietly conservative Richard Bland was applauded when he suggested hanging the governor. Dunmore had anticipated the resentment and armed his servants, then ordered the captains of the British ships in the York River to assemble a military force to defend the governor's palace in Williamsburg. Yorktown was to be shelled if the governor's life was endangered.

Suspicions were such that Lord Dunmore's actions led many to speculate that British reinforcements were waiting just outside the Virginia Capes and that an invasion was imminent.

On April 22 the Williamsburg militia had to be restrained by Peyton Randolph and others from assaulting the palace and capturing the governor. Randolph informed Lord Dunmore that the Williamsburg inhabitants were angered by a report that during the night a large quantity of gunpowder was carried off in the governor's wagon by a detachment of royal marines. Dunmore was reminded that the powder magazine had been erected at public expense for the protection of the colony. The governor replied that, fearing a slave insurrection in the neighboring county, he had removed the gunpowder to a more secure place and did so at night to prevent any alarm.

Dunmore had a different explanation for the British secretary of state:

> The Series of dangerous Measures pursued by the People of this Colony against the Government, which they have now entirely overturned, & particularly their having come to a Resolution of raising a Body of armed Men in all the Counties, made me think it prudent to remove some gunpowder which was in a magazine in this Place, where it lay exposed to any Attempt that might be made to seize it, & I had Reason to believe the people intended to take that Step.

He added that once the people learned the powder had been removed, they assembled, and "during their Consultation, continual Threats were brought to my House, that it was their Resolution to seize upon or massacre me, & every Person found giving me Assistance, if I refused to deliver the Powder immediately into their Custody."

Virginians were mobilizing throughout the colony, from the eastern seaboard to the Shenandoah, demanding return of the powder. Dunmore shrugged and boasted that "with a small

INEVITABLE WAR: 1775

reinforcement of troops and arms he could raise such a body of Indians, negroes, and others as would reduce the refractory people of this colony to obedience." Randolph, Bland, and other conservatives, hoping to avoid violence, urged caution and advised that further action be deferred until the Continental Congress "should adopt a plan of resistance." In May the Congress would resolve to use force, if necessary, "to defend the laws, liberties, and rights of Virginia, or any sister colony, from unjust and wicked invasion." A parody on *God Save the King*, wrote Wirt, concluded the resolution with "God save the liberties of America." This sentiment was echoed abroad by the Earl of Effingham in resigning his commission in the British Army. The Earl said that the king

> has not a subject who is more ready than I am with the utmost chearfulness to sacrifice his life and fortune in support of the safety, honour, and dignity of his Majesty's crown and person. But the very same principles...will not suffer me to be instrumental in depriving any part of his people of those liberties which form the best security for their fidelity and obedience to his government.

When Patrick Henry was informed about the battles of Lexington and Concord he linked them with the Williamsburg episode as part of a British strategy to subjugate the colonies. Determined to take military action against Lord Dunmore, Henry sent riders throughout his native Hanover County to urge volunteers to join him on May 2 at New Castle. Hundreds of volunteers showed up and (wrote Wirt) Henry told them that the moment had come when "they were called upon to decide whether they chose to live free and hand down the noble inheritance to their children, or to become hewers of wood and drawers of water to those lordlings who were themselves the tools of a corrupt and tyrannical ministry." No time was to be lost, he warned. The time to act was now, while the enemy was weak and could be easily overwhelmed by a swift attack to recover the confiscated gunpowder. The Hanover volunteers "would thus have an opportunity of striking the first blow in this colony in the great cause of American liberty." Soon, Henry's corps of volunteers was joined by companies from other counties, amassing a force believed to have been five thousand armed men for the march on Williamsburg.

Even Virginia's patriots were shocked by Henry's boldness. They would stop Henry along the route and "beg him to desist from his purpose, and discharge his men." But Henry was obsessed with his mission to strike a blow before an invading army should enslave the colony. As the march continued Randolph despatched a party from Williamsburg to the crown's receiver-general in King William County to demand three hundred and thirty pounds as compensation for the confiscated gunpowder. The receiver-general complied.

Before Henry arrived at Williamsburg for his confrontation with the royal troops, he was intercepted by Carter Braxton, a member of the Virginia Convention. Braxton was able to persuade Henry to disband his army and deliver the receiver-general's bill of exchange to Philadelphia where it could be used by Congress to purchase gunpowder to defend the colonies against future assaults. Thus, for the moment, revolution was put to rest for the price of three hundred and thirty pounds.

Patrick Henry's rashness earned him the disapproval of the colony's political elite but won him the popularity of the radicals who escorted him in triumph to his Hanover County home. There Henry learned that Governor Dunmore had denounced him and his followers as traitors for taking up arms to incite rebellion.

Dunmore did not go unnoticed by American poet Philip Freneau who wrote: *Deliver us O Lord, not only from British Dependence, but also...*

> *From the valiant Dunmore, with his crew of banditti,*
> *who plunder Virginians at Williamsburg city....*

When a group, led by Richard Henry Lee, sent a pilot boat to the West Indies for gunpowder, Lord Dunmore urged General Gates in Boston to send a warship and troops to Chesapeake Bay to restrain the rebellious Virginians. He then wrote to London, asking Lord Dartmouth, Secretary of State for the Colonies, to rush supplies to arm his band of "Indians, negroes, and others." Dunmore also sent a message to Williamsburg's mayor stating that if harm came to the British officials stationed there, he would "lay the town in ashes [and] depopulate the whole country."

Despite the efforts of Virginia's conservatives to resolve the conflict with Britain by "constitutional" means (described as "ill-judged procrastination" by Eckenrode), the renegade actions of Lord Dunmore had driven the colony to the brink of all-out war.

Elsewhere, over a three-week period from the middle of May to early June, American forces commanded by Ethan Allen and Benedict Arnold captured enemy garrisons at New York's Ticonderoga, the strategic fort on Lake Champlain; patriots in Savannah, Georgia, seized gunpowder from the royal magazine; New York patriots captured another British post ten miles north of Ticonderoga; Arnold occupied St. John's, the key to defense of Montreal, Canada; British law was declared null and void in North Carolina; citizens of South Carolina announced they were "ready to sacrifice their lives and their fortunes" for liberty; Major Generals John Burgoyne and Henry Clinton arrived in Boston to join William Howe as British reinforcements for General Gage.

And in Maryland (as in Virginia) harsh measures were enforced against loyalists—measures described by a holdover of Maryland's proprietary government as "destructive of those very rights they profess to protect, & if generally pursued will probably introduce as much violence & oppression as we can possibly apprehend from the Mother Country." To avoid prison many Maryland loyalists abandoned their estates and either sailed to England, settled in Florida or Canada, or took up arms against the patriots.

John Hancock succeeded Peyton Randolph as president of the Second Continental Congress on May 15. New delegates included Benjamin Franklin and Thomas Jefferson. Congress resolved to put the colonies in a state of defense. Appeals were made to Canada, Florida, and the British West Indies to join the American cause. Canadians were warned that if they refused to be friends of America they would be treated as enemies. They refused, and later in the year the Americans would make a futile effort to take Canada by force. Congress also heard a proposal by the Virginia delegation that the colonies unite for independence.

On June 7, as more and more Virginians prepared for war, Lord Dunmore and his family fled for safety and transferred the seat of government from the Governor's Palace in Williamsburg to the *Fowey*, which then sailed from Yorktown to Norfolk. The governor's flight initiated open hostilities between Virginia patriots and loyalists.

Jefferson, speaking for the House of Burgesses, said he hoped to "see reunited the blessings of liberty and prosperity, and the most permanent harmony with Great Britain." The House tried to make peace with Lord Dunmore, voicing concern for his and his family's safety and urging him to return to Williamsburg. Dunmore refused the offer and charged the House with usurping his executive power. In reply, the Virginia burgesses pledged "faith and true allegiance to our most gracious sovereign, George III, our only lawful and rightful king." As for Governor Dunmore, it was deemed that he had abdicated his office and dissolved the government. A new plan for governing the colony would be organized at the convention called for July 17 at Richmond.

Wirt added this anecdote: Following the session in which the House refused to placate Dunmore, Richard Henry Lee,

standing with two other burgesses, recalled these prophetic lines from *Macbeth*:
> When shall we three meet again?
> In thunder, lightning, and in rain;
> When the hurly-burly's done,
> When the battle's lost and won.

Conciliatory overtures from Lord North in London were rejected in Virginia on June 10. Resolutions written by Jefferson said that the offer simply changed "the form of oppression, without lightening its burthen." North's offer was rejected because

> the British Parliament has no right to intermeddle with the support of civil government in the Colonies...;
> to render perpetual our execution from an unjust taxation, we must saddle ourselves with a perpetual tax...subject to thedisposal of Parliament alone...;
> the Commons only resolve to forbear levying pecuniary taxes on us; still leaving unrepealed their several Acts passed for the purpose of restraining the trade and altering the form of Government of the Eastern Colonies...;
> at the very time of requiring from us grants of Money they are making disposition to invade us with large Armaments...;
> on our agreeing to contribute our proportion towards the common defence, they do not propose to lay open to us a free trade with all of the world...;
> the proposition now made to us involves the interest of all the other Colonies.

Within a few days the British Admiralty stationed ships in Chesapeake Bay to prevent colonial trade with any place other than England, Scotland, Ireland, or the West Indies. The *Otter*, a 16-gun sloop under Captain Matthew Squire, was ordered to sail the lower Chesapeake and the James and York Rivers in search of contraband. When the British ship captured two small vessels in Hampton Roads harbor, a local newspaper declared:

> How miraculous it is, that men of war can overcome, and be the terror of, oyster boats and canoes.

Maryland patriots soon found that militant loyalists (or Tories) were sometimes more menacing than the redcoats. On the Eastern Shore a group of organized loyalists attempted to overthrow or at least inhibit the provisional government's control over the region. The Maryland militia foiled a loyalist plot to kidnap Worchester County officials during the night and deliver them to Dunmore. From a base established by the British on Hog Island, Virginia, tenders and barges manned by loyalist privateers made night raids on the Shore, destroying property and seizing poultry, cattle, hogs, and grain to supply the British warships in the area. The Hog Island base was commanded by the piratical Captain John Kidd whose Tory marauders would terrorize the bay region waters throughout the Revolution.

Loyalists believed that the anti-Parliament cause embraced by the patriots would lead not only to a break with Britain but also to anarchy and economic ruin in America. Adams and Jefferson and other patriots continued to argue that their fight with Parliament was not for separation from the crown but to defend their rights.

Maryland loyalists received no encouragement from the colony's governor, Robert Eden, who was married to Lord Baltimore's sister. Eden was no Dunmore, at least not on the surface. It was said, for example, that Eden had no interest in raiding the Annapolis powder magazine—not simply because he did not want to incite a rebellion but because the gunpowder was twenty years old and useless.

The United States Army was created on June 14. George Washington was nominated "General and Commander in Chief of the forces to be raised in defence of American liberty" by Maryland's Thomas Johnson (who in 1791 would be named by Washington to the Supreme Court). John Hancock wanted to be the army chief, but fellow New Englanders said the choice of a Virginia planter would attract support of southerners yet undecided about America's course. Washington had demonstrated his unique military skills in the French and Indian War. And Washington was the only one of the delegates wearing a uniform, which he had designed himself. Still, after accepting the command, he wrote to his wife Martha:

> *You may believe... that I have used every endeavour in my power to avoid it, not only from my unwillingness to part from you and the Family, but from a consciousness of its being a trust too great for my Capacity.*

Washington felt it was "a kind of destiny" thrust upon him:

> *It was utterly out of my power to refuse this appointment, without exposing my character to such censures, as would have reflected dishonour upon myself, and given pain to my friends.*

Washington took control of the Army at Boston on July 3, and directed the siege against the occupying British troops until they were forced to withdraw to the sea. His Virginia replacement in the Second Continental Congress was George Wythe, who would move that all British vessels be liable to capture anywhere on the high seas.

There would be more to Washington's command than the struggle against better equipped, better trained British forces; there would be a continuing fight with Congress over money, men, and materiel, and bitter battles with his own generals. Even at the outset of his command there was a conspiracy to deny Washington leadership of the Army. The instigator of the plot was a former British officer who had defected to the Americans. Nevertheless, Washington chose that officer, Horatio Gates, to command the American force in Canada.

Congress issued two million dollars in bills of credit to support the army, with all colonies but Georgia pledged to share the burden of redemption in proportion to population. Congress also resolved to raise ten companies of riflemen; the first marksmen to be enlisted into service were from the frontiers of Maryland, Virginia, and Pennsylvania, with orders to join the troops surrounding Boston. A typical recruiting poster appealed to "all brave, healthy, able bodied, and well disposed young men" with the promise of sixty dollars a month plus the prospect of returning as decorated heroes with pockets full of money. As in all wars, the allure would belie the actuality.

Frederick County, Maryland, supplied two companies of riflemen to Washington's army during the siege of Boston. These independent and undisciplined companies of backwoods marksmen marched more than five hundred miles to Boston under the command of Captain Thomas Price and Captain Michael Cresap.

The highest ranking officer to serve in the Continental Army from Maryland was Major General William Smallwood, a veteran of the French and Indian War. During the conflict, he would command the highly regarded Maryland Line, which won commendations in virtually every encounter with British troops.

As did various Virginia regiments; notably companies led by Daniel Boone descendant Daniel Morgan of Fauquier County–except at Boston where Captain Morgan's unruly riflemen, though welcomed by Washington with open arms, would become a Virginia embarrassment described as "damn'd riff-raff–dirty, mutinous and disaffected."

Early in the New York campaign, George Weedon, an ex-tavernkeeper from Westmoreland County and relative by marriage to James Monroe, would command the 3rd Virginia Regiment which he praised as "Noble, Orderly, and Brave." Later Washington formed the 3rd and 1st Virginia Regiments into a brigade under General Weedon.

Virginia's Elizabeth City County, located on the Chesapeake, was acknowledged to be one of the few American counties to supply men for the Continental Army from the war's outset until the Yorktown surrender in October 1781.

On June 17, a band of Massachusetts farmers, armed with muskets, were routed at Breed's Hill, a ridge adjoining Bunker Hill, but the victorious British suffered more than a thousand casualties. As the redcoats took refuge on Bunker Hill, within view of their warships, news of the battle brought thousands of patriots to Boston, where (said one account) they ringed the city with "campfires that would soon become siege lines."

Stunned by the news, the Continental Congress adopted the "Olive Branch Petition" on July 5, professing America's attachment to the king and a desire for reconciliation with Great Britain "in a manner not inconsistent with her dignity and welfare."

But hostilities continued on Chesapeake Bay. Dunmore was now reinforced by British troops sent from St. Augustine, Florida, with a promise that more would arrive by August. HMS *Mercury* appeared in Norfolk waters as relief for Dunmore's flagship, *Fowey*. Radicals in Congress won support for their proposal to create an expedition to drive Dunmore from the Chesapeake.

- 4 -

Military Buildup

1775

Threats of war were no longer rumors or propaganda. Dunmore proved the threats were real. Hostilities spread from Boston harbor to the Chesapeake. The Continental Congress decided to act. A year before the Declaration of Independence was adopted, the delegates agreed to "A Declaration of the Causes and Necessity of Taking Up Arms."

Jefferson's draft for building up America's defense was considered too caustic and had to be modified by William Livingston of New Jersey. But the revision did retain Jefferson's closing paragraphs because of their clarity in stating the colonial position:

> Lest this declaration should disquiet the minds of our friends and fellow-subjects in any part of the empire, we assure them that we mean not to dissolve that union which has so long and so happily subsisted between us, and which we sincerely wish to see restored. —Necessity has not yet driven us into that desperate measure, or induced us to excite any other nation to war against them. —We have not raised armies with ambitious designs of separating from Great Britain, and establishing independent states. We fight not for glory or for conquest. We exhibit to mankind the remarkable spectacle of a people attacked by unprovoked enemies, without any imputation or even suspicion of offence. They boast

of their privileges and civilization, and yet proffer no milder conditions than servitude or death.

In our native land, in defense of the freedom that is our birthright, and which we ever enjoyed till the late violation of it—for the protection of our property, acquired solely by the honest industry of our forfathers and ourselves, against violence actually offered, we have taken up arms. We shall lay them down when hostilities shall cease on the part of the aggressors, and all danger of their being renewed shall be removed, and not before.

With an humble confidence in the mercies of the supreme and impartial Judge and Ruler of the Universe, we most devoutly implore his divine goodness to protect us happily through this great conflict, to dispose our adversaries to reconciliation on reasonable terms, and thereby to relieve the empire from the calamities of civil war.

The Continental Congress appropriated two million dollars in bills of credit for America's defense. The expenses were apportioned to the colonies according to population. Virginia, having the largest population (400,000), had the largest share of the estimated expense: $330,852. Maryland (with a 250,000 population) was billed $206,783.

On July 17 the Virginia Convention in Richmond established a centralized Committee of Safety, with broad executive powers. Its members, all men of means and position, consisted of the following conservatives: Edmund Pendleton (chairman), Richard Bland, Carter Braxton, John Page, Paul Carrington, Dudley Digges, and John Tabb; and the following progressives: George Mason, James Mercer, Thomas Ludwell Lee, and William Cabell. This committee was responsible for Virginia's defense.

One week later the Committee resolved to raise a military force, dividing the colony into sixteen military districts, each to create a battalion of at least five hundred men. Once recruited, the troops were to assemble in Williamsburg. Theirs was to be a defensive mission, wrote Wirt, prepared to "resist any attempt on the liberties" of the colony, while still professing fidelity to the king. Dunmore, however, considered the colony to be in "a state of open and general rebellion." Patrick Henry was named the ranking officer of Virginia forces, with Colonel William Woodford second in command. The need for independent companies was soon to be evident in Hampton Roads where Dunmore would attack the town of Hampton on one side of the harbor and Norfolk on the other.

In the same month the Maryland Convention adopted Articles of Association to form a new provincial government. Then, following a recommendation by the Continental Congress that all able-bodied men enlist in military service, the convention required all free males and indentured servants to join a county militia. Refusal to do so would brand the Marylanders as Tories. Response, nevertheless, was low and the early militia groups were badly organized and undisciplined. To correct the problem, sixteen delegates were appointed to Maryland's Council of Safety with authority to direct and regulate activities of all militiamen, who were to be enrolled and drilled in companies and batteries. Field officers were to be appointed by the council.

On July 26 the Maryland Convention met in Annapolis for the fifth time, still hoping for a reconciliation with Great Britain "on constitutional principals." It resolved that the colony's new government would continue representation of qualified voters and place executive and judicial power in a sixteen-member Council of Safety. The Convention endorsed the Association of the Freemen of Maryland, which had pledged military and financial aid to support forty-five militia companies against British military forces in the colony. The Freemen declared: "We therefore, inhabitants of the province of Maryland, firmly persuaded that it is necessary and justifiable to repel force by force, do approve of the opposition by arms to the British troops." Copies of the document were circulated and those Marylanders who refused to sign it were looked down upon as enemies of the Revolution.

The U.S. was born in a denial of dissent; the bay country no exception. "Slowly, but surely, the Revolution slipped from the hands of the gentry," wrote David C. Skaggs. "They still controlled a majority of the [Maryland] Convention's delegates," but as voting requirements relaxed with the demise of proprietary government, "some of the more radical leaders entered the Convention." Thereafter, Marylanders suspected of pro-British leanings were arrested, fined, imprisoned, or banished from the colony, although most opponents of the Revolution considered themselves as much an American as those who called themselves patriots. Many who hoped to remain neutral finally declared themselves as loyalists, especially on the Eastern Shore where proximity to Dunmore's base offered a refuge.

In August, before adjourning, the Second Continental Congress turned down Virginia's proposal for independence but asserted that Americans were ready to die rather than be enslaved. The Congress followed Virginia's lead in rejecting Lord North's proposal for reconciliation.

Though less dramatic than the destruction of the *Peggy Stewart* a year earlier, the *Totness* and its cargo were burned by a band of Maryland patriots when the vessel ran aground below Annapolis.

That same month Dunmore commandeered several Virginia vessels in Hampton Roads harbor and set up a temporary headquarters aboard the merchantman *William*. Dunmore soon assembled a flotilla of small craft, supported by the frigates, *Mercury* and *Mars*. At the time, the only military force which Dunmore directly controlled was the crew and marines aboard the *William* and the two frigates, but he would be reinforced by three hundred British regulars plus a few untrained Virginia loyalists (a number of people in Norfolk had refused to swear allegiance to America). In the meantime Dunmore set up a new base at Gosport where Andrew Sproule, a British naval agent and wealthy Scottish merchant, owned a shipyard. Gosport, situated on the southern branch of Elizabeth River in Norfolk County and separated from the town of Portsmouth by a small creek, is the site of the vast complex which has become the Norfolk Naval Shipyard. From there Dunmore accelerated his raids on the lower Chesapeake and the river banks, seizing supplies and confiscating slaves. Most of those raids were executed by Captain Squire aboard the *Otter*.

In Norfolk this dispatch appeared in the August 16 issue of John Holt's *Virginia Gazette*:

> Last week several slaves, the property of gentlemen in this town and neighborhood, were discharged from on board the Otter, where... many of them for weeks past have been concealed, and their owners in some instances ill-treated for making application for them. The public, it is generally thought, is indebted for this discharge to a higher power than any on board that vessel.

Holt, a bold and often eloquent defender of freedom of the press, was a nephew of the celebrated editor of the *New York Journal*.

Because the conservatives dominated Virginia's Committee of Safety, military action against the Dunmore raids would be delayed until the committee was forced to respond to Dunmore's proclamation to free the slaves.

Yet Virginians continued to ready for war, as indicated in this letter printed abroad in the *Morning Chronicle and London Advertiser* on August 21:

> It would really surprise you to see the preparations making for our defence, all persons arming themselves, and independent companies, from 100 to 150 in every county of Virginia, well equipped and daily endeavouring to instruct themselves in the art of

war...and I can positively affirm that in a few days an army of at least 7 or 8 thousand well-disciplined men might be got together (well armed) for the protection of this country; and, from the best information I can get, the Northern Colonies have forces far superior to this country, so that you may depend there will be many more bloody battles before the Americans will give up their liberties.... When you traded here you well knew it to be the ambition of the people of this country to endeavour who should be best dressed with the British manufactures, but they are now quite on the contrary extreme, for their glory now is to dress in their own manufacture ...the example is daily followed by all ranks of people here: you may see from this how scandalous our [Governor Dunmore] has been in informing the ministry that we could not subsist more than one or two years without the assistance of the British manufactory.... Instead of our fields being planted with tobacco, as usual, they are now flourishing with cotton and flax, and our pastures well stored with sheep; so I think there will not be the least danger of our suffering for want of clothes.

On August 23, the same day that an American peace proposal was to be presented to George III, the king issued his Proclamation of Rebellion which read in part:

Whereas many of our subjects in divers parts of our Colonies and Plantations in North America, misled by dangerous and ill designing men, and forgetting the allegiance which they owe to the power that has protected and supported them; after various and dissorderly acts committed in disturbance of the publick peace, to the obstruction of lawful commerce, and to the oppression of our loyal subjects carrying on the same; have at length proceeded to open and avowed rebellion, by arraying themselves in a hostile manner, to withstand the execution of the law, and traitorously preparing, ordering and levying war against us: And whereas, there is reason to apprehend that such rebellion hath been much promoted and encouraged by the traitorous correspondence, counsels and comfort of divers wicked and desperate persons within this realm: To the end therefore, that none of our subjects may neglect or violate their duty through ignorance thereof, as though any doubt of the protection which the law will afford to their loyalty and zeal, we have thought fit, by and with advice of our Privy Council, to issue our Royal Proclamation, hereby declaring, that not only all our Officers, civil and military, are obliged to exert their utmost endeavours to suppress such rebellion and to bring the traitors to justice, but that all our subjects of this Realm, and the dominions thereunto belonging, are bound by law to be aiding and assisting in the suppression of such rebellion, and to disclose and make known all traitorous conspiracies and attempts against us, our crown and dignity....

In Philadelphia the Continental Congress's response to the Royal Proclamation was to disclaim any intent of denying the king's sovereignty while disavowing allegiance to Parliament.

Elsewhere, in recent months, Maine patriots seized the British cutter, *Margaretta*, and killed the captain; Georgia sent out the first patriot vessel commissioned for naval warfare; New York patriots seized royal stores on Manhattan Island; patriots raided Nantasket Point in Boston harbor; the British sloop *Falcon* chased an American schooner into Gloucester, Massachusetts, harbor, but next day patriots drove the ship away after wounding thirty-five British crewmen and confiscating twenty-six; patriot ships raided Bermuda, capturing forts and carrying away all the gunpowder in the

British magazines; British Navy bombarded Stonington, Connecticut; British hired thousands of German mercenaries to fight Americans.

Hurricane winds on Chesapeake Bay on the night of September 2 drove a number of vessels ashore, including the *Otter's* tender commanded by Captain Squire while cruising the lower bay region in search of plunder. The British tender was wrecked and abandoned on Back River near Hampton. Squire and his crew, fearing capture by Virginians incensed by the raids, sought refuge in the woods and for two days wandered around lost. The captain was able to escape, but some of the men were captured and the tender was confiscated.

Harsh terms used by John Holt in describing the incident in Norfolk's *Virginia Gazette* drew this response from Squire:

> Sir,
> You have in many papers lately taken the freedom to mention my name, and thereto added many falsities. I now declare, if I am ever again mentioned therein with any reflections on my character, I will most assuredly seize your person and take you on board the Otter.

When Holt printed the letter, he noted that "it needs no comment." Nevertheless, he added:

> The Printer cannot forbear as to say that he has always endeavoured to keep an open and liberal press, as free for Captain Squire as for anyone else. If there have been any mistakes, they have been the result of the popular voice, and although it would always have given the Printer pleasure to be in any degree instrumental to the strictest harmony between his Majesty's subjects in this colony and the gentlemen of the navy, yet he does not conceive that his press is to be under the direction of anyone but himself, and while he has the sanction of the

law, he shall always pride himself in the reflections that the liberty of the press is one of the grand bulwarks of the English constitution.

On September 10 Captain Squire sent this letter from the *Otter* to the Hampton Town Committee:

Gentlemen,
> Whereas a sloop tender, manned and armed on his majesty's service, was on Saturday the 2d instant, in a violent gale of wind, cast ashore in Back river, Elizabeth county, having on board the under mentioned king's stores, which the inhabitants of Hampton thought proper to seize; I am therefore to desire that the king's sloop, with all the stores belonging to her, be immediately returned, or the people of Hampton, who committed the outrage, must be answerable for the consequence.

The captured stores included swivels, musquets, cutlasses, powder horns, swivel shot, fishing net, rope, anchor, cables, lead, and an iron stove.

On the same day Thomas Roberts, a Norfolk merchant, wrote to his good friend St. George Tucker in Bermuda:

> Every thing is in Grate Confusion & a Much Heavyer Cloud seemes to hang over us then when you was here. The Man of War Tender got Burnt the other Day at Hampton, & they seem to Threaten Very Much...God knows how Long the Town will Stand. For my part I could wish my Self with You...Almost Every Body is moov'd their things out of Town.

In the recent storm Roberts had lost a ship, seven crew members, and cargo valued at one thousand pounds sterling, but "had the Good Luck to Save one of our Vessells in 13 fathoms Water, with upward of 100 hhds of Rum & Sugar."

About one hundred Virginia volunteers, under Major James Innes, were prepared to repel the threatened invasion by

Captain Squire. But for the present Squire focused on Hampton Roads harbor where, wrote Wirt, "he seized the passage boats, with the negroes in them, by way of reprisal, as he alleged, for the stores, etc., taken out of his tender when driven ashore in the late storm."

In Williamsburg Alexander Purdie's *Virginia Gazette* (one of four newspapers by that name) made the playful observation

> that the renowned Captain Squire, of his majesty's sloop Otter, is gone up the bay for Baltimore in Maryland; on his old trade, it is to be presumed, of negro-catching, pillaging the farms and plantations of their stock and poultry, and other illustrious actions, highly becoming a Squire in the king's navy. Some say, his errand was to watch for a quantity of gunpowder intended for this colony; but that valuable is now safely landed where he dare not come to smell it.

A letter addressed to Captain Squire on September 16 from the Committee of Elizabeth City County and the Town of Hampton called his charge "injurious and untrue." Squire was told that the tender had not been "in his majesty's service" but was "on a pillaging or pleasuring party." The letter went on to say that

> although it gives us pain to use indelicate expressions, yet the treatment received from you calls for a state of facts in the simple language of truth, however harsh it may sound. To your own heart we appeal for the candour with which we have stated them; to that heart which drove you into the woods in the most tempestuous weather, in one of the darkest nights, to avoid the much injured and innocent inhabitants of this county, who had never threatened or ill used you, and who would, at that time, have received you, we are assured, with humanity and civility, had you made

yourself and situation known to them. Neither the vessel or stores was seized by the inhabitants of Hampton; the gunner, one mr. Gray, and the pilot, one mr. Ruth, who were employed by you on this party, are men, we hope, who will still assert the truth. From them divers of our members were informed, that the vessel and stores, together with a good seine (which you, without cause, so hastily deserted) were given up as to one Finn, near whose house you were drove on shore, as a reward, for his entertaining you, &c. with respect and decency.

The Committee offered to deliver to Squire "every article left on our shore" upon his compliance with the following demands:

First. We, on behalf of this community, require from you the restitution of a certain Joseph Harris, the property of a gentleman of our town, and all other our slaves whom you may have on board; which said Harris, as well as other slaves, hath been long harboured, and often employed, with your knowledge (as appeared to us by the confession of Ruth and others, and as is well known to all your men) in pillaging us, under cover of night, our sheep and other live-stock.

Secondly. We require that you will send on shore all boats with their hands, and every other thing you have detained on this occasion.

And Lastly. That you shall not, by your own arbitrary authority, undertake to insult, molest, interrupt, or detain the persons or property of any one passing to and from this town, as you have frequently done for some time past.

Next, the Committee extended the town's "most hearty thanks to Major James Innes, the other gentlemen officers, and to the several volunteer companies now under their command, for so expeditiously and cheerfully marching to our assistance and defence on the alarm occasioned by the threats and several insolent letters of a certain Matthew Squire, commander of his majesty's ship the Otter."

Squire's heart did not respond well to the candor expressed by the Committee of Elizabeth City County and the Town of Hampton, according to this report in Holt's *Virginia Gazette* dated Norfolk, September 20:

> We are informed from good authority that a system of justice similar to that adopted against the devoted town of Boston, is likely to be established in this colony, by the renowned [Captain Squire]. He has, in the course of this week, as a reprisal for the loss of his tender, seized every vessel belonging to Hampton that came within his reach, and thereby rendered himself the terror of all the small craft and fishing boats in [Hampton] river; especially the latter, having brought some of them under his stern, by a discharge of his cannon at them. He has likewise seized a vessel belonging to the Eastern shore, and having honoured the passengers so far with his notice, as to receive them on board his own vessel, took the liberty of sending one of their horses as a present to Lord Dunmore. This act of GENEROSITY we doubt not, will gain him considerable interest with his Lordship, it being an instance of his industry in distressing a people who have of late become so obnoxious to his Excellency for their spirited behaviour. We hope that those who have lived under and enjoyed the blessings of the British constitution, will not continue tame spectators of such flagrant violations of its most salutary laws in defence of private property. The crimes daily committed by this plunderer we would not willingly brand with the odious name of piracy, but we are confident they come under those offences

to which the English laws have denied the benefit of clergy.
We are just informed that he sent, some days ago, a message to the inhabitants of Hampton, with a proposal that if they would return the stores, &c. taken on board the tender, he would molest them no longer, but retire peaceably to his old station. This proposition being taken under consideration by the principal inhabitants, an answer was returned promising a compliance with the Captain's request, provided he would deliver up a negro slave belonging to Mr. Henry King, who has long acted as a pilot to the Otter; but this the honest Captain, as well on account of the fellow's knowledge of the rivers as his singular ATTACHMENT and LOYALTY to his sovereign, refused, and, after damaging the IMPUDENCE of these people in demanding his Ethiopian director, swore he would make them no other reply than what his cannon could give them; Accordingly he has taken his station between the two bars to be more convenient for the business.

In Williamsburg Purdie's edition of the *Virginia Gazette* reported "that Lord Dunmore is called home, with what view we have not yet learned, but probably it is to render an account of his sagacious and *spirited* conduct in Virginia; which can hardly fail to attract the *admiration* of Lord North [the prime minister]...His lordship has this satisfaction upon his departure, that he will leave the colony with the *universal consent* of the inhabitants, of all ranks and denomination."

In Norfolk's *Virginia Gazette* Holt enraged both Squire and Lord Dunmore in his September 27 editorial, which called Squire "a stealer of sheep and hogs" and referred to an occasion in 1746 when Dunmore's father was found guilty of treason and sent to prison for life. Dunmore's response was not surprising.

Within a week the renegade governor of Virginia ordered the marines, sailors, and grenadiers stationed aboard the *Otter* to destroy the print shop where Holt published his *Virginia Gazette*. Dunmore then informed British authorities: "The public prints of this dirty little Borough of Norfolk has for some time past been wholly employed in exciting, in the minds of all Ranks of People, the spirit of sedition and Rebellion." As reported by Williamsburg's *Virginia Gazette*, between two and three o'clock in the afternoon, about thirteen soldiers and sailors landed at the Norfolk wharf "under cover of the men of war (who made every appearance of firing on the town, should the party be molested)." They then marched up the main street to Holt's shop where

> without the smallest opposition or resistance (although there were some hundred spectators), they deliberately carried off the types and sundry other printing implements with two of the workmen, and after getting to the water side with their booty gave three huzzas, in which they were joined by a crowd of negroes. A few spirited men in Norfolk, justly incensed at so flagrant a breach of good order and the constitution, and highly resenting the conduct of Lord Dunmore and the navy gentry (who have now commenced to be down-right pirates and banditti) order the drum to beat the arms, but were joined by few or none; so that it appears Norfolk is at present a very insecure place for the life or property of any individual, and is consequently deserted daily by numbers of inhabitants with their effects.

The news account continued:

> We hear that Lord Dunmore is exceedingly offended with the Virginia printers for presuming to furnish the publick with a faithful relation of occurrences, and now and then making a few strictures upon his lordship's own conduct...It seems

his lordship has it much at heart to destroy every channel of publick intelligence that is inimical to his designs upon the liberties of this country, alleging that they have poisoned the minds of the people, or, in other words, laid open to them the tyrannical designs of a weak and wicked ministry, which have been supported, in character, by most of their slavish dependents.

The *Gazette* concluded that "so diabolical a scheme...never could have been devised but by a person of the most unfriendly principles to the liberties of mankind."

Dunmore seized the Norfolk press but failed to silence Holt, who escaped to Williamsburg where he used Purdie's *Virginia Gazette* to ridicule his lordship:

> Mr. Holt presents his compliments to lord Dunmore, and begs leave to inform him that he has, as a partial retaliation for the loss he has sustained by his lordship's seizure of his types, and other effects, taken possession of several of his lordship's horses....

Richard Henry Lee, now a Virginia delegate to the Continental Congress, failed to see the humor in Dunmore's behavior:

> Lord Dunmore's unparalleled conduct in Virginia has, a few Scotch excepted, united every man in that Colony. If [the king's ministers] had searched thro the world for a person the best fitted to ruin their cause, and procure union and success for these Colonies, they could not have found a more complete Agent than Lord Dunmore.

Virginia patriots were intolerant of anyone not totally devoted to the cause. In Norfolk, where a British naval officer described the inhabitants as "earnestly desirous of living in harmony with his majesty's servants," a man was beaten, stripped, and nearly tarred and feathered after the local safety committee denounced him as "an enemy to American liberty." In October Norfolk's large loyalist population (notably the Scottish mercantile community), having lost hope that the Assembly in Williamsburg would protect their interests, asked Lord Dunmore (a Scot) to take control of the city. The patriots quickly mustered several hundred militia from Norfolk and Princess Anne counties, but they were easily dispersed by a Dunmore army that had grown in strength with more help on the way. On October 5 John Hancock told Washington that Rear Admiral Molyneaux Shuldham of the Royal Navy was ready to support Lord Dunmore "with a number of Frigates, Cutters &c. which are to be employed in obstructing all communication by water inland between the Carolinas, Virginia, Maryland, Pennsylvania & the northern colonies." The expedition was ordered to burn Chesapeake towns "and spread devastation over the plantations bordering on the navigable rivers" to prevent Virginia and Maryland from providing assistance to New York or Massachusetts.

Now that the communities near the mouth of the Chesapeake were in jeopardy, minutemen from King and Queen County under Captain George Lyne were sent to Hampton on October 7 by the Virginia Committee of Safety. A few days later a militia company commanded by Captain George Nicholas also joined the Hampton defenders who now numbered more than five hundred men, including the local riflemen.

Wrote Mapp: "Obviously more in earnest about defense than Norfolk, on the other side of Hampton Roads, the Hamptonians had sunk several vessels in the channel of the Hampton River to impede a British advance."

Dunmore's assaults on lower Chesapeake intensified. Fear led to flight. George Mason wrote to Washington: "Many of the principal Families are removing from Norfolk, Hampton, York & Williamsburg, occasioned by the Behaviour of Lord

Dunmore & the commanders of the King's Ships & Tenders upon this Station."

From October 12 to October 14 Dunmore's army, under Captain Samuel Leslie, conducted a series of raids, capturing or destroying seventy pieces of ordnance in Norfolk County, and harassing other towns on the lower Chesapeake. A militant response had to be taken.

At Williamsburg, on October 24, the Virginia Committee of Safety ordered Colonel William Woodford and his troops to march to the Norfolk area. The following is an extract from the colonel's instructions:

> You are to use your best endeavours for protecting and defending the persons and properties of all friends to the cause of America, and to this end, to attack, kill, or capture all such as you shall discover to be in arms for the annoying of those persons, as far as you shall judge it prudent to engage them.

Woodford's force consisted of his own militia troops plus five companies of minutemen from Culpeper County wearing green hunting shirts bearing the motto "Liberty or Death." Among his troops was twenty-year-old John Marshall, and the future Chief Justice's father, Major Thomas Marshall. Woodford would pick up two more companies of minutemen at Smithfield, on the James, and at Kemp's Landing, just south of Norfolk.

At the time a British marine aboard the *Otter* wrote to a friend in England: "I cannot forbear laughing at the false opinion you have of the courage of the Americans, mere poltroons, I assure you...a set of wretches who will take every opportunity of attacking you by surprise, but if you make a show of openly attacking *them*, depend on it, they will always make good those verses of [Samuel Butler's] Hudibras: '...they that fight and run away will live to fight another day.'" His words would return to haunt him.

While Woodford was en route to Norfolk, Dunmore sent Captain Squire with an armed schooner, a sloop, and three tenders, with troops on board, to Hampton. Squire sent a message ashore informing the Hamptonians "that he would that day capture and burn the town." Those were the words that introduced the war to the Chesapeake.

On the first day militia riflemen drove off a British landing party and, with the addition of another rifle company, repelled the second day's attack. The British suffered casualties and loss of a tender. Wilson Miles Cary, Hampton's militia colonel and formerly a naval officer for British customs, was described by Dunmore as "one of the most active and virulent of the Enemies of Government." Cary said he belonged "to the Country and not to the Crown."

During a fiery exchange with Squire's tenders on October 25 a company of Virginia regulars was joined by Captain Lyne's minutemen in Hampton's defense at a point of land near the sunken vessels. On the scene was John Page who wrote:

> Cannon Balls, Grape Shot and Musket Balls whistled over the Heads of our Men, Whilst our Muskets and Rifles poured Showers of Balls in their Vessels and they were so well directed that the Men on Board the Schooner in which Capt. Squire himself commanded were unable to stand to their 4 Pounders which were not sheltered by a Netting, and gave but one Round of them but kept up an incessant firing of smaller Guns and Swivels, as did 2 Sloops and 3 Boats for more of an Hour and 1/4, when they slipt their Cables and towed out except the Hawk Tender a Pilot Boat they had taken some Time before from a Man of Hampton.

In late afternoon British marines from the tenders went ashore and burned one of the farmhouses on a plantation near the mouth of Hampton River. On hearing the news, Colonel Woodford redirected his troops from Norfolk to Hampton.

Woodford arrived at Hampton between seven and eight o'clock in the morning of October 26. By nine the British had broken through the barricade of sunken vessels in Hampton River and begun firing on the town. Woodford's riflemen and the local militia returned the enemy fire from windows and from behind hastily constructed breast-works. Some defenders, under command of Hampton's Captain Samuel Barron and Colonel John Nicholas, stood unprotected on the wharf and fired on the British vessels. As the press reported, "brave young officers, at the head of their men, without the least cover or breast-work, on the open shore, stood a discharge of 4 pounders, and other cannon, from a large schooner commanded by captain Squire himself, and from a sloop and two tenders, which played on them with all their guns, swivels, and muskets. They stood cooly till the vessels were near enough for them to do execution, when they began a brisk and well directed fire, which forced the little squadron to retire." Other militiamen were ordered to pull back to intercept British marines who might land on the banks of Back River and attack Hampton from the rear.

Because British cannoncers aboard the *Otter* were constantly seeking shelter from the steady barrage of musket and rifle fire from the Hampton defenders, Squire's ship managed to fire only one round from its cannons. When it appeared the attack was futile, the British captain ordered his ships to withdraw. All escaped except the pilot boat *Hawke*. The Virginians captured a gunner and seven seamen, along with one white woman and two black males, one of whom "was shot by a Rifle Man across the Creek at 400 yds. distance." The boat's commander jumped over the side and swam away.

Hampton suffered no casualties and only minor property damage, although British guns did make a direct hit on St. John's Church, America's oldest continuous Episcopal parish (still possessing its 1618 communion silver). The Virginians, despite the scorn expressed by the young marine on the *Otter*, had stood their ground, and it was the British cannons which had retreated in the face of Virginia rifle fire. Some of the defenders despatched the following message:

> The rifle-men and soldiers of Hampton desire their compliments to captain Squire and his squadron, and wish to know how they approve the reception they met with last Friday.

The editor of Williamsburg's *Virginia Gazette* wrote: "Lord Dunmore may now see he has not cowards to deal with." He described the battle as action "becoming freemen and Americans, and must evince that Americans will die, or be free." The editor noted that Hampton could expect Squire's raiders to make another visit soon, adding: "If they should, we hope our brave troops are prepared for them; and we can with pleasure assure the public, that every part of them ...are wishing for another skirmish."

A local historian declared that "America's Revolution began in Virginia in the proud port town of Hampton." The claim might find disagreement in the proud port town of Boston, but the attack on Hampton did prove that America's "newly raised troops with little training could defeat the greatest military power in the world."

Thomas Jefferson, in Philadelphia, wrote that Lord Dunmore's attempt to burn Hampton had stirred the local people "into perfect phrensy." It sparked a bitter attack on the king in a letter to his cousin in England, John Randolph, in which Jefferson declared that "we must drub you soundly before the sceptered tyrant will know we are not mere brutes, to crouch under his hand and kiss the rod with which he deigns to scourge us."

George III, in an October speech before Parliament, sharpened his opposition to American actions:

> The object is too important, the spirit of the British nation too high, the resources with which God hath

blessed her too numerous, to give up so many colonies which she has planted with great industry, nursed with great tenderness, encouraged with many commercial advantages, and protected and defended at much expence of blood and treasure.

During debate in the House of Commons, Lord Wedderburn summed up the general view of Parliament:

> Sir, we have been too long deaf; we have too long shown our forbearance and long-suffering; faction must now be curbed, must be subdued and crushed; our thunders must go forth; America must be conquered.

Again Jefferson expressed his rage to his English cousin John Randolph: "Believe me Dear Sir there is not in the British empire a man who more cordially loves a Union with Gr. Britain than I do. But by the god that made me I will cease to exist before I yield to a connection on such terms as the British parliament propose and in this I think I speak the Sentiments of America."

Theodorick Bland (who could trace his American heritage back to Pocahontas) announced that Virginians "are, to a man, determined that the day which deprives them of their liberties, shall also deprive them of their existence."

The thought of building a fleet to take on the British Navy was "the maddest idea in the world," said Samuel Chase, a Maryland delegate to the Continental Congress. But it was the influence of Virginia delegate George Wythe's classical background that helped shape Washington's thesis: that "no maritime power near the sea-coast can be safe without it. Had not Rome built a fleet for the Carthaginian war? Why should we not take counsel from the example?" Washington had already commissioned the schooners *Hannah* and *Lee* to intercept British vessels for munitions needed at the Boston siege.

The Continental Navy, authorized by Congress on October 13, was to be created by the Naval Committee whose members were Stephen Hopkins, Rhode Island; Joseph Hewes, North Carolina; Richard Henry Lee, Virginia; and John Adams, Massachusetts. Their mission was to build a navy for "protection and defense of the United Colonies." For months British naval vessels had been harassing the shipping in Chesapeake Bay, New York Harbor, and Narragansett Bay.

Esek Hopkins, brother of Stephen Hopkins, was appointed the naval commander-in-chief. Jack Coggins wrote that the main recommendation for the 57-year old Hopkins "was that he had commanded a privateer in the French and Indian War."

In November Congress appropriated a fund of $500,000 to build thirteen frigates. To handle immediate needs Congress had already approved the transformation of merchant vessels into warships at Philadelphia, including conversion of the ex-London packet *Black Prince* into the *Alfred*, which would serve as flagship for Commodore Esek Hopkins. Other conversions: two 14-gun brigs, *Andrew Doria* and *Cabot*; two sloops, the 12-gun *Providence* and 10-gun *Hornet*; and two 8-gun schooners, the *Wasp* and *Fly*. Those first ships were manned by crews assembled by press gangs; the infant naval service held no attraction for volunteers. Enlistment was encouraged by offering crews a bounty that amounted to half the value of all the warships and a third of all the merchant vessels captured. Thus America's Navy was born in the same spirit of privateering which had enabled Elizabeth I to create the fleet of the British empire.

Incidentally, Britain and its loyalist allies would capture or destroy all the converted vessels within two years and all thirteen frigates by 1780.

In the selection of officers and crew, a preference was shown for Chesapeake Bay watermen. Of the twenty-four captains initially commissioned by Congress, James Nicholson of Kent County, Maryland, was designated the ranking officer. Nicholson had been educated in England and served in the

Royal Navy during the French and Indian War. When the Revolutionary War started he served briefly in the Maryland Navy and supervised the construction of the brig *Defence*, built by George Nells of Baltimore. He took command of the vessel in early 1776. After being commissioned in the Continental Navy, Nicholson lost the frigates *Virginia* and *Trumbull* and later saw Chesapeake action with the Maryland galleys.

Maryland's Joshua Barney, who would command the *Wasp*, earned his greatest victories against the British as a privateer.

None perhaps were so intrepid as Maryland's Thomas Boyle, the captain of the 16-gun brig *Chasseur* who made a foolhardy attempt to blockade the entire British Isles and succeeded in capturing prizes valued at a million dollars.

Actually, Britain had little to fear from America's newly created fleet. By 1776 America would have but twenty-seven poorly equipped vessels to go against 270 heavily armed warships in a Royal Navy which had long enjoyed supremacy of the seas. And it would get no better. By the end of the war the British fleet would have nearly five hundred ships compared to twenty in the United States Navy.

Far more devastating to British shipping were the American privateers, whose raids were authorized by Congress to intercept ships carrying supplies to British forces. Within two years these independent seamen would take five hundred merchant vessels. By 1781 they would seize or destroy nearly two thousand ships, capture more than twelve thousand sailors and prizes valued at eighteen million dollars, forcing British merchants to call for an end to the war.

Unfortunately, the privateers which inflicted so much damage on British shipping also helped wreck America's fleet by depriving the Continental Navy of manpower and materials. Nearly two thousand American privateers would be commissioned during the war, carrying crews totaling at least eleven thousand men (with multiple enlistments estimated as high as sixty thousand).

Privateering impact was described by Milo M. Quaife:

> No sailors in the world excelled American seamen of the Revolutionary War period. Sailing under a great variety of flags, [they] brought terror and destruction to Britain's far-flung ocean trade, and presently it became a matter of concern to neutral European governments how to identify the country to which [these vessels] claimed allegiance.

The American flag to receive the first salute was made by Margaret Manny, Philadelphia milliner. It had thirteen red and white stripes and was first flown aboard the flagship *Alfred*. The flag's stripes, representing the union of the thirteen colonies, also displayed the crosses of St. Andrew and St. George retained from Britain's Union Jack, suggesting that the American colonies were hesitant about separating from the British crown. Another version, as reported by Jack Coggins, has it that the flag bore a rattlesnake and was hoisted by John Paul Jones who questioned "why such a venomous serpent should be the combatant emblem of a brave and honest folk, fighting to be free."

Lambert Wickes of Kent County, Maryland, was the first of America's naval commanders to capture enemy vessels in British waters. He would transport Franklin to France aboard the *Reprisal*, and in 1777 would go down with his ship on the Newfoundland Banks.

On November 10, about a month after the Navy was created, the Marine Corps was established and placed under Washington's command.

The anticipated destruction of Norfolk was discussed by Page in a letter to Jefferson:

> The People at Norfolk are under dreadful Apprehensions of having their Town burnt....They know they deserve it, but we seem to be at a Loss

what to do...Many of [the loyalists] deserve to be ruined and hanged but others again have acted dastardly for Want of Protection. But at all Events rather than the Town should be garrisoned by our Enemies and a Trade opened for all the Scoundrels in the County, we must be prepared to destroy it.

Conditions in Norfolk were described by James Gilchrist in a letter to a friend at the British Admiralty:

> Times grow worse & worse here – & happy are they who are at the time out of the Vortex of these disturbances. I wish from my Soul I was with you.
>
> Troops are collecting very fast at Williamsburg, where the Committee of Safety now reside. Five hundred men are at Hampton & the Minute Men in Motion all over the Colony. Lord Dunmore has lately got a Reinforcement from St. Augustin, & we expect a Visit...very soon. So much for Politicks which to me are very far from agreeable...
>
> All the Cannon & small arms in & about this Town have been seized by his Lordship. He even had the Impudence to send a small Party as far as Kemp Landing....

The Kemp's Landing event was the topic of a November 1 letter sent to British Major General Howe in New York from Captain Samuel Leslie in Gosport:

> On the 17th of October his Lordship [Dunmore] was informed that there was a great quantity of Artillery, small arms and all sorts of ammunition, concealed in different stores at a place called Kemp's Landing, in consequence of which I [and a party of naval, marine, and army personnel] embarked at 2 o'Clock in the afternoon in boats & a Schooner in which some Guns were mounted to cover our landing, and proceeded seven or eight miles up the eastern

branch of Elizabeth river to Newtown, where we landed without opposition notwithstanding above two hundred of the rebels were at exercise near that place the same evening, and marching three or four miles through the Country we arrived at Kemp's landing a little after it was dark, where we searched several stores and could discover nothing but a good many small arms, musquet locks, a little powder & ball, two Drums, & a quantity of Buck shot, all which we either brought off or destroyed; and returning pretty near the same road we went we reembarked about 2 o'Clock the next morning without interruption. We likewise took several prisoners, one of whom was a Captain of Minute men and another a Delegate of the Convention at Richmond....

Many great guns, small arms, & other implements of war have been taken since by small parties, so that there has been in all at least seventy seven pieces of ordnance taken & destroyed since my Detachment arrived here without the smallest opposition, which is a proof that it would not require a very large force to subdue this Colony. There are about eight hundred of the rebels now at Williamsburg & four hundred at Hampton. We are in possession of a large store on the banks of the Southern branch of Elizabeth river, under cover of the Otter sloop of war, so that we are not very apprehensive of an attack tho' the Rebels often threaten to pay us a visit....

On November 7 Dunmore placed Virginia under martial law and issued his Proclamation which read in part:

As I have entertained Hopes that an Accommodation might have taken Place between Great Britain and this Colony, without being compelled by my Duty to this most disagreeable but now absolutely necessary Step, rendered so by a Body of armed men, unlawfully assembled, firing on His Majesty's Tenders, and the formation of an Army, and that Army now on their march to attack His Majesty's Troops, and destroy the well-disposed Subjects of this Colony: To defeat such treasonable Purposes, and that all such Traitors, and their Abettors, may be brought to Justice, and that the Peace and good Order of this Colony may be again restored...I do in Virtue of the Power and Authority to ME given, by His Majesty, determine to execute Martial Law, and cause the same to be executed throughout this Colony: and to the end that Peace and good Order may the sooner be restored, I do require every person capable of bearing Arms, to resort to His Majesty's STANDARD, or be looked upon as Traitors to His Majesty's Crown and Government, and thereby become liable to the Penalty the Law inflicts upon such Offences; such as forfeiture of Life, confiscation of Lands, etc. etc. And I do hereby further declare all indented Servants, Negroes, or others (appertaining to Rebels) free, that are able and willing to bear Arms, they joining His Majesty's Troops as soon as may be, for the more speedily reducing this Colony to a proper Sense of their Duty to His Majesty's Crown and Dignity.

Dunmore would inform General Howe that the Proclamation "has had a Wonderful effect as there are not less than three thousand that have already taken and signed the enclosed Oath. The Negroes are flocking in also from all quarters which I hope will oblige the Rebels to disperse to take care of their families and property, and had I but a few more men I would March immediately to Williamsburg, my former place of residency, by which I should soon compel the whole Colony to Submit."

Dunmore's recruitment of blacks was so successful that he was able to organize his Ethiopian Regiment, which was comprised of three hundred blacks serving under white officers and noncommissioned officers. Their shirts bore the motto "Liberty to Slaves." It was Dunmore's answer to the "Liberty or Death" slogan of the Culpeper minutemen and other patriot organizations. The Revolution was fought as much for slogans as for principles.

When Jefferson was told that "Numbers of Negroes and Cowardly Scoundrels" were responding to Dunmore's promise of freedom, he was concerned about the safety of his family, whom he urged to keep "at a distance from the alarms of Ld. Dunmore." Twelve of the runaway slaves were from Jefferson's Monticello. He told Richard Henry Lee that Dunmore could become "the most formidable enemy America has" unless he were crushed immediately.

Propagandists tried to warn the runaway slaves that Dunmore had no intention of keeping his promise and planned to sell them in the West Indies. The charge was untrue. The slaves were threatened by reports in the *Virginia Gazette* which warned that the women and children of runaways would face the vengeance of backwoods riflemen "who never wish to see a negro, and will pour out their vengeance upon them whenever it is desired." Most of Dunmore's slaves would die of smallpox; some would go to England with him.

Robert Carter Nicholas of Williamsburg, in a letter to the Virginia delegates in the Continental Congress, called Dunmore's Proclamation "an Object worthy of the most serious Attention of the Congress, since all the Colonies are more or less likely to be materially affected by it." Nicholas named the Norfolk Tories as ringleaders in the scheme to destroy Holt's printing press, adding that

> many of our Natives it is said have been intimidated and compeld to join them and great Numbers of Slaves from different Quarters have graced their Corps. The Tenders are plying up the Rivers, plundering Plantations and using every Art to seduce the Negroes. The Person of no Man in the Colony is

safe, when marked out as an Object of their Vengeance; unless he is immediately under the Protection of our little Army.... Engaged, as we are, in one general Cause, I submit to your Consideration whether it will not be prudent and necessary to make it a Point with General Washington to retain proper Hostages for the Security of any Persons that may be seized on any part of the Continent. I fear no time is to be lost, as we understand the Gentlemen and others taken here are to be sent to Boston to undergo what is infamously call'd a Trial.

On November 10 a local Tory wrote that Williamsburg militia planned to destroy both Norfolk and neighboring Portsmouth because "they think them places of refuge for those who are Inimical to what they call the Liberties of America; & it is true there are many so Inhabitants now in both Towns but what are avowed Tories & have publicly declared themselves friends to Government & willing to take up arms in its defence."

Four days later Dunmore's army, commanded by Captain Leslie, set out to occupy Norfolk. At Kemp's Landing these highly trained British regulars and embittered loyalist volunteers routed three hundred armed farmers and fishermen who had hidden in the woods to defend the wooden bridge spanning a branch of the Elizabeth River just twenty miles south of Norfolk. The easy victory over unprepared colonials led Dunmore to underestimate the strength and will of his adversary—to the point that he ridiculed the locals and declared martial law, ordering all the able men to support the crown or be punished as traitors. The incident became known as the First Battle of Great Bridge. There the British claimed they found an American colonel "dead drunk" on the battlefield, shouting "We'll die in the bed of honor!"

When Colonel Woodford at Williamsburg learned that Dunmore's force had assembled at Norfolk, he immediately called for Virginia Regiment reinforcements and about two hundred minutemen to recover the city. Dunmore, hearing of their approach, took a strategic high-ground position on the north side of the Elizabeth River to stop Woodford at the bridge; Dunmore "had erected a small fort on a piece of firm ground surrounded by a marsh, which was accessible, on either side, only by a long causeway," wrote Lieutenant John Marshall who was there. "Colonel Woodford encamped within cannon-shot of this post, in a small village at the south end of the causeway; across which, just at its termination, he constructed a breast-work; but, being without artillery, was unable to make any attempt on the fort." Two days passed before Dunmore ordered his troops to attack Woodford's encampment. By then Woodford had been reinforced by a company of North Carolinians under Colonel Robert Howe, and the enemy would face about nine hundred trained militiamen—a dedicated force of patriots far superior to the ragtag army of farmers and fishermen.

At sunrise on the morning of December 9, a British regiment of sixty grenadiers "advanced along the causeway with fixed bayonets, against the breast-work." When Woodford's troops were alerted by British artillery, "the bravest rushed to the works, where, regardless of the order, they kept up a heavy fire on the front of the British column." Even supported by cannons the column broke and retreated, with the patriots in pursuit, taking a number of captives and two guns. The battle had lasted thirty minutes, and every British grenadier was killed or wounded. Colonel Woodford did not lose a man.

Later recalling the British charge along the causeway, one of the Virginia participants recorded: "I then saw the horrers of war in perfection, worse than can be imagin'd."

Dunmore may have been tricked into the charge that was bound to end the slaughter of his British grenadiers–according to a tale described by Virginian historians T. Triplett Russell and John K. Gott as "a masterpiece of deception, brilliant coordination and a courageous and clever black hero." Woodford informed the Virginia Convention on December 10 that supposedly a young servant owned by Major Thomas Marshall had deserted to Dunmore and "completely taken his Lordship in" by minimizing colonial strength at Great Bridge. Though Russell and Gott found the story hard to believe, it was suggested at the time that Marshall's runaway slave not only lied about the size of the colonial force but also told a gullible Dunmore that the Americans "were out of ammunition, had no powder and had been obliged to melt up their shore buckles for shot."

Russell and Gott had a more plausible explanation for the British defeat: "Dunmore was the victim of his own propaganda." The Americans were neither as weak nor as cowardly as he anticipated.

The night following the Second Battle of Great Bridge, the British fort was evacuated and Woodford's troops crossed the bridge and proceeded to Norfolk, the town which Lee had described as "that infamous nest of Tories." Dunmore took refuge on board his vessel, there to await his next move: the bombardment of Norfolk, which he threatened to burn to the ground. The threat was recorded in the journal of a British midshipman on board the *Otter:*

> The rebels, having now nothing to obstruct their passage, arrived and took possession of Norfolk, and in the evening saluted us with a volley of small arms; [on] the next morning, I was sent ashore to their commander to inform him that if another shot was fired at the Otter, they must expect the town to be knocked about the ears.

Woodford, in a report dated December 10, called Great Bridge "a second Bunker Hill affair, in miniature, with this difference, that we kept our post and had only one man wounded in the hand."

On reading of Hampton's "chastisement" of Dunmore's "Banditti" in Lee's letter of November 28, Washington wrote: "I am glad to find that our Noble Govr has, at length, met with a Check." He added that should Lord Dunmore be struck by "one of our Bullets... the World would be happily rid of a Monster without any person sustaining a loss, this is my opinion at least."

Wirt reported that Patrick Henry, as chief of the Virginia military forces, was unhappy that he was not given the command at Great Bridge. His anger increased when Colonel Woodford refused to acknowledge Henry's military superiority. "This gentleman," wrote Wirt, "after his departure from Williamsburg, on the expedition against Dunmore, considered himself as no longer under Mr. Henry's authority, and consequently addressed all his communications to the convention when in session, and when not so, to the committee of safety."

Thus soon after Woodford's triumph at Great Bridge, Patrick Henry resigned his Virginia command and also refused a commission in the Continental Army. Shortly after his resignation, Henry was elected a delegate to the Virginia Convention which, now that Lord Dunmore was no longer recognized as governor, had assumed the role of governing the colony. Convention delegates, with Henry in the lead, vowed never to submit to the crown's denial of their rights, but to "hand down to their children the birthright of liberty which they had enjoyed, or perish in the attempt."

In late Autumn, with Marylanders on one shore of the Potomac and Virginians on the other, a plan was devised to make the river less vulnerable to the British fleet. As described by Jean B. Lee, it called for the scuttling of vessels in the channel "so that no ship of Force could get up the River." But the Potomac was either too deep or too wide to make the tactic workable. The alternative was to erect a system of warning beacons along the river from the Chesapeake to Alexandria, a distance of one hundred miles. It was decided that beacons would signal the approach of enemy ships more speedily than could be done by hand. To coordinate the system, a delegation of Marylanders and Virginians met at Port Tobacco. They planned for twenty beacons, spaced about five miles apart, and each would be "a kind of Iron Gate suspended by a Chain on the end of a Sweep fixed with a Swivel so as to be turned." Since the beacons would be visible only in clear weather, lookout boats would have to patrol the river when the area was cloaked in fog or heavy mist. The system was approved by the Maryland Council of Safety but never installed. The alert of enemy raiders became a responsibility of the patrol boats which fired warning shots upon impending danger.

On December 2 Congress sent Virginia's Benjamin Harrison to Baltimore to acquire armed vessels for the Continental Navy. He procured the sloop *Hornet* and the schooner *Wasp*, both of which would be outfitted and ready for immediate convoy duty. Congress also passed the following resolutions pertaining to protection of the Chesapeake area:

> Resolved, That the Committee for fitting out armed vessels be instructed and directed to confer with Captain Stone, and engage him and his vessel, on the most reasonable terms, in the service of the Continent, for the purpose of taking or destroying the cutters and armed vessels in Chesapeake Bay, under Lord Dunmore.
>
> Resolved, That Colonel Harrison do immediately proceed to Maryland, and be empowered in conjunction with the delegates of that colony to this Congress, or any one or more of them, [to] take such measures, as appear to them most effectual to procure, with all possible despatch, on continental charge, two or three armed vessels to proceed immediately to cruize on, take or destroy as many of the armed vessels, cutters, and ships of war of the enemy as possible.

At the same time, Congress was told that Ethan Allen had been captured near Montreal and "confined in irons on board a vessel in the river St. Lawrence." Washington was asked to apply to General Howe for Allen's exchange. In May Allen and his Green Mountain Boys of Vermont had teamed up with Benedict Arnold in scoring America's first victory at Fort Ticonderoga in New York, opening an invasion route to Canada. It was during an attempt to invade Canada that Allen was taken prisoner. He would be held until 1778, and in four years would publish a pamphlet entitled *Reason the only Oracle of Man, or a Compendious System of Natural Religion*, which declared that the Holy Bible was not the Word of God. Later, when Congress refused Vermont's petition for statehood, Allen tried to get Great Britain to make Vermont a British province. In the very early days of the Revolution, his brother Seth had hoped to annex the American colonies to Canada.

Subversive loyalist activities on Virginia's Eastern Shore now required Continental Army soldiers to support Virginia militia in guarding the Shore's creeks and inlets. Watched closely, Eastern Shore loyalists were tried for treason if found engaged in acts hostile to the patriot cause. Winston Churchill described it as a "hideous strife in which American slew American and each man suspected his neighbor." Should a man on the Shore show support for the British, his first name would be preceded by the word *Tory*, as in *Tory* Tom or *Tory* William. Most Tories were men of property who knew their property would be confiscated by patriots if they had to flee to Canada or England to escape oppression.

As indicated earlier, many of the loyalists located in the Norfolk area were the Scottish merchants whose livelihood depended upon trade with Great Britain. They openly took a stand against the patriots and sought protection from Lord Dunmore. In remaining true to the king, their persecution by Virginia's Committee of Safety caused the colony to lose a major segment of its needed commercial community and left the organization of the Revolution largely in the hands of wealthy planters. Not all Scots, of course, were Norfolk Tories. Many had built splendid estates along the rivers feeding the Chesapeake and were active patriots who bore arms against the British. Dr. James Craik, a Scot of Charles County, Maryland, helped set up the Continental Army's hospital department. Alexander Purdie, from Edinburgh, was the editor of Williamsburg's *Virginia Gazette*.

Loyalists in Virginia may not have been as numerous or as active as those in other colonies, but they included men of great prominence who expected Britain to win the war; such as Jefferson's cousin John Randolph who resigned as Virginia's attorney general and went to England; William Byrd, called "the first gentleman of Virginia," who refused a command in the Continental Army and spent the war at his Westover plantation; Washington's friend Lord Thomas Fairfax who sat out the war at his vast estate in western Virginia; Reverend John Camm, President of William and Mary, the college that produced many of the Virginia revolutionaries; and Andrew Sprowle, Norfolk merchant and one of Virginia's richest men who, because of his association with Lord Dunmore, would lose his estates and his shipyard at Gosport and die in exile on Gwynn's Island.

John Boucher, an Anglican minister and bay region loyalist from 1759 to 1775, preached that "government authority is derived from God, not from the consent of the governed." And therefore it "requires obedience," wrote Merriam and Chalberg. Boucher denied that all men are equal. He believed "It would be unreasonable to suppose that God, having created men, should turn them loose in the world with no other guide than their own passions." All monarchs, though they govern for the benefit of the people, govern by divine right. Thus Boucher denied the right of resistance to authority and equated democracy with anarchy. What he said was: "Obedience to government is every man's duty [and] it is particularly incumbent on Christians, because it is enjoined by the positive commands of God." To protect himself, Boucher preached with a brace of loaded pistols in his pulpit.

There were a few Virginians for whom the Tory label was a convenience, to be worn only when the British were around, but Joseph Whelan was an obvious exception. This native of Virginia's Eastern Shore commanded four barges and made Toryism a highly profitable way of life, conducting most of his raids in Maryland along the Patuxent, Wicomico, Potomac, and St. Mary's Rivers. When captured and charged with treason, Whelan escaped from a Baltimore jail and found refuge in the marshes near Tangier Island where he starved to death. Still another notorious Virginia Tory was Josiah Phillips of Princess Anne County; his band of fifty privateers so terrorized bay country patriots that some thought the hanging he got was too good for him.

John Paterson, a Kent County minister, told Maryland's sixth convention in December 1775 that there was "more liberty in Turkey than in this province." That convention instructed delegates *not* to support any proposition declaring the colonies independent and re-affirmed Maryland's loyalty to the crown:

> That the people of this province, strongly attached to the English constitution, and truly sensible of the blessings they have derived from it, warmly impressed with sentiments of affection for, and loyalty to, the house of Hanover, connected with the British nation by the ties of blood and interest, and being thoroughly convinced, that to be free subjects of the king of Great Britain, with all its consequences, is to be the freest members of any civil society in the known world, never did, nor do entertain any views or desires of independency.

The convention also defended colonial rights, declaring that Marylanders were descendants of Briton, "entitled to the privileges of Englishmen." Yet, these loyal people of Maryland "have seen with the most extreme anxiety the attempts of parliament to deprive them of those privileges, by raising a revenue upon them, and assuming a power to alter the charters, constitutions, and internal policy of the colonies without their consent."

By mid-December Lord Dunmore had assembled a formidable naval force consisting of the 22-gun *Eilbeck* (which had replaced the *William* as flagship and been renamed *Dunmore*), the 16-gun *Otter*, the 20-gun *Mercury*, the 28-gun frigate *Liverpool*, the *Arundel* and three other schooners, three pilot boats, the *King's Fisher* and two additional sloops, and several tenders attached to the larger ships. The large schooner *Magdalen* had returned to England with Lady Dunmore aboard. Despite the costly setback at Great Bridge, Dunmore and his agents continued to terrorize the bay region inhabitants.

In a deposition dated December 1, Solomon Butler of Worcester County, Maryland, testified that a company of men led by the Tory Levin Townsend kidnapped and pressured a number of Marylanders "to enlist under Lord Dunmore, and told them they should have a Guinea and a Crown advanced, and standing pay allow'd them with a Suit of Regimentals, a Gun & Bayonet [but] that this Deponant and several others refused to Enlist." Butler also said that Townsend "intended to fit out a Tender to cruise in the Bay and take all the prizes they could and then proceed up Pocomoke River to take the Committee of Worcester County prisoners and carry them to Lord Dunmore."

Dunmore agents were everywhere, terrifying the privileged few and agitating their indentured servants and slaves to revolt. Poor whites, feeling they had nothing to lose, became bolder in their vocal attacks on the governing elite. A Frederick County, Maryland, farmer wrote: "It was better for the poor people to lay down their arms and pay the duties and taxes laid upon them by the king and Parliament than to be brought into slavery and to be commanded and ordered about as they were." A Baltimore farmer agreed: The people should support the king because "the American opposition to Great Britain is not calculated or designed for the defence of American liberty or property, but for the purpose of enslaving the poor people thereof."

One of the Virginia Lees was a Marylander, Richard Lee, Jr., who exiled himself on his Charles County estate in 1775 and accused the revolutionaries of "imposing the greatest and most disgraceful of all slavery, a restraint on the human mind."

There were of course men with different ideas about liberty and the cost of pursuing the American cause. Such a man was John Page, a close friend of Jefferson's since college days at William and Mary. In a November 1775 letter to Jefferson, Page wrote: "We care not for our Towns, and the Destruction of our Houses would not cost us a Sigh. I have long since given up mine as lost....I can declare without boasting that I feel such Indignation against the Authors of our Grievances and the Scoundrel Pirates in our Rivers and such Concern for the Public at large that I have not and cannot think of my own puny Person and insignificant Affairs." John Page, a native of Gloucester County, would serve as a colonel at Yorktown and as Virginia governor after the war.

On November 25 Robert Carter Nicholas of Williamsburg notified the Virginia delegates in Congress "that great Numbers have flocked to L. D's Standard. The Tories of Norfolk are said to be the Ring-leaders; many of our Natives it is said have been intimidated and compeld to join them and great Numbers of Slaves from different Quarters have graced their Corps. The Tenders are plying up the Rivers, plundering Plantations and using every Art to seduce the Negroes. The Person of no Man in the Colony is safe, when marked out as an Object of their Vengeance."

MILITARY BUILDUP: 1775

At year's end the Continental Congress resolved to send armed vessels to Chesapeake Bay to take or destroy Dunmore's fleet. It called on bay region inhabitants to resist Dunmore's demands and urged the Virginia Convention to hold elections for the purpose of establishing a new government. When a Dunmore squadron commanded by Captain Squire attempted to land at Jamestown, it was driven away by a local group which included about twenty riflemen.

The Maryland Convention met again to reorganize the colony's defenses. First, by disbanding the minutemen, then by proposing a battalion of regular troops that would be paid and supported by a Maryland fund dedicated to "the defense of the liberties thereof." The battalion, raised by Colonel William Smallwood, succeeded the Baltimore Independent Cadets, a volunteer company of "gentlemen of honor, family and fortune" formed in 1774 by Mordecai Gist, a young Baltimore merchant. The Smallwood battalion would be composed of eight regular infantry companies and one light infantry company, two companies of artillery and one company of marines. It would become one of the best fighting units in Washington's army and win instant fame as the Maryland Line in the battles in New York where Smallwood was wounded. Washington's admiration for the battalion inspired him to nickname Maryland *The Old Line State*. Smallwood and Gist, along with Maryland's Otho Holland Williams and John Eager Howard, would rank among the outstanding military leaders of the Revolutionary War.

In Virginia, during an inspection tour of Hampton defenses, Patrick Henry initiated the action which created the colony's navy. When drawn to two suspicious ships in the bay, Henry commissioned James Barron, a Hampton sea captain, to outfit a small vessel and bring the ships in. Within days, James and his brother Richard captured ten "suspicious" vessels and put an end [temporarily] to the freedom with which the British had harassed colonial shipping on the bay.

The Virginia Convention expanded the powers of the Committee of Safety on December 19, acknowledged its supremacy in military affairs, and authorized the establishment of the Virginia Navy.

Three days later a royal proclamation prohibited trade with America and authorized the British Navy to seize colonial vessels as prizes. One week later Maryland and Virginia were encouraged by Congress to trade with any nation for arms and needed supplies.

In a dispatch to Great Britain's Secretary of State for the colonies, Lord Dunmore called for a blockade of Chesapeake Bay. On New Year's Day Norfolk would be in flames.

- 5 -

A City Aflame

1776

Dunmore was unable to obtain needed provisions from people living along the southern shore of Hampton Roads harbor. His revenge was to bombard Norfolk. Naval cannons opened fire between three and four in the afternoon on January 1, 1776. Rumors that the city was to be invaded had prompted loyalist merchants to invest heavily in supplies that would be needed by the British troops.

For a while Lord Dunmore's ships drew rifle fire from the patriots stationed along the waterfront, but these defenders were forced to withdraw when Dunmore dispatched a party of sailors and marines to set fire to the buildings near the water. The cannons continued into the early hours of morning, leaving the largest of Virginia's cities ablaze. Old St. John's Church, built in 1739, would be the only building to survive, with an English cannonball still embedded in one wall. Many men on both sides were killed or wounded.

The event was recorded by the British midshipman on board the *Otter*:

> The detested town of Norfolk is no more! Its destruction happened on New Year's Day. About four o'clock in the afternoon the signal was given from the Liverpool, when a dreadful cannonading began from the three ships, which lasted till it was too hot for the rebels to stand on their wharves. Our boats now landed, and set fire to the town in several places. It

burned fiercely all night, and the next day; nor are the flames yet extinguished; but no more of Norfolk remains than about twelve houses which have escaped the flames.

Across the harbor in Hampton, the conflagration was recorded by a Virginia soldier named William Campbell:

> At night the fire was so great the Clouds above the Town appeared as red and bright as they do in an evening at sun setting.

Lord Dunmore was not the only culprit. What he started, the patriots finished. Apparently Norfolk inhabitants made no attempt to arrest the flames which Mapp called "a small imitation of hell." Worse were the reports of drinking and looting by troops described by a British observer as "a backwoods mob of American soldiery." These patriots torched the buildings which had not been destroyed by Dunmore's raiders, many of them still occupied. This was denied by Edmund Pendleton, president of the Committee of Safety, who said the rumors had

> been propagated without having the least foundation in truth, it having been determined, and the army aforesaid being instructed, particularly to support and protect the persons and properties of all friends to America, and not wantonly to damage or destroy the property of any person whatsoever.

It was not Virginia's shining hour. Officials had decided the colony would be better off without Norfolk and its Tories. They had reasoned that should the town fall into the hands of the British, its sympathies and location at the mouth of James River would give the enemy control of the lower Chesapeake and its access to the sea. When a militia colonel announced that Norfolk was entirely destroyed, he thanked God.

Though Virginia troops were ordered to sack Norfolk because of its strategic value to the enemy if occupied, propagandists made it appear the town was leveled by a spiteful Dunmore who saw Norfolk as a hotbed of revolutionary fervor (despite the patriot claim that it was a "nest of Tories"). Of such stuff are legends made. Below is an excerpt from a letter to the Virginia Convention on January 2:

> The cannonade of the town began about a quarter after three yesterday, from upwards of one hundred pieces of cannon, and continued till near ten at night, without intermission; it then abated a little, and continued till two this morning. Under cover of their guns they landed and set fire to the town in several places near the water, though our men strove to prevent them all in their power; but the houses near the water being chiefly of wood, they took fire immediately, and the fire spread with amazing rapidity. It is now become general, and the whole town will, I doubt not, be consumed in a day or two. Expecting that the fire would throw us into confusion, they frequently landed, and were every time repulsed, I imagine with loss....
>
> I cannot enter into the melancholy consideration of the women and children running... to get out of town, some of them with children at their breasts; a few have, I hear, been killed. Does it not call for vengeance, both from God and man?

Dunmore claimed that the British destruction of Norfolk was limited to the waterfront. In a report which appeared in his own *Virginia Gazette* printed aboard ship on the press he captured from Holt, Dunmore blamed "the rebels" for the ruin.

Though Jefferson thought Norfolk should be burned, the town's destruction was pure folly, occurring at the one site in Virginia where the king had a significant number of loyal supporters. But it was a radical coup. Not only did Norfolk's destruction all but end Tory sentiment in the colony, but it also provided the propaganda opportunity the patriots needed to put down conservative resistance and rally the people to the revolutionary cause.

The actual cost of Norfolk's damage would not be known until late 1777. In a report commissioned by the Virginia Assembly, Lord Dunmore was held responsible for destruction of nineteen buildings at a cost of 1,616 pounds plus personal property of 1,305 pounds. American patriots accounted for the destruction of 863 houses worth in excess of 110,807 pounds and personal property valued at more than 8,085 pounds. One man whose property was destroyed was Thomas Claiborne, a member of the Norfolk Safety Committee who had moved to the city in 1770; Claiborne (related to George Wythe) was among the "friends to the American cause" who by Act of Assembly were to be compensated for their losses.

Washington, in a letter written at the end of January, felt that a few more such "flaming arguments" would "not leave numbers at a loss to decide upon the propriety of a separation" from Great Britain. He lashed out again at Dunmore as "that Arch Traitor to the Rights of Humanity" and warned that if he "is not Crushed before Spring, [he] will become the most formidable Enemy America has." Yet much of the American army would sit and wait elsewhere.

In 1916 Eckenrode made this observation about the destruction of Norfolk:

> If there had been towns of any size in Virginia, with royal forces to occupy them, or if there had been at Norfolk a fifth part of the army Howe wasted in idleness at Boston in the winter of 1775-76, the history of the Revolution in Virginia and of the Revolution in general might have been different.

In other words, the American Revolution may have been saved because Virginia, an agrarian colony whose largest town had a population of only six thousand, was not perceived as the key to British victory over the colonies until it was too late.

With Norfolk in ruins, actions toward anti-revolutionaries in bay country increased in severity and forced loyalist families to find sanctuary not only in the swamps and the Tory enclaves on the Eastern Shore, but also aboard Dunmore's ships where many became ill from lack of water and malnutrition. So bad were conditions aboard the crowded ships that when some of the loyalists died of fever, they were dumped into the bay to stop the contagion from spreading throughout the fleet.

Thus, for now, most Tory activities in the bay area would be limited to privateering raids, many of which were conducted by the Goodrich family which owned a plantation in Virginia's Isle of Wight County. John Goodrich was widely known as a merchant sea captain and smuggler. He and his four sons incurred the displeasure of Virginia authorities by transporting British goods disguised as Dutch to evade the nonimportation agreements. When they joined up with Dunmore their knowledge of Chesapeake tributaries made them extremely invaluable in leading British raids against the plantations and storehouses. Eventually, the five Goodriches were captured by the patriots and imprisoned. But one by one the family members escaped to New York, bought a fleet of privateers, and proceeded to capture cargo vessels up and down the Atlantic coast from New Jersey to the Carolinas. Other vessels, also privately owned and operated by Tories, would continue to raid Chesapeake waters from Maryland's Eastern Shore.

Much of Norfolk's trading activity shifted across the Elizabeth River to Portsmouth, a deep water port and location of the busy Gosport shipyard. On the opposite side of Hampton Roads harbor, the town of Hampton was the official port of entry for the lower James River customs district, but a sand bar made Hampton's river too shallow to handle all but small vessels. Another important port close to the lower Chesapeake was Suffolk, located on the Nansemond River which entered the James just west of the Elizabeth. Yorktown, with waters deep enough to accommodate the largest merchant and naval vessels, was official customs port for the York River district and an active market center for tobacco, flour, and lumber. At the head of James River, Richmond merchants prospered on tobacco and wheat loaded at this port from farms above the falls. The official port of entry on the Rappahannock was Urbanna. Fredericksburg, also on the Rappahannock, was a major commercial center close to the ironworks at Falmouth. The Potomac River region was served by the port of Alexandria, the second largest town in Virginia and the most active following the Norfolk holocaust. Most of Maryland's shipping was conducted out of Baltimore and Fells Point on the Patapsco River and Oxford on the Eastern Shore. All Chesapeake ports and rivers were vulnerable to Lord Dunmore's fleet, which had become a terrifying "Floating Town" of more than one hundred vessels.

Dunmore's war on the Chesapeake's major rivers—ransacking the plantations, seizing slaves, and burning homes—increased the fear with which he was held throughout bay country. The people who lived along waterways usually had to fend for themselves and complained of the lack of resources to protect them "against the Enemy Barges that are now in our Bay & Rivers, plundering the inhabitants on the Shores and keeping the whole of them in constant alarm and dread."

When news of the Norfolk burning reached the upper Chesapeake communities, the Maryland Convention quickly mobilized the marines. Norfolk's impact on Maryland patriots caused a member of Governor Eden's staff to write: "This unhappy event has given fresh alarm to our citizens, many of whom are preparing to quit Annapolis." The governor, concerned that Marylanders were "extremely agitated" by Dunmore's threat to free the slaves, prohibited all correspondence with Virginia by land or water.

By January 5, as the new Continental Navy was being readied for sea at Philadelphia, the Naval Committee had to determine where to use the fleet most effectively. When all the options had been carefully considered, the Committee issued orders to John Burroughs Hopkins, captain of the *Cabot*, to command a fleet of eight ships to Chesapeake Bay to destroy Dunmore's flotilla. Then he was to cruise the seacoast of the southern colonies and capture any enemy ships or privateers he confronted. Once these missions were completed, Hopkins was to head north and clear the waters at Rhode Island.

For a fleet with less than one-third the ships and guns of the British presence in American waters—deployed from Boston Harbor, Narragansett Bay, New York, the Chesapeake, Charleston, and other Atlantic ports—the odds were overwhelming. So, as Barbara Tuchman wrote, it was no surprise that some Americans, when offered officer commissions, "declined on the grounds that 'they did not choose to be hanged.'" It was known that captured soldiers "were treated as prisoners, but sailors as pirates."

As a political maneuver, Washington invited to his headquarters three members of Congress—Benjamin Franklin, Benjamin Harrison, Thomas Lynch—to discuss the commissioning of armed vessels. In a gesture to win their support, the general announced that three of the new vessels would be named *Franklin, Harrison*, and *Lynch*. Two others would be named after John Hancock and Richard Henry Lee.

There was always the threat that the British would gain control of the Chesapeake waters. It was essential therefore that the two bay colonies build their own navies. Prior to the split with Britain, wrote Ernest McNeill Eller, "Chesapeake shipwrights were noted for their swift schooner and sloop types."

Virginia's Navy was officially established on January 11 "for the protection of the several rivers in this colony." It began with the acquisition of the pilot boats *Liberty* and *Patriot*, commanded by the brothers James and Richard Barron. James would be appointed the fleet's first commodore and Hampton would serve as the navy's home port throughout the war; the commodore's son Samuel would distinguish himself at seventeen by capturing an enemy ship whose crew greatly outnumbered his own.

A shipyard located near Hampton's public wharf built many of the Virginia frigates, brigantines, schooners, sloops, and pilot boats. Other shipbuilding centers were at Gloucester Point on the York, Cumberland on the Pamunkey, Carrotman Creek, and Alexandria on the Potomac. Perhaps the most distinctive vessel to come out of the Revolution was the Chesapeake Bay clipper-schooner, originally known as a Virginia-built schooner but later the popular Baltimore Clipper.

The pilot boat *Patriot* was the first Virginia vessel to see action against the British fleet. The *Liberty* engaged in twenty naval encounters and was one of the few Virginia ships to survive the war.

The Maryland Navy was directed by the Council of Safety and its first commodore was Thomas Grason. Key shipyards were located at Baltimore, Fells Point, Chester River, and Choptank. Aside from New England, the two Chesapeake colonies "represented the largest shipbuilding area" in America, wrote Middleton, "exceeding the combined production of New York, New Jersey, and Pennsylvania."

Maryland was divided into eight naval districts as follows:

> That the River Potowmack be accounted the first district; the River Patuxent the second; the City of Annapolis, with all the waters above the river Patuxent to the river Magothy inclusive on the Western Shore, the third; Baltimore town including the river Patapsco and all the waters above it to the river Susquehannah inclusive, the fourth; the inlets in the County of Worcester, the river Pocomoke including the river Wicomico and all the waters between them, the fifth; the river Nanticoke including

all the waters to the river Choptank on the Eastern Shore, the sixth; the river Choptank including all the waters to the river Chester on the Eastern Shore, the seventh; the river Chester including all Waters above it to the river Susquehannah, the eighth district.

Maryland launched its navy with the purchase of the merchant ship *Sidney* from John Smith of Baltimore. This vessel was then converted into the frigate *Defence* and armed with eighteen six-pound cannons and two four-pounders. Its first commander, Captain James Nicholson of Chestertown, would win honors in several major encounters with the British before receiving a Continental Navy commission. His brother Samuel Nicholson would gain command of the Continental Navy and oversee construction of two of America's most famous fighting ships, the *Constitution* and the *Constellation*.

Though there were early successes in which the *Liberty* and *Patriot* captured several prizes on the Chesapeake, including two of Dunmore's tenders, a personnel shortage made it difficult for the two colonies to man but a small number of naval vessels at any one time. A problem was the Continental Navy's success in recruiting so many of the bay region's best seamen. It would be left to the *Lafayette* and other Chesapeake Bay privateers to harass the British ships which had been ordered to "take, burn, and destroy" all colonial vessels. "Drawing little water," wrote Eller, "and manned by crews familiar with the deeps and shallows of the Bay, [these craft] had the odds on their side for slipping by patrolling warships."

Later in the war, Maryland and Virginia would have to defend the Chesapeake against a far superior British force with galleys and other small vessels. Attempts to construct larger war vessels were always stopped by British raiders who burned them before they reached the water. Thus to help protect the Maryland and Virginia waterways against British raiding parties, galleys were stationed in the lower Chesapeake at Hampton Roads harbor and on the Eastern Shore. Typically, these galleys were armed with two to four cannons and as many as fourteen swivel guns. They were propelled both by sails and by long double-banked oars, ten on a side and two men on each oar. Large galleys were seaworthy and capable of holding their own against privateers and tenders. The smaller galleys were well adapted to the Chesapeake and able to elude enemy ships by slipping into shallow waters. The ideal galley crew was about 160 men, but rarely managed to assemble more than half that number.

The Maryland and Virginia Navies, always short of funds, were unable to attract enough seamen to properly man their vessels. Yet the mere presence of these naval vessels inhibited the movement of British ships. Dunmore said it was dangerous "to trust one of his Majesty's Sloops alone in the Bay."

Elsewhere in the colonies, patriots had chased the redcoats toward Quebec and occupied Montreal; radical voices in Congress had denied again British government authority over the colonies and declared the king a figurehead; New Jersey patriots had captured a British supply ship off Sandy Hook; North Carolina's royal governor urged loyalists to collaborate with the British, just as General Henry Clinton left Boston to lead an offensive against southern patriots; about nine hundred loyalists would be captured in the battle at Moore's Creek Bridge, near Wilmington, South Carolina; a British attack on Savannah would be turned back by Georgia patriots.

In bay region naval operations in early 1776, an armed British tender was captured off Bowler's Wharf in the Rappahannock River; the Virginia brig *Liberty* captured the British merchant vessel *Jane* with a valuable cargo off the Virginia coast. Commodore Barron's cruisers captured a British tender carrying Alexander Ross, a Scot who had been commissioned by Dunmore to sail down the Mississippi with a band of Indians to block the supply route from New Orleans; Ross's instructions from Dunmore were confiscated.

Ashore, four companies of Maryland troops, from Kent and Queen Anne's Counties, were stationed on Kent Island. There they prepared to join Virginia militiamen in defending the lower Eastern Shore from a threatened invasion by Dunmore and his loyalists. The Marylanders were placed under command of Captains Thomas Barnes, Thomas Elliot, John Dean, and Greenbury Goldsborough.

After some of the militia companies completed their training on Virginia's Eastern Shore peninsula, they were organized into the Ninth Virginia Regiment of the Continental Army. Later that year they would march to New York to join Washington's decimated troops as they headed south through New Jersey and across the Delaware to spend a bitter cold winter in Pennsylvania.

When General Clinton sailed into Chesapeake Bay with his troop transports in early February, Dunmore thought that his long-awaited reinforcements had arrived. He was dismayed to learn that Clinton was on his way to meet Lord Charles Cornwallis, a general en route from Great Britain with additional troops for the planned attack on North Carolina. With the aid of local loyalists, Clinton expected to subdue the Carolina rebels quickly and then return to New York to plan the northern campaign with General William Howe. Dunmore expressed his disapproval to London, convinced that the Chesapeake offered the ideal location to establish a naval base to control the southern and middle colonies.

Dunmore was somewhat mollified on February 10 when Captain Andrew Snape Hammond, aboard the British frigate *Roebuck*, arrived at Hampton Roads with a contingent of marines. Hammond instructed his ships to blockade the Chesapeake and "annoy the Rebels by every means in your power [and] seize and detain all American vessels you may meet with, as well as those of any other Country that may be trading with the Americans."

The Americans responded two days later. The Continental Navy ships *Hornet* and *Wasp*, after convoying merchant vessels safely out of the bay, joined a squadron commanded by Commodore Hopkins and proceeded to Philadelphia. There, Hopkins was informed by the Naval Committee of Hammond's arrival in the Chesapeake and instructed to "search out and attack, take or destroy all the naval forces of our enemies that you may find there." Instead, the commodore used heavy storms as an excuse to bypass the Chesapeake and take his fleet to the West Indies, where he hoped to pick up a supply of gunpowder.

Squire had an eye on the upper Chesapeake on February 26. He had been ordered by Hammond to depart Hampton Roads with the *Otter* and two tenders, *Samuel* and *Edward*, and sail to Baltimore. His mission: to search out and destroy the *Wasp* and *Hornet*, which had been escorting merchant vessels down the bay to the sea. Squire was also instructed to capture any vessels "having the appearance of being proper for Arming"— the object being "to prevent their conversion into American warships." He was told to avoid unnecessary risks.

On March 5 Maryland had its first taste of war. As a storm built up, the small squadron under Squire's command reached the mouth of the Patuxent River where the *Edward* captured a New England schooner. Two Maryland pilot boats sighted the squadron and raced to Annapolis to alert the Council of Safety. Drums sounded a warning and militia companies, hampered by wind and rain, assembled to defend the town. Merchants closed their shops and families fled inland to safety. Annapolis officials also alerted the Baltimore inhabitants to "be on your Guard and make all Preparations in your Power for your Defence."

Maryland militia and a few Continental Army regulars marched into Baltimore just as cannons were being positioned aboard the newly built *Defence*. Small craft were commandeered to support the frigate in her expected engagement with the seasoned *Otter*.

Squire's squadron appeared in the bay opposite the Annapolis harbor on the afternoon of March 7. There, based on reports in the *Maryland Gazette*, the *Otter* "burnt a shallop

A CITY AFLAME: 1776

laden with oats, and in the evening anchored near the mouth of the Patapsco." The two tenders then captured a Baltimore trader which, during the storm, had run aground north of Kent Island. At daybreak the *Otter*, while attempting to maneuver Baltimore's Patapsco River with a Virginia pilot unfamiliar with the area, went aground off Bodkin Point. This allowed Baltimore patriots time to erect a battery at Fells Point and block the channel at Whetstone (future site of Fort McHenry).

On learning of the *Otter's* mishap, James Nicholson in command of the *Defence* set sail on the morning of March 9 in the hope of reaching the British warship while still stranded on the shoals. But because the 22-gun *Defence* was considered essential to the protection of Baltimore, Nicholson received orders similar to those given to Squire: beware foolish risks. He was told not to attempt an assault on the *Otter* unless the ship appeared helpless.

When rain and fog subsided Squire was surprised to see the size of the convoy escorting the *Defence* down the Patapsco. Already under heavy fire from the shore, he immediately ordered the two tenders *Samuel* and *Edward* to abandon the grounded Baltimore vessel and return to the *Otter*. Thus Squire was able to free his frigate and escape before the cautious Nicholson reached the scene. The anticipated battle that would never take place made Nicholson a Maryland hero and left Squire the freedom to continue Dunmore's pillaging raids on the lower Chesapeake.

Later when Squire requested Maryland Governor Robert Eden to supply provisions for the *Otter*, Eden passed the request along to the Annapolis Council of Safety which replied:

> Your Excellency will be pleased to inform Captain Squire that the Time has been, when we should have thought it an Honor, and would with pleasure have supplied any of His Majesty's Ships with Provision; and are still not destitute of Hope, a Time may yet come, when we may enjoy that satisfaction.

> We have always considered Captn Squire as a Man of Humanity, and a Gentleman, and as such cannot account for the burning of a Vessel in full View of the People of this City, as if meant to add Insult to Misfortune already too severely felt by the People of this Province, who were always attached to his Majesty and his Family.

Prior to the standoff at Baltimore, Commodore Hopkins landed a party of sailors and marines at New Providence in the Bahamas for an attack on Fort Nassau, which was taken without resistance. The fort yielded seventy-one cannons, twenty-four barrels of gunpowder, and fifteen brass mortars—a plunder which so delighted Hopkins that he was convinced he would be rewarded by a grateful Congress. Though he did receive congressional congratulations, bay region members were unhappy that America's Navy had abandoned Chesapeake Bay to the continuing harassment of Lord Dunmore's raiders.

It appeared the Chesapeake would have to depend on its own naval protection. And soon the *Defence* was joined by other Maryland vessels, ready for battle. They included the brigs *Friendship* and *Amelia*, the sloop *Hebe Johnson*, and a fleet of barges and galleys that were ideal for shallow waters yet large enough to carry cannon and armed men. The Continental Navy brig *Lexington*, formerly owned by Maryland, took the British tender *Edward* in Hampton Roads.

On March 29 Washington sent Major General Charles Lee to Williamsburg to command all the Continental and militia forces in Virginia. Lee was a native Englishman and adventurer whose ideas about the glories of war would be echoed by General George Patton in World War II. Lee wrote to Patrick Henry: "I used to regret not being thrown into the world in the glorious third or fourth century of the Romans." He even proposed that Virginia form two "Roman Legion" companies of its tallest men armed with thirteen-foot spears.

Disdainful of Washington, Lee saw himself as rightfully the American commander-in-chief. He was exasperated by Washington's inaction on the battlefield and by the hesitancy of the delegates at the Continental Congress to move for separation from Britain. Lee complained that the Philadelphia delegates seemed to be "as desperately and incurably infected with this epidemical malady as the provincial Congress of Maryland, or the quondam assembly of Pennsylvania."

Lee's anti-Dunmore policy began with terrorizing assaults on Tory-dominated Portsmouth. His letter to the chairman of Virginia's Committee of Safety declared that "it wou'd (strictly speaking) be perhaps right and politick to destroy it totally." In addition to burning two merchant vessels to keep them from the British, Lee had torched the houses of several prominent loyalists "with the view of intimidating the neighborhood from trifling any longer or flying in the face of your ordinances."

While Portsmouth burned, one of Dunmore's tenders operating out of Gosport captured a New England schooner in the Rappahannock River. The tender was attacked by Virginia small craft and forced to abandon its prize.

Captain Richard Barron of Hampton, adhering to resolutions of the Continental Congress making all British ships and cargoes in American waters liable to capture, seized two merchant vessels at Fredericksburg, Virginia, and one at nearby Port Royal.

In April General Lee was meddling in Maryland affairs, urging the arrest of the colony's proprietary governor for collaborating with the enemy. Captured Dunmore despatches revealed that Governor Eden had been sending British Colonial Secretary Lord George secret information on the practicality of military landings in the two bay colonies. Lee's demand for action had bypassed Maryland's Council of Safety and gone directly to Samuel Purviance, chairman of the Baltimore Committee of Observation; he considered Purviance more aggressive than the Council leaders whom he called "namby pambys." Purviance sent Lee's letter together with the captured documents to John Hancock, President of the Continental Congress, who authorized a scheme to seize Eden and his personal papers. The attempt to kidnap Eden did not succeed. Purviance was chastised for assuming powers beyond his authority, Hancock was chided for his attempt to subvert the Maryland government by seizure and imprisonment of the governor, Eden had to promise that he would not leave the province.

In a directive to Edmund Pendleton, chairman of Virginia's Committee of Safety, General Lee ordered (among other things) that Portsmouth be destroyed, that Eastern Shore defenses be improved and that livestock there be destroyed to keep it from the British, that Virginia's rivers be fortified, that a Virginia cavalry be raised, that sterner discipline be effected for the militia, and that stronger measures be taken against the loyalists. Then he left Virginia for the campaign in the Carolinas, joined by Colonel John Peter Gabriel Muhlenberg and the eighth Virginia Regiment.

Spring arrived with another attempt by the Continental Congress to win Canada's support. George Wythe was named head of the committee responsible for drafting an appropriate solicitation. The mission to Montreal consisted of Benjamin Franklin and Maryland delegates Samuel Chase and Charles Carroll. Because a promise of religious freedom was extended to Canada's Catholics, Charles Carroll was urged to take along his cousin, a priest. The mission was furnished a printing press for the dissemination of revolutionary propaganda. The mission failed.

America lost Canada but gained France on May 1 when Louis XVI supplied munitions to the colonies through a fictitious company run by a French secret agent, Pierre de Beaumarchais. After Spain took similar action, the two nations combined would supply Washington's armies with more than eighty percent of their gunpowder, plus other supplies, for the next two years. Wrote Gelb, the irony of the war was that

Americans, in "their struggle for liberty and justice," turned for assistance to the king of France, "a tyrant far more despotic than the English monarch they so persuasively castigated."

In May a letter to Jefferson in Philadelphia from his close friend John Page concluded on this urgent note: "For God's sake declare the Colonies independant at once, and save us from ruin."

Independence

1776

Formation of a state government was the business at hand when the Convention of Delegates of the Counties and Corporations of the Colony of Virginia convened at Williamsburg on May 6. Randolph, Bland, and other leading conservatives regretted their failure to find a peaceful solution to the dispute with Britain and had to be dragged into the Revolution. It was Henry, Jefferson, Mason, Wythe, and the other progressives who mobilized enough votes to defeat the obstructive tactics of the conservatives who wanted to maintain the status quo and simply declare the colony independent.

Though most Virginians who led the independence movement were not (as yet) all that concerned about the common man, they sought a new form of government which recognized the equal and natural rights of the people to be free. At that time, "the people" constituted that six percent of Virginians qualified to vote. Still, representative government was advanced in the new state constitution by providing for a Senate and House of Delegates composed of one member elected from each county. Virginia was the first of the colonies to adopt as a preamble to its constitution a Declaration of Rights, written by George Mason in language that has become familiar:

> That all men are by nature equally free and independent, and have certain inherent rights...namely, the enjoyment of life and liberty, with the means of

acquiring property, and pursuing and obtaining happiness and safety.

Mason believed that government's role was to *protect* the life and liberty of its people. He warned that "all power is derived from the people," that the people "cannot be taxed without their own consent, nor bound by any law to which they have not assented for public good." Aside from the fact that he owned a plantation of five thousand acres and hundreds of slaves to work it, Mason like Jefferson was as much a democrat as his class and times allowed.

Abolishment of the monarchical system was unmistakably articulated in Jefferson's third draft of the Virginia constitution. By the authority of the *people*, George III was to be removed "from the kingly office within this government and absolutely divested of all its rights, powers and prerogatives; and that he and his descendants and all persons claiming by or thorough him, and all other persons whatsoever shall be & for ever remain incapable of the same; and that the said office shall henceforth cease and never more either in name or substance be re-established within this colony." The text as amended by the more conservative members of the Virginia Convention struck Jefferson's language and simply dissolved "the Government of this Country, as formerly exercised under the Crown of Great Britain."

The state constitution was adopted on June 29. George Wythe was elected Speaker of the House over conservative opposition, giving the progressives control of the new government. The capital was moved from Williamsburg to Richmond, a village up the James that was said to be secure from British raids. Actually, the move was a progressive ploy to further weaken the conservative faction, which was drawn largely from the eastern tidewater area. Patrick Henry was elected first governor of the Virginia Commonwealth.

Disputes over differing political philosophies would persist, but as the separation from Great Britain became a reality, the conservatives—no less than the progressives—proved themselves active and dedicated patriots.

George Mason and Thomas Jefferson were frequent collaborators, and the young Jefferson drew heavily upon Mason's principles in drafting the Declaration of Independence and the Virginia Statute for Religious Freedom. Other states borrowed from Mason when they drew up their constitutions; and when Maryland copied Mason's handiwork, it prohibited future legislatures from making any changes in the state's bill of rights.

An unsung hero of the American Revolution, Mason was one of the few spokesman for the poor. He called for a government that "would provide no less carefully for the rights and happiness of the lowest than of the highest order of citizens." Though he was instrumental in drafting the Virginia constitution and declaration of rights, Mason refused to sign the constitution. By reasoning which must have confused his fellow Virginians, this man who owned hundred of slaves said he strongly opposed the "infernal traffic" of slaves. He blamed "the avarice of British merchants." Thus when delegates to the 1776 Virginia Convention postponed the abolition of slave trade, Mason declared that that postponement was the key factor in the decision to withhold his signature. When he died in October 1792, Jefferson honored him as "a man of the first order of wisdom among those who acted in the theater of the Revolution."

The Virginia delegation had been instructed on May 15 to urge the Continental Congress "to declare the United Colonies free and independent states, absolved from all allegiance to, or dependent upon, the crown or parliament of Great Britain." Edmund Randolph reminded Congress of the militant actions of Lord Dunmore which had enraged Virginians:

> The king's representative in this colony hath not only withheld all the powers of government from operating

for our safety, but, having retired on board an armed ship, is carrying on a piratical and savage war against us, tempting our slaves by every artifice to resort to him, and training and employing them against their masters. In this state of extreme danger, we have no alternative left but an abject submission to the will of those over-bearing tyrants, or a total separation from the crown and government of Great Britain, uniting and exerting the strength of all America for defence, and forming alliances with foreign powers for commerce and aid in war.

Randolph urged that the delegates agree to

whatever measures may be thought proper and necessary by the Congress for forming foreign alliances and a confederation of the colonies, at such time, and in such manner, as to them shall seem best; Provided that the power of forming government for...the internal concerns of each colony, be left to the respective colonial legislatures.

The idea that thirteen colonies would settle upon a uniform plan of government that would serve as a model for all the colonies was rejected by the delegates at the Virginia Constitutional Convention. Of course, in view of political differences existing from colony to colony, Virginia was right in proposing that each colony's form of government be decided by its own legislature.

Virginia's resolution did not reach Philadelphia until May 27. By then the Congress had adopted a John Adams resolution, prompting Adams to declare: "Great Britain has at last driven America to...a complete separation from her, a total absolute independence."

Delegations from Pennsylvania, New York, and South Carolina called for caution in declaring independence prematurely, warning that to do so before establishing a national government would give "our Enemy Notice of our intentions before we had taken any steps to execute them." That problem would not be resolved until ratification of the Articles of Confederation in 1781. All the colonies (except Rhode Island and Connecticut which had already structured a new form of government) would adopt state constitutions, and most would be conservative documents reserving power to the political elite that had always ruled the colonies. The Maryland Convention, which would not adopt a new constitution until November, was now under pressure to endorse the independence issue before the Continental Congress severed relations with Great Britain.

The standstill on independence in Maryland was frustrating to many patriots because Maryland had been one of the first colonies to rebel against the new taxes imposed by Parliament and one of the first to move toward military preparedness. Not only was there the resistance of Maryland loyalists and the hostility of poor whites to contend with, but also the growing number of militia recruits who were deserting or openly rebelling against authority and the social structure. Fearful of insurrection, the Maryland Council of Safety ordered militant patriots to use force to prevent slaves, servants, deserters, and others among the disaffected from going over to the British. The situation was acute in Eastern Shore counties where the poor would remain antagonistic to the Revolution until the end of the war, and where large Tory concentrations had already declared allegiance to Lord Dunmore. Chief among Maryland Tories was wealthy planter James Chalmers, a Scotsman who organized the First Battalion of Maryland Loyalists on the Eastern Shore.

Even as late as June independence seemed a risky proposition in Maryland, at least among conservatives who had gained control of the Convention and were pushing for reconciliation with the British government. "With all its imperfections," wrote Chalmers in his pamphlet *Plain Truth,* the British constitution "is, and ever will be, the pride and envy of mankind." Maryland delegates at the Continental Congress were forbidden to agree to resolutions for independence or to alliance with a foreign power against Britain. This led Virginia's Richard Henry Lee to express disdain for Maryland's timidity. But Maryland conservatives were not timid in attacking the radical elements who were willing to plunge the province "fatally deep in schemes of independence." Though the Maryland Convention was in the hands of the antirevolutionary faction, the Sons of Liberty had taken over the Maryland streets, terrorizing those who opposed separation from Great Britain.

The expectation of "a formidable fleet of British ships, with a numerous army of foreign soldiers" persuaded a group of angry freeholders in Charles County to renounce allegiance to Britain. A spokesman for the freeholders said they feared the British would "force us to yield the property we have honestly acquired, and fairly won, and drudge out the remainder of our days in misery and wretchedness, leaving us nothing better to bequeath to posterity than poverty and slavery."

Pressured by leaders of the Continental Congress the Maryland delegates returned home to campaign for independence. Samuel Chase, Charles Carroll, Thomas Johnson, Matthew Tilghman, Daniel Jenifer, along with other revolutionaries both moderate and radical, went from county to county selling the cause. That the campaign worked was due in large measure to Chase's skills of persuasion. Success was evident in the instructions sent from Anne Arundel County to the Maryland Convention. County representatives were told to

> move for and endeavour to obtain a resolution in Convention, that this province be united with the other twelve colonies represented in Congress and that the deputies of this colony be authorized and directed to concur with the other united colonies, or a majority of them, in Congress, in declaring the United

Colonies free and independent states, and in forming such further compact and confederation between them, in making foreign alliances, and in adopting such other measures as shall be adjudged necessary for securing the liberties of America, provided the sole and exclusive right of regulating the internal government and police of this province be reserved to the people thereof.

There was no mistaking the "Declaration of the Delegates of Maryland," which urged the people of Maryland to form a union with the other colonies, and concluded:

...we appeal to the Almighty Being who is emphatically styled the searcher of hearts, and from whose omniscience nothing is concealed. Relying on his divine protection and affiance, and trusting to the justice of our cause, we exhort and conjure every virtuous citizen to join cordially in defence of our common rights, and in maintenance of the freedom of this and her sister colonies.

Chase, Carroll, and the other Maryland delegates returned to Philadelphia with instructions to vote for independence. They got there just in time to mollify John Adams and other unhappy members of Congress who had been ready to let the obstinate Maryland colony stand alone. Adams had called Maryland "so eccentric...sometimes so hot, sometimes so cold; now so high, then so low—that I know not what to say about it or to expect from it." He said he wished that Maryland "could exchange Places with Halifax." To Edmund Pendleton, Marylanders had behaved badly. "We build our Government slowly," he said. "I hope it will be founded on a Rock."

In voting for independence the convention also put an end to proprietary government in Maryland. The 150-year reign of the Lords Baltimore was over. Such leaders as Charles Carroll, worried that independence might result in a leveling process and diminish their political power, made sure that the rights of privilege were safe-guarded in the formation of a new government. Thus the adoption of Maryland's state constitution later in the year would include provisions that were "shrewdly framed in Annapolis by the wealthy for the wealthy," wrote Maryland historian Carl Bode.

This fact disputes the belief that by 1776 the colonies had reached a consensus on what Americans stood for: just governments based on the consent of the governed. And these governments, wrote David Hawke (in his essay "The American Revolution: Was it a Real One?"), were based on principles reflected in the covenants between the rulers and the ruled. The problem was, the rulers drafted the covenants to protect *their* interests. It would take years before the constitutional principles applied to *all* Americans.

Charles Carroll was a successful planter, businessman, politician. Born in Annapolis and educated by Jesuits as a child, he studied law in England and France. After building Carrollton Manor, a ten thousand acre estate in Frederick County, he extended his name to "Charles Carroll of Carrollton" in order to distinguish himself from his Charles Carroll relatives.

Though denied membership in Maryland's legislature because of his religion, Carroll emerged a champion of the colony's patriots through newspaper attacks on the proprietary governor. He supported nonimportation measures, attended Maryland Conventions, served on Committees of Correspondence and the Council of Safety.

Carroll was elected a delegate to the Continental Congress in 1776 and became the only Roman Catholic to sign the Declaration of Independence. He had supported separation because he was convinced that the colonies must either be totally independent or totally dependent on the whims of the British government. But he despised the "clamor of the mob." Carroll felt that radical schemes of the populists could erupt into anarchy and involve Maryland "in all the horrors of the ungovernable and revengeful Democracy...dyed with the blood of its best citizens."

Carroll would help form the Baltimore & Ohio Railroad, become the richest man in America and last of the signers to die.

Virginia's resolution in favor of independence, foreign alliances, and a confederation of American states was offered by Richard Henry Lee to the Continental Congress on June 7:

> Resolved, that these United Colonies are, and of right ought to be, free and independent States, that they are absolved from all allegiance to the British Crown, and that all political connection between them and the State of Great Britain is, and ought to be totally dissolved.
>
> That it is expedient forthwith to take the most effectual measures for foreign Alliances.
>
> That a plan of confederation be prepared and transmitted to the respective Colonies for their consideration and approbation.

The Virginia resolution was seconded by John Adams. In debate it was strongly supported by George Wythe, who asked the delegates not to look upon the resolution as a new policy but as confirmation of existing truth. He argued that it was a "certain position in law that allegiance and protection are reciprocal, the one ceasing when the other is withdrawn." Adams applauded. Earlier, in admiration of Wythe's wisdom, Adams had written:

> You and I, dear friend, have been sent into life at a time when the greatest lawgivers of antiquity would have wished to live. How few of the human race have ever enjoyed an opportunity of making an election of government for themselves and their children! When, before the present epocha, had three millions of

people full power and a fair opportunity to form and establish the wisest and happiest government that human wisdom can contrive?"

A committee—consisting of Jefferson, Adams, Franklin, Robert Livingston, and Roger Sherman—was appointed to draft a declaration of independence as war on the Chesapeake continued.

Following General Lee's attack on Portsmouth, Pendleton wrote to Jefferson:

> We have had repeated Accounts lately from Norfolk by deserters that Dunmore and his Fleet were reduced to half allowance and were preparing to depart....By letter from Hampton yesterday we are informed they were Collecting just below the Mouth of James River and they expected an Attack.

When Dunmore received word that Virginia patriots were going to ram his fleet with burning rafts, he sought advice from Captain Hammond who was still aboard the *Roebuck* in Hampton Roads. Hammond confirmed the danger, and Dunmore decided to abandon the harbor and escape to the north with his shrinking army of regulars, loyalists, and slaves. His destination was Gwynn's Island, east of Matthews County, Virginia, where the Piankatank River emptied into the bay. Dunmore had been told the island was "inhabited by many Friends of Government [and] could easily be defended from the Enemy." Before leaving Hampton Roads, his guns destroyed "between 40 and 50 sail of small vessels," wrote a correspondent for Purdie's *Virginia Gazette*, adding that Dunmore "suffered all the salt on board to go to the bottom."

By Dunmore's account, when his fleet (accompanied by Hammond on the *Roanoke*) arrived off Gwynn's Island, he began to erect a Fort against the Enemy, who began to gather from all quarters: and fired with musquetry upon the People at work but without doing us the least mischief: Being covered by Foweys Guns on one side, and by two small Tenders (which I had sent into the Haven) on the other. The Otter & her Tender immediately returned to cruize off the Capes, to prevent any of the Rebels Vessels from getting in or out....

Dunmore's plan was to use Gwynn's Island as a base from which to direct punishing raids on the Virginia mainland five hundred yards away, but the island was "much too large for us to defend in our present weak situation," wrote Captain Hammond on June 10 in his request for additional armament.

Pendleton reported the situation to Jefferson:

Dunmore with 400 half starved motly soldiers on Gwyns Island, and 2000 of Our men on the Main[land] are looking at each other as two Tenders are in the thoroughfare between Milford haven and Piankatank to stop the Passage and the Fleet in the River to Protect the Island.

Dunmore's plight was described in Purdie's *Virginia Gazette*: "It is an undoubted fact that all the Tories who were in Lord Dunmore's service have left him, there not being half the fleet now at Gwyn's Island; where they are gone to is uncertain." The newspaper suggested that it "was occasioned by a fever which has raged with great fury amongst them for some time past."

Two weeks later the Virginia Navy brothers James and Richard Barron, posing as pilots and joined by the crew of the Continental Navy brig *Andrew Doria*, boarded the British transport *Oxford* and captured more than two hundred kilted Scottish Highlanders. The Scots were marched through

Williamsburg with high celebration. "Everyone here," wrote Page, "looks upon the wonderfull Manner in which the great Number of Highlanders have fallen into our Hands as truly providential."

At the same time, Page described Virginia's defense needs:

> Col. Stephen is fortifying Portsmouth but we are in Great Want of Cannon to mount on the Works necessary to command the whole Harbour of Norfolk. Our Cruizers and Gallies have taken up all the good Cannon we had except 1 at Jas. Town and those at Gwyn's Island. We want 6 or 8 24s or 18s for our Fort at Jas. Town, as many more for a floating Battery to be anchored opposite the Fort, the like Number for every other River, and 3 or 4 for the Works at Burwells Ferry.

Page would assert later that if Virginians had possessed "only 2 more 18 Pounders and Powder and Ball in plenty" they might have "taken or utterly destroyed" Dunmore's flagship and all supporting tenders. Page concluded that "4 18s and as many 9 Pounders" would have saved Norfolk.

Maryland's Council of Safety, having discovered that Governor Eden was secretly supporting Dunmore, ordered the governor to leave the province. Eden contacted Captain Hammond in Hampton Roads and asked for transportation from Annapolis. The *Fowey*, commanded by George Montagu, arrived on June 22. Following a tense period in which five servants from the area were granted sanctuary aboard the ship, Eden was permitted to depart. The *Fowey* delivered him to Lord Dunmore at Gwynn's Island.

In a surprising move the Council of Safety attempted to boost the Maryland military morale by granting suffrage to all militiamen regardless of rank or social status. This made it possible for many men outside the propertied gentry class to move into positions of local leadership. The move also extended opportunities for social advancement to the ethnic and religious minorities that previously had been victimized by discrimination. "Merit should be the only recommendation to office," proclaimed the Maryland radical leader Rezin Hammond. Though special privilege was under assault because of agitation in the militia ranks, it would continue to thrive in Maryland politics during and after the war.

Elsewhere, General William Howe replaced Gage as Commander of the British Army in America; Congress established a Board of War and Ordnance, forerunner of the War Department; a British expeditionary force of two thousand men and nine warships attacked Charleston but had to withdraw with all ships damaged and two hundred casualties; a Tory plot to assassinate Washington and other patriot generals was uncovered, and Washington's personal guard was executed in New York City for "sedition and mutiny;" British troops camped at New York (Staten Island) numbered nearly thirty-two thousand men, the largest single military force in America during the war; the first Continental Navy engagement in foreign waters would take place at Martinique between the *Reprisal*, under Captain Lambert Wickes, and the British sloop *Shark*.

In the Declaration of Independence Jefferson turned the language of George Mason into poetry:

> When in the Course of human events, it becomes necessary for one people to dissolve the political bonds which have connected them with another, and to assume among the Powers of the earth, the separate and equal station to which the laws of Nature and of Nature's God entitle them, a decent respect to the opinions of mankind requires that they should declare the causes which impel them to separation.
>
> We hold these truths to be self-evident, that all men are created equal, that they are endowed by their Creator

with certain unalienable Rights, that among these are Life, Liberty and the pursuit of Happiness. That to secure these rights, Governments are instituted among Men, deriving their just powers from the consent of the governed.

Jefferson's words were read to the Continental Congress on July 2 in a slow and ponderous voice in keeping with the weighty frame of Benjamin Harrison (the Fifth). Afterwards, this Virginia delegate turned to Eldridge Gerry of Massachusetts, a man of slight build, and said "When the time of hanging comes, I shall have the advantage over you. It will be over with me in a few minutes, but you will be kicking in the air for half an hour after I am gone."

For two days the delegates debated the form and content of Jefferson's document, some of which was indebted not only to Mason but to the seventeenth-century English philosopher, John Locke. In opposing England's tradition of the divine right of kings, Locke had defined government (the legislative) as "only a fiduciary power to act for certain ends, [while] there remains still in the people the supreme power to remove or alter the legislative when they find the legislative act contrary to the trust reposed in them."

Virginia delegate Carter Braxton, a wealthy planter, was concerned about "the tumult and riot incident to simple Democracy." Without England, who would protect the colonists from themselves? He proposed the English system as the proper model for America's government:

> However necessary it may be to shake off the authority of arbitrary British dictators, we ought, nevertheless, to adopt and perfect that system which England has suffered to be grossly abused, and the experience of ages has taught us to venerate.

Franklin compared Great Britain to "an old mother [who] forgets we've grown up and have sense of our own." The Braxton proposal was rejected.

Conservatives representing the middle colonies and lower south argued that independence would require the continuity of a strong national government. The New England and Virginia moderates, who opposed monarchy and any form of central authority, considered themselves *republicans* and advocated a system which separated the "powers of government that would prevent one branch from gaining too much control." The words "republicanism" and "republic" were often used in derisive attacks on patriots who opposed Britain's form of government and the English Constitution. The *Providence Gazette* would find it necessary to define a democratic republic:

> By a democracy is meant, that form of government where the highest power of making laws is lodged in the common people, or persons chosen out from them. That is what by some is called a republic, a commonwealth, or free state, and seems to be most agreeable to natural right and liberty.

Scholars have written that a system in which citizens elect representatives to manage the government is probably the nearest thing to pure democracy that a large country can expect.

In Philadelphia the republicans would carry the day and create a government in which the power of the people was indeed exercised by qualified representatives—qualified, that is, by education and the ownership of substantial property. Republicans championed the fight for that "body of natural rights antedating the existence of government and superior to its authority." It was in the framework of human nature that natural rights were founded, said John Adams.

But no system that set out to preserve the political elite and disregard majority rule could be called *democratic*. When

Adams said there is "no good government but what is republican," what he meant was a political system similar to the representative government he already had: one which (in his words) denied the right to vote to women, to "lads from twelve to twenty," to the "man who has not a farthing," and to others without property or position. Adams would proclaim that a "democratic" system would "confound and destroy all distinction and prostrate all ranks to one common level."

Adams was not alone in his distaste for political or social equality. Most delegates, moderate or conservative, held the view that power belonged to men like themselves: cultured gentlemen of wealth and leisure. "The ambiguity of the Revolution's philosophy lay in affirming personal liberty while at the same time linking it to private property and economic self-interest," wrote Staughton Lynn. But more progressive delegates warned that such a government would collapse under the weight of its egocentricity; and a few, including Jefferson, would attempt to expand voter participation by modifying the property-owning requirement.

Virginia, Pennsylvania, and Massachusetts were the only states which adopted a bill of rights including the principle of equality. Pennsylvania's was virtually the same as Virginia's, "that all men are by nature equally free." Massachusetts declared "all men are born free and equal," with the controversial exception of the town of Hardwick, which proposed that "all men, whites and blacks, are born free and equal."

Hardwick was perhaps closer in spirit to Thomas Paine:

> The principle of equality of rights is clear and simple. Every man can understand it, and it is by understanding his rights that he learns his duties; for where the rights of men are equal, every man must finally see the necessity of protecting the rights of others as the most effectual security for his own....
>
> If property is to be made the criterion, it is a total departure from every moral principle of liberty,

because it is attaching rights to mere matter, and making man the agent of that matter...I maintain the principle, that when property is used as an instrument to take away the rights of those who may happen not to possess property, it is used to an unlawful purpose, as fire-arms would be in a similar case.

In a state of nature all men are equal in rights, but they are not equal in power; the weak cannot protect themselves against the strong. This being the case, the institution of civil society is for the purpose of making an equalization of powers that shall be parallel to, and a guarantee of, the equality of rights. The laws of a country, when properly constructed, apply to this purpose.

About slavery, Thomas Paine wrote: "Certainly one may, with as much reason and decency, plead for murder, robbery, lewdness, and barbarity, as for this practice."

Paine was not a man that many of the Founders liked. Though Adams agreed with Paine on slavery and angrily opposed the deletion of the slave clause from the Declaration of Independence, he called Paine's *Common Sense* "a poor ignorant, malicious, short-sighted, Crapulous Mass."

The first time that African captives were brought to English America was in 1619 when a Dutch ship docked at Port Comfort, Virginia, and discharged a cargo of "20 and odd Negroes" from the West Indies. The blacks, mostly male between the ages of fourteen and twenty, were sold at Jamestown to English planters, not as slaves but as indentured servants required to serve a specified number of years, after which they would be entitled to protection of English law. As America's needs for labor increased so did the import of Africans and the concern by the English colonists about the growing number of Africans being admitted into their society as freemen with the right of naturalization. At that point the colonists decided that the Africans could be admitted only under a permanent status of servitude. In short, as slaves. The practice expanded beyond Virginia to Maryland, the Carolinas, Georgia, and even to abolitionist New England. It became so profitable to the slavers that many of the English shipowners entered the trade. Britain's king owned stock in a company that purchased captive Africans and sold them into slavery in the American colonies. Hence, Jefferson's reference to George III in the slave clause the delegates deleted from his original draft of the Declaration. Jefferson had accused the king of waging

> cruel war against human nature itself, violating its most sacred rights of life & liberty in the persons of a distant people who never offended him, captivating & carrying them into slavery in another hemisphere, or to incur miserable death in their transportation thither. This piratical warfare...is the warfare of the CHRISTIAN King of Great Britain, determined to keep open a market where MEN should be bought and sold....

As president, Jefferson would succeed in pushing legislation through Congress abolishing the slave trade. And his draft of the Virginia Constitution provided that "No person hereafter coming into this country shall be held in slavery under any pretext whatever." But he would fail to free his own slaves in his will, as Washington and other Virginians had done. Though he forbade his overseers at Monticello to whip his slaves, Jefferson noted the economics of slavery in his Farm Book: "I consider the labor of a breeding woman as no object, and that a child raised every 2 years is of more profit than the crop of the best laboring man."

The inability to separate slaves from property was a problem that confronted more than half the Founders who were slaveowners. Washington shipped an "unruly slave" to the West Indies in exchange for "a hogshead of rum and other commodities."

Even the egalitarian Franklin, while debating the Articles of Confederation, would observe that slaves were property that should be counted in population figures no more than sheep, but that sheep would strengthen the economy and "never make any insurrections."

Maryland's Samuel Chase would call slavery contrary to the natural rights endorsed by the Continental Congress, and stress that no government could "make right wrong, or wrong right." But Chase would underestimate the omnipotence of both the state and federal legislatures he helped to shape.

Jefferson, Adams, and Franklin symbolized the paradox that was America to outsiders like Baron Wilhelm von Knyphausen, a British mercenary who could not understand the colonials:

> Why were these people, so well treated, enjoying so much freedom, ungrateful enough to rebel against their king? Why, while they ranted about freedom and liberty, did they treat their black slaves worse than animals were treated in Germany?"

On July 4 the amended Declaration of Independence was adopted without dissent by 56 signers.

Virginia signers: Richard Henry Lee, Thomas Jefferson, George Wythe, Benjamin Harrison, Carter Braxton, Thomas Nelson Jr., and Francis Lightfoot Lee.

Maryland signers: Samuel Chase, William Paca, Thomas Stone, and Charles Carroll.

Copies of the Declaration were prepared and delivered to all thirteen states and read before Washington and his troops in New York City, announcing:

> The Continental Congress has declared the thirteen United States of America free and independent.

Nearby, a crowd of patriots in a park at Bowling Green pulled down the statue of George III. The statue would be cast into more than forty thousand bullets to be used against the British Army.

American independence was broadcast to the world on July 9. But of course it was independence with strings. It was not entirely grievances over callous and arrogant treatment by the British government that led to Revolution. A more realistic reason was good old self-interest—America's rich aspired to get richer.

The rich enjoyed privileges denied the poor, and were careful to perpetuate those privileges. As Norman Gelb noted, the power elite sought to gain more power while many among the disenfranchised poor moved westward beyond the mountains to challenge the frontier wilds and British territorial proclamations to acquire the land they had been denied in the civilized east—where a tenth of all the white males owned most of the land.

Thus, based on the plan approved by the revolutionaries, equality for all Americans was an unexpected result. An anonymous writer pointed out in the *Pennsylvania Evening Post* that the rich had been so used to governing they thought it was their right. Prior to Revolution, wrote Forrest McDonald, not many Americans "espoused the doctrines about to be set forth in the Declaration of Independence, and hosts of divergent opinions were perfectly tolerable; but once the Declaration was made, it became not only immoral but virtually unthinkable to hold any other position."

Today, after more than two centuries, we continue to enshrine the Founders, most of whom expressed opinions that many of us would find distasteful and unAmerican. Of course, even then the Founding opinions were not the majority view. Adams estimated that one-third of the colonists favored independence, one-third bitterly opposed it, and one-third were indifferent. This French observation would be recorded in the following year: "There is a hundred times more enthusiasm for the revolution in any Paris cafe than in the whole of the United

States put together." To British Army historian Sir John Fortescue, it was "unquestionable that the American Revolution was, as is generally the case, the work of a small but energetic and well organized minority, towards which the attitude of the mass of the people, where not directly hostile, was mainly indifferent."

Yet George Mason would write:
There has never been an idler or a falser Notion than that which the British Ministry have imposed upon the Nation "that this great Revolution has been the Work of a Faction, of a Junto of ambitious Men, against the Sense of the People of America."

In two years time an over-zealous Lafayette would attest that all Americans were on the same level: "In America, there are no poor....Each individual has his own honest property."

Following the signing of the Declaration of Independence, more than eighty thousand American loyalists abandoned their homes to begin anew in Great Britain or Canada. At least fifty thousand became British soldiers. And freedom of dissent became one of the war's early victims. A press editorial raged against the loyalists: "Banishment, perpetual banishment, should be their lot!" Of those who stayed at home, some continued to wage war on American patriots under Lord Dunmore's command.

Dunmore's ships, anchored in the channel off Gwynn's Island, came under heavy fire on July 5 from a battery of guns installed on the mainland by General Andrew Lewis of the Virginia militia. Dunmore, who had sworn to reduce the colony to obedience, sent a flag of truce to Lewis proposing "an exchange of prisoners," reported the *Virginia Gazette*. The general was told that if Dunmore did not have a sufficient number of Virginia captives, he would give him credit and pay him when he could. The *Gazette* report concluded:

General Lewis, we hear, answered his lordship's very witty and ingenious proposal as it deserved... a furious attack upon the enemy's shipping, camp and fortifications.

Having been wounded when his flagship was hit, Dunmore left Gwynn's Island accompanied by the *Roebuck* and the *Otter* under the steady barrage of General Lewis's guns. The flotilla, now reduced in size, was handicapped by rampant disease which Captain Hammond described as a "violent bilious intermitting fever, together with a most inveterate scurvy."

The following is an extract from the July 10 report filed by General Lewis after he and two hundred Virginia troops commanded by Colonel Alexander M'Clanahan landed on Gwynn's Island:

> On our arrival, we found the enemy had evacuated the place with the greatest precipitation, and were struck with horrour at the number of dead bodies, in a state of putrefaction, strewed all the way from their battery to Cherry point, about two miles in length, without a shovelfull of earth upon them; others gasping for life; and some had crawled to the water's edge....I myself counted 130 graves [one containing the remains of Andrew Sprowle of Gosport]. Many were burnt alive in brush huts, which, in their confusion, had got on fire. In short, such a scene of misery, distress, and cruelty my eyes never beheld; for which the authors, one may reasonably conclude, never can make atonement in this world.

Dunmore's force reached Maryland on July 14 and for three days plundered homes along the St. Mary's River, eventually anchoring at St. George's Island in the mouth of the Potomac. From there, several vessels sailed upriver to the village at Occoquan Falls in search of water and food supplies. Before

INDEPENDENCE: 1776

being driven off by militia, they burned a mill and William Brent's plantation before returning to St. George's Island. In a letter to Jefferson, Richard Henry Lee said "we have no reason to be sorry for the disgrace of our African Hero at Qwins [Gwynn's] Island. He is now disturbing us in [the] Potomac having attached himself to St. Georges Island on the North side. But it seems the brave spirit of the Marylanders will not Permit these folks to remain long where they are now." George Wythe was more philosophical about the situation in his letter to Jefferson:

> Lord Dunmore, driven from Gwins, retreated to St. George's island in Potomack, a station we hear he found no less unquiet than what he left, so that he hath gone up that river, distressed, it is imagined for want of water. Ought the precept, "if thine enemy thirst give him drink," to be observed towards such a fiend, and in such a war? Our countrymen will probably decide in the negative; and perhaps such casuists as you and I shall not blame them.

On July 20 the 44-gun *Roebuck*, along with three other ships, two tenders, and an oar-propelled galley, proceeded up the Potomac terrorizing colonials on both banks and cutting off transportation between Maryland and Virginia.

On July 23 three inexperienced militia companies from Charles County watched from the Maryland side of the Potomac as Dunmore's raiders on the other side surprised a group of Virginia militiamen in a "drinking Frolick" and burned a house and its grain supply. Maryland's militia took a defensive position on the Potomac shore at the base of a hill. When the *Roebuck* and *Otter* began firing on them they were directed "to scatter as they retreated through the old fields." In the confusion the men retreated uphill to the edge of the woods without firing a shot.

The British warships lay offshore until July 26 and did not open fire again. After they sailed away Maryland officials praised the militia companies for preventing "the Enemy from landing or plundering if they intended it." But the view was different from the other side of the Potomac, where Virginia observers accused the poorly prepared Marylanders of cowardice. Colonel William Harrison called the charge "malicious, infamous falsehood." False or not, it was through such encounters with the British that Maryland militia "learned to soldier," wrote Jean Lee. They would recall the "Sundry great guns" and the shot "grounded within a few paces of us."

In Pendleton's report to Jefferson, there was dismay at the lack of militia action of both sides of the river:

> Dunmores Squadron were Pirating up Potowmack last week. I am not informed of any particular damage they did, except to Mr. William Brent of Stafford, in burning his dwelling House and Stable, some Stacks of Hay and wheat. They set fire to every House, but the Matches went Out and they were saved except the two above. I would willingly conceal the shame of some of our Militia on that Occasion, who departed from the Dignity of Men, in Rude behavior to the Enemy 'til they provoked them to come on shore and then in runing away from them.

Adam Stephen's account was only a bit more sanguine:

> Lord Dunmores fleet went up Potowmack untill they found the Water fresh enough to drink. Irritated by Some Blackguards of the Stafford Militia, they landed at the House of Mr. William Brent, Situated on Potowmack about ten Miles below Dunfries. The Poltroons, the Militia of Stafford, run, and the Enemy Set fire to the House. They were on their way to burn a fine Mercht. Mill at a Small distance, but 30 of the P. William militia happily arrivd, advancd with good Countenance, and drove him on board.

It was common knowledge that Dunmore had his mind set on the destruction of Mount Vernon. Washington had been informed by his Mount Vernon manager: "I believe we must defend our plantations upon Potowmack with our Musquets." He said "the gentlemen are ready & willing to turn out & defend any mans property—but the common people are most Hellishly frightened." In addition to looting towns and destroying warehouses and estates on both sides of the Potomac, Dunmore was continuing to liberate slaves and preach insurrection.

On July 28 the Maryland ship *Defence* and Virginia's *American Congress* attacked Dunmore's vessels at St. George's Island and were repelled by the *Roebuck* and bad weather. While the ships fired at each other, diseased Tories and slaves were dying so fast that one account described the St. Mary's shoreline as "full of Dead Bodies chiefly negroes." Fever had ended the war for Dunmore.

Having failed to find refuge on the Potomac River, the remnant of Dunmore's fleet headed for the lower Chesapeake, escorted by the *Roebuck*. The last of Virginia's royal governors was accompanied by the last of Maryland's proprietary governors, Sir Robert Eden. When the news reached Williamsburg, Pendleton expressed his concern in a letter to Jefferson: "I hear Ld. Dunmore and his Fleet are now in Hampton road waiting I suppose a favourable Opportunity of striking at some prey." Pendleton and his fellow Virginians could relax on August 7 as Dunmore cleared the Capes, where his vessels scattered, some sailing south to Florida, some to England, and some to join the British fleet at New York.

On August 20, Page reported:

> Ld. Dunmore is at Staten Island. His sick he sent to Halifax, his effective men he carried to Staten isld. and the blacks he shipped off to the West Indies. Two gentlemen who had been taken prisoners by the enemy have made their escape.

Dunmore's departure from the Chesapeake was noted in Purdie's *Virginia Gazette*:

> By advices from Hampton, we learn that last Wednesday morning the Right Hon. the Earl of Dunmore...after dividing his fleet, and burning ten or a dozen vessels, took leave of the Capes of Virginia, where he has, for more than a twelvemonth past, perpetuated crimes that would even have disgraced the noted pirate BLACKBEARD.

For sixteen months the Dunmore campaign was a microcosm of the war at large, a bloody struggle fought on both land and water with a handful of spirited but poorly-equipped patriots on one side and Great Britain's mighty army and navy on the other, supported by loyalist fanatics and runaway slaves. Had Lord Dunmore succeeded in his war on the Chesapeake, the northern colonies may well have been isolated from southern support and unable to withstand the full brunt of the British military power in America.

The convention of Maryland delegates which assembled in Annapolis on August 14 to draft a state constitution resolved unanimously to "maintain the freedom and independency of the United States with their lives and fortunes." It was dominated by the conservative faction of the patriot coalition, namely Matthew Tilghman, William Paca, Robert Goldsborough, Thomas Johnson, George Plater, Charles Carroll of Carrollton, his father Charles Carroll of Annapolis, and the borderline conservative Samuel Chase. They were leaders of the Whigs, the party of privilege that favored a system restricting the vote and concentrating power in the economic and political elite. These men, who distrusted a government that would place the vote in "the hands of the very lowest people," came from Eastern Shore and the lower western counties where the majority of the tobacco plantations and slaves were located. Their control of the Convention guaranteed that none of the radical element would be appointed to the committee to draft a declaration of rights or a constitution for Maryland.

The radical element, favoring expanded suffrage with no significant property qualification, was led by Rezin Hammond of Anne Arundel County, a planter and owner of more than five thousand acres and seventy slaves who advocated democracy and usually wound up on the losing side.

Other opposition to the "Whiggish" leaders came from the Baltimore County delegation of Charles Ridgely, John Stevenson, Thomas Cockey Deye, and Peter Shepherd; William Fitzhugh of Calvert County; Walter Bowie and Osborn Sprigg of Prince George's County; Elisha Williams of Frederick County; and John Archer of Harford County. Ridgely believed the success of any government created by the convention would need the support of "the relatively poor men who served in the militia." The purpose of Fitzhugh's opposition was simply to obstruct "a revolutionary movement with which he had little or no sympathy."

Though the opposing factions were polarized on the political issues they were remarkably similar in background. The leadership of both groups was composed of prominent planters, merchants, and lawyers.

In the August 15 issue of the *Maryland Gazette* an essayist who called himself the Watchman argued that the convention resolution calling for a new form of government denied half the freemen "the enjoyment of their inherent right of free suffrage." He wanted a government "where equal liberty can be enjoyed [and] the interest of the people promoted." It has been suggested that Watchman was a pseudonym for Rezin Hammond or his brother Matthais, both of whom were active members of the Sons of Liberty and supporters of the disenfranchised poor. Charles Carroll characterized the brothers and their followers as men of "desperate & wicked designs" who endeavored "to introduce a leveling scheme, by which they, these evil men, are sure to profit."

Most of the land was held by the old families, representing no more than twelve percent of population; and the diminishing supply of land left less fortunate Marylanders without a political voice.

But petitions from county after county, urging the right to vote regardless of property qualification, were rejected. When the Anne Arundel County petition asked the convention to support the plan, Samuel Chase was one of the county's three delegates to resign. He called the plan "incompatible with good government, and the public peace and happiness." Chase was re-elected to the convention and praised in the press for his leadership in avoiding the unicameral system adopted by Pennsylvania. Typically a political elitist as well as a zealot for independence, Chase opposed Pennsylvania's single-chamber legislation because it tended to have a leveling influence on the electorate.

Though the proposed constitution would preserve the right of privilege it would eliminate ethnic and religious restrictions by opening the Maryland voting booth to Germans and Roman Catholics. The Maryland Declaration of Rights, in more than forty articles, would secure the rights of all white males. No similar action was taken to acknowledge the rights of women, servants, and blacks.

When it was reported that legislators were required to own property worth one thousand pounds, the gentry was ridiculed in a poem printed in the *Maryland Gazette* on October 24. It opened:

> Alas! we've lost our liberty.
> When thousand pounds must bear the sway,
> While men of merit's cast away;
> Because they thousands can't produce,
> They're render'd quite unfit for use,
> While naves and fools may strut and flutter,
> About their money make a sputter,
> Persuading people all they can
> It is the money makes the man....

Only six percent of Maryland's households in 1776 had taxable fortunes of one thousand pounds or more. Yet no change was made in the high-property qualification for office holders, and political control was left in the hands of an aristocratic clique.

Some progress was made, however in the eligible voter issue. Currently, Maryland voters were "freemen above twenty-one years of age, being freeholders of not less than fifty acres of land or having visible property [worth] forty pounds sterling at least." The convention delegates agreed to a compromise that reduced the forty-pound sterling requirement to thirty pounds in Maryland currency, thus increasing the voter qualification among household heads from fifty-five to sixty-three percent. As noted by Philip A. Crowl, "the break with Britain [would prove to be] a break with the whole concept of tradition, of aristocracy, of privilege. The voice of the people—the declassed and the discontent—once given a hearing would not again be easily silenced."

The Maryland Constitution was adopted on November 11. Thomas Johnson of Calvert County was elected the first state governor.

Property and education qualifications to suffrage and public office were fixtures in all state constitutions, creating protests and demands for reform among a vocal minority. The modest societal reforms enacted in most states, in order to gain general support for the Revolution, worried some leaders but the gentry continued to rule throughout the war and after America had become a republic. The only constitution to grant the vote to every adult male, with no qualification, was adopted by the territory of Vermont, which thought of itself as the fourteenth state. Another quarter century would pass before the leveling ideas expressed by Maryland's and Virginia's egalitarian leaders would begin to reshape the basic rights of the bay region society. It was the conclusion of Howard Zinn, in *A Peoples History of the United States*, that most leaders of the

American Revolution were members of a colonial elite who used the war for independence "to create a consensus of popular support" for their continued rule at the expense of social change.

Elsewhere, during the late months of 1776, ten thousand Americans routed twenty-two thousand British and Hessian troops to push into Brooklyn Heights; Congress resolved that commissions and documents be issued in the name of *United States* instead of United Colonies; Franklin, Silas Deane, and Arthur Lee (a replacement for Jefferson) were named commissioners to France, charged with securing military assistance and French recognition of the United States (at the time America had no major industry, no acceptable currency, no unifying government; no allies); peace talks between a congressional delegation and Admiral Lord Richard Howe on Staten Island failed when it was learned that Howe lacked the power to negotiate; an American fleet commanded by Benedict Arnold on Lake Champlain was defeated; Washington had to evacuate New York City and retreat across New Jersey, without the expected support of Major General Charles Lee who had been captured while attempting to attack the rear guard of British General Cornwallis's army; the British established a naval base at Newport, Rhode Island; Washington made his first crossing of the Delaware River en route to the defense of Philadelphia; the Continental Congress, fearing an enemy attack on the city, fled to Baltimore; two weeks later Washington's army recrossed the Delaware to surprise and take one thousand Hessians at Trenton.

The British peace overture had been praised in a letter published by William Goddard, a Baltimore printer, in *The Maryland Journal*. As a result, a Baltimore vigilante society brought Goddard before its council and banished him from the town. Goddard appealed to the General Assembly, which urged the governor to protect both Goddard and the state from anarchy and to condemn all vigilante groups for usurping the powers of government.

On the Chesapeake the Virginia galleys interrupted their protection of merchant vessels to escort Continental Army troops up the bay to the landing at Head of Elk, Maryland. From there the troops would march through Delaware into Pennsylvania to reinforce Washington. By year's end, most of Virginia's recruits were fighting elsewhere, not only up north in Washington's struggle to restrain the British march across New Jersey but also in the south to defend the Carolinas. Virginia was forced to remind Congress that the Continental Army had cannibalized its military units and destroyed its ability to protect its citizens along the state's many vulnerable waterways.

By contract, Washington's army also depended upon farm commodities grown in Virginia and Maryland and transported to the upper Chesapeake, where they were carried by wagons to small craft that sailed up Delaware Bay to Philadelphia. The food supply line never had to venture outside the Virginia Capes to reach the army.

General William Smallwood was in command of a division charged with protecting military supplies at the Head of Elk depot and with observing British movements in the bay. Later, Smallwood's division would put down a Tory rebellion on the Eastern Shore.

But there was still the danger of British ships and loyalist privateers cruising the bay. To protect their commerce, as well as the military supply line, Virginia and Maryland assembled a fleet of brigs and barges armed by Baltimore merchants. Maryland's House of Delegates passed an "Act for the Defence of the Bay," ordering the evacuation of small islands and the removal or destruction of everything that could be of use to the enemy.

A petition was sent to the Virginia Convention by patriots in Princess Anne (just south of Norfolk) protesting loyalists raids:

Plantations have been ravaged, and our wives and children stripped almost to nakedness, our bedchambers invaded, at the silent hour of midnight, by ruffians with drawn daggers and bayonets; our houses not only robbed of plate, specie, and every valuable but wantonly reduced by fire to ashes; our persons treated with every indignity that elated insolence and cruelty could suggest.

Adam Stephen's report to Jefferson from New Jersey suggested that rape and other forms of abuse were to be a pattern of British behavior: "The Enemy like locusts Sweep the Jerseys with the Besom [broom] of destruction. They to the disgrace of a Civilisd Nation ravish the fair Sex, from the Age of Ten to Seventy."

It should not be surprising therefore that a Virginia militia colonel, Charles Lynch, was compensated by the Assembly for hanging Tories without a trial. The practice came to be known as lynching.

Continued opposition to the Revolution by Tory merchants in the Norfolk-Portsmouth area led the Assembly to expel "all the natives of Great Britain, who were partners with factors, agents, storekeepers, assistant storekeepers, or clerks here, for any merchant or merchants in Great Britain, [to be effective] on the First Day of January 1777."

The Anglican Church dominated Maryland and Virginia prior to the Declaration of Independence, but now the Protestant movements were gaining strength, especially on Maryland's Eastern Shore. Quakers had increased in number on both shores. Roman Catholics, however, were still victims of harsh discrimination in Maryland, where laws forbade the erection of Catholic churches and employment of Catholic teachers, and banned Catholics from public office and the voting booth. The law refusing public office to Jews would not be removed until 1826. In Virginia it would be ten years before the General Assembly enacted the Statute for Religious Freedom, which Jefferson regarded as one of his most important accomplishments. In the meantime, religious opposition to the Revolutionary War was cause for imprisonment. Passivism was equated with treason. The conclusion to Tory James Chalmers's *Plain Truth* pamphlet cried out in capital letters: INDEPENDENCE AND SLAVERY ARE SYNONYMOUS TERMS.

One of Thomas Jefferson's correspondents after the war would be Dr. Richard Price, and English clergyman who shared his views on human rights but was more hostile toward slavery. A letter from Price on July 2, 1785, would inform Jefferson that he had been discouraged by an account from South Carolina which criticized his pamphlet recommending "measures for preventing too great an inequity of property and for gradually abolishing the Negro trade and Slavery." "It appears," he wrote, "that the people who have been Struggling so earnestly to save themselves from Slavery are very ready to enslave others, mortifying America's friends of liberty and humanity in Europe."

In response from Paris on August 7, Jefferson would agree that "Southward of the Chesapeak" Price's pamphlet "will find but few readers concurring with it in sentiment on the subject of slavery." But, he continued, "From the mouth to the head of the Chesapeak, the bulk of the people will approve it in theory, and it will find a respectable minority ready to adopt it in practice, a minority which for weight and worth of character preponderates against the greater number, who have not the courage to divest their families of a property which however keeps their conscience inquiet."

Jefferson noted that in Maryland he did "not find such a disposition to begin the redress of this enormity as in Virginia. This is the next state to which we may turn our eyes for the interesting spectacle of justice in conflict with avarice and oppression: a conflict wherein the sacred side is gaining daily recruits from the influx into office of young men grown and growing up. These have sucked in the principles of liberty as it were with their mother's milk, and it is to them I look with anxiety to turn the fate of this question. Be not therefore discouraged."

America's future would not embrace Jefferson's optimism and, ironically, he would have to include himself among "the greater number" who refused to free their slaves, even in their wills.

Blockade

1777-1779

On orders from General Howe on January 20, 1777, British Commodore William Hotham positioned his small force at the Virginia Capes to blockade Chesapeake Bay. The force—including the 50-gun Preston, the 20-gun Brune, the 44-gun Phoenix, and the 32-gun Emerald—was able to capture two merchant vessels, one coming to Virginia with rum and other supplies, the other bound for France from Baltimore with 550 hogsheads of tobacco.

Newspaper accounts from Williamsburg reported that the British blockade make it "almost impossible for vessels bound in or out to escape." Not only was there no way to prevent enemy warships from entering the Capes, but the defensive batteries at Norfolk and Portsmouth were no longer able to defend those important forts or the bay against attack. Most of the captured cargoes were aboard inbound vessels which had not been informed about the blockade. And the loss would have been heavier had the British blockade been larger. When Hotham sailed for Delaware Bay in February, he left only the *Phoenix* and the *Emerald*, permitting at least some vessels to get in and out of the Chesapeake with cargoes intact.

Now a fifty-foot flagstaff was erected on Cape Henry to alert incoming merchantmen. If Virginia's Capes were safe to enter during the day a large red and white flag would be flown; a lantern would replace the flag at night.

The Continental Congress learned on February 13 "that the Enemy mediates an Expedition to the Bay of Chesapeak."

Because the Eastern Shore was considered to be "the first object or Place of Landing," Virginia and Maryland were asked to remove supplies from the Shore to keep them from falling into British hands. As disturbing to bay region authorities as the blockade were the enemies of the patriot cause who sold supplies and information to the British—the Tories operating in the remote regions of the Eastern Shore and in a few isolated areas in the western part of the state. In early 1777 a rebellion by four hundred loyalists in Somerset and Worcester counties failed when anticipated British naval support failed to appear. Maryland's legislature immediately authorized two thousand militia troops for duty on the Shore to suppress future attempts at insurrection. A county lieutenant was created to supervise the militia and coordinate defense efforts in each of the counties. In addition, these lieutenants would work with Continental Army recruiters to help maintain the state's troop quotas, as well as training and quartering the troops until they reported to one of the Continental camps.

The military manpower situation in Virginia was so desperate that George Mason, author of the state's bill of rights, proposed a resolution in the House of Delegates that "for the Preservation of the State...the usual forms of Government shou'd be suspended, during a limited time, for the more speedy Execution of the most vigorous and effectual Measures, to repel the Invasion of the Enemie." Mason's intent was to permit Governor Patrick Henry to use his powers to raise an army without waiting for Assembly approval. Though Jefferson was worried that this "dictatorial" move might influence future state governments to alter the constitution at will and weaken the representative system, Henry's independent army did not materialize and Mason's resolution was rescinded. Despite the inadequacy of its own defenses and its resistance to the draft as "the last of all oppressions," Virginia continued to raise troops for the Continental Army—although it was unable to meet the quotas imposed by

Congress, a problem that existed in all states. For in May 1777, Washington reported that Virginians represented a third of his main army in New York. Only Massachusetts, closer to the New York scene, supplied more troops.

Indian tribes had been attacking American settlements in Kentucky and elsewhere in the northwest. A group of Virginians—Jefferson, Wythe, Mason, Governor Patrick Henry—worked out a plan that would protect the settlers as well as Virginia's claim to the Northwest Territory. The plan called for George Rogers Clark, an experienced surveyor and Indian fighter, to lead a raiding party against the British outposts north of the Ohio River. Once he was commissioned a Virginia colonel and authorized to raise seven companies of men, Clark decided it would be easier to defend "the dark and bloody ground" of the northwest if he first captured Detroit, which the British were using as a base to supply the Indians. But Clark was unable to reach Detroit, and the Indians (and Tories) continued to terrorize the Ohio and Indiana country under the leadership of the renegade American Simon Girty, who lived the life of an Indian and sided with the British.

It would take two years for Clark to complete his campaign and force a British surrender at Fort Sackville in Vincennes, Indiana. Later, when speaking of the obstructions en route to the capture of Vincennes, Clark said they would have been enough to stop "any set of men not in the same temper" as he. Before the war was over, the settlers would move freely over Daniel Boone's Wilderness Road and down the Ohio into the Kentucky and Tennessee regions.

When Washington was informed that Major General Charles Lee was a British prisoner in New York, he sent a dispatch to General Howe which threatened retaliation upon "the lives and liberties" of captured British officers if there were any violence done to Lee. The danger to Lee was real; he had once served in the British Army and could be hanged as a deserter. But Lee had ingratiated himself with Howe on March 29 by offering the following scheme intended to end the war for the British:

> If the Province of Maryland, or the greater part of it, is reduced, or submits, and the people of Virginia are prevented or intimidated from marching aid to the Pennsylvania army, the whole machine is divided, and a period put to the war; and if [the plan] is adopted in full, I am so confident of success that I would stake my life on the issue.

Lee recommended that four thousand British troops "be immediately embarked in transports, one-half of which should proceed up the Potomac and take post at Alexandria; the other half up Chesapeake Bay and possess themselves of Annapolis."

On April 4 Howe informed Lord George Germaine, minister for the American colonies, that he would invade Pennsylvania from the Chesapeake rather than the Delaware Bay as planned, and avoid the difficult march through New Jersey. Germaine approved the change and told Howe to execute the invasion "in time for you to cooperate with the army ordered to proceed from Canada, and put itself under your command."

The original strategy planned for the army in Canada, under Lieutenant General John Burgoyne, to move south in the spring of 1777, and separate New England from the lower colonies, permitting Howe to capture the American capital of Philadelphia and trap the Washington army in New Jersey. According to this scenario, colonies in the south would be stranded and forced to surrender by winter.

That strategy would fail with the defeat of Burgoyne's army at Saratoga in September—a major colonial victory that would convince France to actively support the American cause. This boon to America was rooted in a French hatred of the English summarized by James Breck Perkins:

> There was no strong desire to win back the lost possessions in North America, especially in Canada

[lost in the French and Indian War]....But if there was no desire to recover Canada, there was a strong wish to humiliate England, and it was thought that the loss of her American colonies would be a ruinous blow to her prosperity.

Meanwhile, as the summer of 1777 neared, Howe was preparing to embark from New York with thousands of seasoned troops destined for the Chesapeake. Elsewhere, Maryland's Lambert Wickes, in command of the *Reprisal* and two smaller ships, *Lexington* and *Dolphin*, conducted raids in the Irish Sea and captured eighteen enemy vessels; the Continental Congress left Baltimore for Philadelphia; Cornwallis's two thousand troops attacked the New Jersey post at Bound Brook, manned by five hundred Continentals under General Benjamin Lincoln who managed to escape with a loss of thirty-five men; Washington, after a series of New Jersey victories, set up winter headquarters at Morristown; the French ship *La Victorie*, owned by the twenty-year old Marquis de Lafayette, anchored off South Carolina where Lafayette was put ashore to claim the army commission promised by America's envoy in Paris, Silas Deane; the American commissioner to Spain offered that country the rights to Pensacola, Florida, in return for Spain's declaration of war against Britain; at the same time, France was promised Canadian fishing grounds to enter the Revolutionary War on America's side.

Impressment was still an important means of manning American naval vessels. In Maryland one of the most dramatic reactions to impressment involved Captain James Nicholson while serving as commanding officer of the Continental Navy frigate *Norfolk*. In spring 1777, he was ordered to remove the ship from Baltimore harbor, where it had been inactive since its launching in 1776, and then "proceed to sea at the first favourable opportunity." Of late, Nicholson had been lampooned in the Baltimore press as "Captain Snug in Harbor." The ridicule led him to impress Baltimore seamen into *Norfolk's* crew, whereupon Governor Johnson demanded that Nicholson "instantly" release the seamen who had been wronged by the press gang. Johnson also announced that Nicholson's actions were bad for business: "injurious to the town," he said, "in deterring people from going to market there, for fear of being treated in the same manner." Nicholson expressed his anger at the town council and informed the governor that his activities were endorsed by Congress. Governor Johnson passed on the Nicholson letter to Congress for response. Congress held that Nicholson "had gone beyond impressment" and reprimanded him. Baltimore's kidnapped seamen were released.

In April the Maryland Assembly was under attack by a number of the state's prominent citizens. The Assembly had passed an act that made paper money legal tender for all transactions, including those debts contracted in sterling before the separation from Britain. Charles Carroll of Annapolis, worried that a depreciation in paper currency would make it worthless, urged his son, Charles Carroll of Carrollton, to organize a protest. The son, recently elected to the state senate, resisted the father's pressure rather than create unnecessary unrest. He described the paper money issue as "the price of Revolution." This action (or lack of action) by Carroll was his way of protecting the political and social order so carefully preserved in the state's obviously undemocratic constitution.

The first United States flag was adopted by Congress on June 14, 1777. It displayed thirteen stripes, alternating red and white, with a blue field of thirteen white stars representing the union and "a new constellation." Despite the claims of Francis Hopkinson (who designed various state and national emblems) and the heirs of Betsy Ross, there is no evidence of who designed the flag. Early claims that the design was derived from the George Washington family coat of arms, as suggested in Martin Tupper's 1876 drama *Washington*, are now considered mythology.

It was not out of patriotic passion that the flag was born but out of the need to identify American naval vessels in foreign waters. The man-of-war *Ranger*, commanded by John Paul Jones, was the first ship to show the flag abroad, exchanging salutes with the admiral of the French fleet in Quiberon Bay on the coast of France. The *Ranger* was also the first ship to fly the flag in battle, when Jones defeated the British sloop *Drake* off the English coast in the spring of 1778.

The flag was not called "Star Spangled Banner" until Francis Scott Key did so in the War of 1812, during the bombardment of Fort McHenry at Baltimore. By dawn's early light, he wrote a ballad that by Act of Congress would become the United States national anthem. The tune was from an old Masonic drinking song *Anacreon in Heaven*, which celebrated wine and love.

Lafayette left his ship at South Carolina, traveled through North Carolina into Virginia, slipped by the British fleet guarding the Chesapeake, crossed the Potomac River into Maryland, and arrived at Annapolis on July 23, 1777, to learn that Fort Ticonderoga in New York had fallen to the British. Three days later this young noble who had deserted the French army and defied his government's orders not to come to America, was in Philadelphia offering his military services to Congress.

Lafayette's offer was rejected. Congress was already swamped with applications from foreigners. In Paris, Deane had written: "I am well-nigh harassed to death with applications of officers to go out for America." And Washington, who feared that the acceptance of foreign officers would replace a like number of American officers, preferred that the war be conducted and won by his own countrymen.

The general had told his regimental commanders: "You will therefore send me none but natives."

Urging Congress to reconsider his offer, Lafayette had this note read to the delegates:

> After the sacrifices I have made, I have the right to exact two favours: one is, to serve at my own expense; the other is, to serve at first as a volunteer.

On July 31, Congress passed the following resolution:

> Whereas, the marquis de la Fayette, out of his great zeal to the cause of liberty, in which the United States are engaged, has left his family and connexions, and, at his own expence, come over to offer his service to the United States, without pension or particular allowance, and is anxious to risque his life in our cause:
>
> Resolved, that his service be accepted, and that, in consideration of his zeal, illustrious family and connexions, he have the rank and commission of major general in the army of the United States.

In many histories of the Revolutionary War, Lafayette rivaled the heroic stature of George Washington and contributed to the plan of action that ultimately defeated the British at Yorktown. Had it been otherwise he might have been tracked down and arrested by the French and returned home a fugitive. But the marquis would prove himself a man of courage and vanity, a man ambitious for glory on the battlefield. He was bold enough to think that he could drive the British from America. Jefferson would say that he had "a canine appetite for popularity and fame." But Lafayette was prophetic in his admiration for America:

> The happiness of America is linked to the happiness of all humanity; she will become the sure asylum of virtue, honesty, tolerance, equality and a peaceful liberty.

On the day that Lafayette met Washington (July 31), Howe was reported off the capes of Delaware Bay. The Americans had retaken Fort Ticonderoga and Washington's aim was to defeat General Howe in New York and take control of Canada. But Howe, commanding between fifteen and eighteen thousand men, had been seen near Sandy Hook, New Jersey, in a naval task force commanded by his brother, Admiral Lord Richard Howe. Washington heard that General Howe's expedition would be moving up the Delaware Bay for an attack on Philadelphia, so he placed his army at Chadd's Ford on Brandywine Creek, blocking the Delaware approach to the city. The destination was right, but Howe did not appear in the Delaware. Howe had decided to approach Philadelphia via the Chesapeake because Delaware Bay was too well defended.

General Howe was sighted near the Virginia Capes on August 11. Delayed by strong winds, he entered Chesapeake Bay three days later en route to Head of Elk (Elkton), near the Delaware-Pennsylvania border and only fifty miles south of Philadelphia. Howe's plan was "to bring the enemy to an action [which] General Washington was studious to avoid...unless under most favorable circumstances." On hearing the news, Congress immediately called out the militia of New Jersey, Pennsylvania, Delaware, and Maryland.

When the British sailed through the Capes, an alarm spread so rapidly across Virginia that within days a militia company of four thousand men had mustered on the lower peninsula near Williamsburg. The governor of Maryland ordered that Annapolis be evacuated of "Women, Children, Servants, and Slaves." He then sent two companies of militia up the bay to the Susquehanna River and concluded: "God save the STATE."

Washington, told that nearly "200 sail" were at anchor in the upper Chesapeake, quickly advanced his army to a position between Philadelphia and General Howe. Now numbering about fifteen thousand regulars and militia, Washington's army was badly in need of training, discipline, and uniforms. But

America's treasury was short of funds. And the paper currency printed by the Continental Congress, amounting to $200,000,000, had become so worthless in buying power that it sparked the snide expression, "Not worth a Continental."

Meeting no opposition from Maryland's undermanned Navy, the fleet of twenty-five warships escorting the British army did not threaten hostile actions against Virginians or Marylanders during the eight-day voyage from the Capes to the Head of Elk. The troops disembarked on August 25 in poor condition after a cramped six-week voyage from New York; some had died along the way. Howe would not be reinforced until the middle of September.

The British commander issued a proclamation to "The Province of Pennsylvania, the Lower Counties on the Delaware, and Counties of Maryland on the Eastern Shore of the Chesapeak-Bay," promising protection and a pardon to "all men who disavowed the rebellion and supported George III." Residents on the western shore were warned "that if they, in any manner, molest (either in their persons or property) the inhabitants of the Eastern Shore, who may be disposed to return to duty and allegiance, they may expect to feel the full force and weight of retribution and resentment from his Majesty's forces."

Howe's proclamation and the presence of the Royal Navy in the bay did renew activity among Maryland Tories, especially on Eastern Shore where James Chalmers recruited more than three hundred men for the Maryland Loyalist Regiment. In Virginia, the Queen's Loyal Virginia Regiment was formed by John Ellegon, a planter and former member of the House of Burgesses. Guerilla bands were organized in both Maryland and Virginia, as exiled Tories and deserters from the Continental Army banded together to raid patriot plantations and prey on Chesapeake Bay shipping.

On September 3 Washington's light infantry troops tried to delay Howe's advance. Five miles to the northeast of the Head of Elk landing, near Cooch's Bridge, Delaware, saw its only land combat during the war in spirited action in which the outnumbered American troops were driven back by the Hessians.

A week later, Washington's attempt to stop Howe's march on Philadelphia failed at Brandywine Creek, south of the city where Pennsylvania meets Delaware. In action so intense that guns could be heard twenty-five miles away, Howe attacked the American center and Cornwallis surprised Washington with a flanking maneuver. The Americans were forced to retreat toward Chester, and Howe proceeded to Germantown where he stationed nine thousand troops to hold off Washington. The British occupied Philadelphia on September 25.

British casualties at Brandywine were less than five hundred killed or wounded. The Americans lost three hundred killed, six hundred wounded, and four hundred captured. Among the American wounded was Lafayette; he had been shot in the leg but managed to escape. Bay country was represented at Brandywine and later at Valley Forge by the Maryland Line and the six Virginia regiments under the command of Brigadier General J.P.G. Muhlenberg.

Again the Continental Congress fled Philadelphia; this time reconvening in Lancaster, Pennsylvania, on September 18.

A British historian Reginald Hargreaves described an incident near Brandywine in which a Tory major, Patrick Ferguson, concealed in the undergrowth, had in his rifle sight an American "rider in buff and blue." The rider was "mounted on a bay horse and crowned with 'a remarkable large cocked hat'...an officer of exceptional distinction who apparently had ventured out from his lines on a mission of personal reconnaissance." When the American turned to ride away, Ferguson said he refused to shoot because "it was not pleasant to fire at the back of an unoffending individual who was acquitting himself cooly of his duty." Of course, the man in the cocked hat, who was saved by a sense of honor, was General George Washington. Major Ferguson would die in battle at Kings Mountain, South Carolina, in October 1780.

Elsewhere, Congress, after meeting briefly in Lancaster, reconvened at York, Pennsylvania; following the fall of Philadelphia, American troops, confused by fog, were defeated in the battle at Germantown; in New York a combined force of redcoats, Hessians, and loyalists attacked and took Forts Clinton and Montgomery near Bear Mountain, securing the Hudson River; Lafayette's first command, a detachment of four hundred militia and rifle corps, attacked British pickets in New Jersey, earning Lafayette a Congressional appointment as a division commander in the Continental Army; France agreed to sign the treaty recognizing American independence; one of the final congressional actions in 1777 was to proclaim the first national day of Thanksgiving; and Washington's army camped at Valley Forge, where, according to some reports, nobody froze and nobody starved, and according to others, one in every four died there; Washington praised the "incomparable patience and fidelity" of the troops at Valley Forge and Lafayette called their endurance "a miracle."

The Articles of Confederation were agreed to by the Continental Congress on November 14, after intermittent debate since June 1776, when Richard Henry Lee had proposed that "a plan of confederation be prepared and transmitted to the respective colonies for their consideration and approbation." The Confederation considered the former colonies now an alliance of sovereign states to deliberate as equals on common concerns. Article I declared "this confederacy shall be 'The United States of America'." In Article II, each of the states would retain its sovereignty in all instances "not expressly delegated to the United States." One quaintly historic note appeared in Article XI:

> Canada acceding to this confederation, and joining in the measures of the United States, shall be admitted into, and entitled to all advantages of this Union: but no other colony shall be admitted into the same, unless such admission be agreed to by nine States.

It would be March 1, 1781, before the Articles were ratified by all thirteen states, the last being Maryland which had refused to ratify until Virginia and other states claiming frontier lands ceded them to the United States.

Maryland's James Nicholson, now a captain in the Continental Navy, entered 1778 true to character when his frigate, *Virginia*, was seen at the York River by the 36-gun British frigate *Emerald* and chased back up the Chesapeake to Baltimore. The *Virginia* would remain at anchor for three months, to the displeasure of the Marine Committee of the Continental Congress. Then, during the night of March 31, as the ship was about to run the British blockade at the Virginia Capes with a pilot inexperienced in those waters, Nicholson tried to sail past a British brig unnoticed. But the *Virginia* pilot put the ship on a shoal near the mouth of the bay. Lashed by wind and tides, the frigate lost her rudder and slipped into deep water where Nicholson said he "thought it advisable to come to an anchor until daylight, [having] found one of the enemy's ships about two gun shots abreast ...and another further up the Bay." After the captain and some of his crew managed to reach shore at Cape Henry by barge, a British crew boarded the *Virginia* and accepted the frigate's surrender. Back in Baltimore, Nicholson held his rank as senior officer and prepared to fight another day.

The British captive whose insubordination had tried Washington's patience, Major General Charles Lee, was exchanged in March for British General Richard Prescott, who had been captured by the Rhode Island militia in a bordello near Newport in the spring of 1777. Not until later would Washington learn that Lee had advised General Howe that British control of the upper Chesapeake would divide the colonies and lead to America's collapse. He believed the plan influenced Howe's decision to march on Philadelphia. In four months, a New Jersey court-martial would try Lee for disobeying orders, misbehaving before the enemy, and showing disrespect for his commander-in-chief. Though Lee would deny his guilt on all counts, twenty-eight persons would testify against him. In August he would be found guilty and dismissed from the army for a period of one year.

The day that France signed a treaty of commerce and alliance with Benjamin Franklin ended any hopes that George III had entertained about an early victory over the colonials. Two radicals who had sparked the revolution responded differently to the news. Sam Adams warned against forming the French alliance, referring to America's new ally as the "papist French." Patrick Henry wrote: "I look at the past condition of America as at a dreadful precipice from which we have escaped by means of the generous French, to whom I will be ever-lastingly bound by the most heartfelt gratitude." Congress ratified the treaty on May 4, 1778, and refused the peace overtures recently offered by a British commission.

The Continental Congress had escaped Philadelphia, Washington had eluded the British trap in New Jersey, Clinton had replaced Howe as commander of British forces in America and was convinced that the occupation of Philadelphia was a hollow triumph after Burgoyne had been stopped at Saratoga in September 1777. Forces under Benedict Arnold and Daniel Morgan had been responsible for the Saratoga victory but General Horatio Gates ignored their feat and chose his aide, a young Maryland officer named James Wilkinson, to receive Burgoyne's sword (an affront that would influence Arnold's decision to defect to the British). The defeated Burgoyne returned home to severe criticism and retired to private life; he would be elected to the House of Commons and later write several plays, the most successful being *The Heiress*.

Saratoga was celebrated with parades, cannons, and bells in Williamsburg and Annapolis. The *Virginia Gazette* announced that the Williamsburg guardhouse was emptied except for those "who cannot be ranked amongst the friends of the Thirteen United States."

Clinton's evacuation of Philadelphia on June 18, 1778, led some of the state legislatures to speculate that the war was at an end. But Clinton, having been informed that a powerful French fleet under the command of Comte d'Estaing was approaching the Atlantic coast, decided to strengthen his New York fortifications. En route, he was pursued by Washington as far as Princeton. There, Lafayette took command of a Continental detachment with orders to halt the British withdrawal in New Jersey. The American assault was easily turned back at Monmouth Court House by a British rear guard under General Cornwallis.

The French fleet did not reach Sandy Hook until July. By then Clinton was safely encamped on the Hudson. French inaction over the next four months exasperated the Americans. D'Estaing blamed it on the weather and took his fleet to the West Indies.

The success at Saratoga was not enough to offset the humiliation of Philadelphia, and Washington's leadership was under attack again by Gates. This ambitious general, whose military competence would be discredited in the Carolina campaign, secretly sought Congressional support to have himself named army commander-in-chief. But his aide James Wilkinson revealed the scheme while in his cups—a stroke of good fortune for both Washington and the American Revolution.

Elsewhere, Georgia was being overrun by British troops supported by a large loyalist population, and Savannah would fall at year's end as twenty loyalist militia companies and fourteen hundred Georgians declared their allegiance to the crown; Congress appointed General Benjamin Lincoln commander of the Southern Department and urged Virginia and North Carolina to come to the immediate aid of South

Carolina and Georgia with men and supplies; Washington ordered the Maryland Line and Delaware Regiment, under command of Major General Baron de Kalb, to rescue the Carolinas; Spain asked Great Britain to recognize American independence and began supplying war materiel to the former colonies; the combined French and Spanish fleets would deny the British command of the sea; supplies failed to arrive and conditions at the 1779-80 winter encampment of Washington's army in Morristown proved to be much worse than the corresponding period at Valley Forge in 1777-78.

Fort Nelson was a Virginia fortification constructed on the west side of the Elizabeth River and garrisoned by about 150 militiamen. It was designed to safeguard military supplies stored at Norfolk and Portsmouth, located on each side of the river, and the navy stores and cargo ships at the Gosport marine yard. Thus the destruction or capture of Chesapeake supplies and vessels was a primary object of British amphibious assaults conducted in May 1779 under command of Commodore George Collier and Major General Edward Matthew.

Collier was convinced that the most feasible way to end the American rebellion was to cut off all resources needed to continue the war—not just army and navy arms and equipment but also farm commodities that could be exchanged for military materiel, these being "principally drawn from Virginia, and principally tobacco." The British attacks on bay region vessels, warehouses, and supply depots would come to be called the "tobacco wars." Since 1775, all of the square-riggers that cleared Chesapeake Bay carried tobacco as the main cargo, much of it destined for France or Spain where it was used as currency to build the American arsenal. Prior to the war, Virginia and Maryland tobacco accounted for about ninety-eight percent of the tobacco exported to England, which sold most of the crop to other European nations. And even during the war, loyalist agents were able to smuggle millions of pounds of American tobacco into England and Scotland.

Collier believed that interruption of Chesapeake navigation would wreck America's trade relations abroad and also "drive the Rebels to infinite inconvenience and difficulty, especially as [the Continental] army was constantly supplied by provisions sent by water through the Chesapeake."

The commodore's flagship, the 64-gun *Raisonable*, appeared off Cape Henry on May 8 with a fleet that included warships, gunboats, flat-bottom boats, barges, tenders, and several transports carrying about two thousand troops commanded by General Matthew plus artillery. The fleet anchored off Norfolk in the Hampton Roads harbor, where it was joined by loyalist privateers.

On May 9 Collier transferred from the *Raisonable* to the barge *Rainbow* so that he could lead the smaller craft up the Elizabeth to Fort Nelson. "Everything was prepared for attack," he wrote, "but the Enemy with great cowardice abandoned [the fort] in the night and fled, leaving the 13 stripes flying." The British did take Fort Nelson without opposition, but the fact that the small garrison was facing a vastly superior foe might suggest that "cowardice" was the better part of valor.

Before abandoning the fort, wrote Collier, the Virginians "set fire to a fine ship of war of twenty guns ready for launching, and also two large French merchant ships, one of which was laden with baled goods and the other with one thousand hogsheads of tobacco." But soon the entire southern shore of the James was in possession of General Matthew, who set up headquarters at Portsmouth while his troops seized Norfolk, destroyed Gosport, burned a Continental Army depot at Suffolk, and captured or destroyed 137 vessels.

As a detachment of Royal Highlanders seized arms and stores at Kemp's Landing, the privateers and many of the smaller British vessels sailed up branches of the Elizabeth and the James, and to the upper bay, spreading devastation well beyond initial targets. News accounts mentioned "the cruel and horrid depredations and rapine committed on the unfortunate and defenceless inhabitants."

The raids were called "a savage display of savage brutality!" in the *Pennsylvania Gazette*. The writer described how a "gentleman of consequence" and his daughters were dragged from their house and carried aboard a British warship. There "the wretched father was loaded with chains [while] the still more wretched daughters... became victims to the lust of those monsters of Hell."

Commodore Collier described the damage at Suffolk: "Nine thousand barrels of salted pork which were in store there for Washington's army, eight thousand barrels of pitch, tar and turpentine with a vast quantity of other stores and merchandise were all burnt and destroyed together with 7 vessels in the harbor richly laden." According to Campbell's account, the contents from the barrels of tar, pitch, turpentine, and rum "commingled" on the Suffolk wharves and flowed in "torrents of liquid flame" to the river, where...

> wind blowing violently, the splendid mass floated to the opposite shore in a conflagration that rose and fell with the waves....The broad sheet of fire, the crackling flames of the town, the lurid smoke, and occasional explosion of gunpowder in the magazines, projecting ignited fragments of timber like meteors in the troubled air, presented altogether an awful spectacle of the horrors of civil war.

Collier blamed the "cruel and horrid depredations of rapine" and other assaults on the privateers who "had no idea of order or discipline." The privateers had been ordered, he said, "to do no wanton acts of cruelty, not to burn houses or in any shape molest innocent people; but in spite of every endeavour to prevent it, some little irregularities happened." Though the raids succeeded in striking a blow at vital resources and

Chesapeake commerce, they failed to bring the patriots to their knees. Rather, the violence and ruin reinforced the passionate hatred of all things British in the lower bay region.

True to Britain's military behavior, the Chesapeake invasion was a brief in-and-out operation that failed to enlarge upon its success and establish a naval base at Portsmouth—but it did carry away needed supplies, more than five hundred slaves, and forty-four loyalist women and children who had sought refuge in the swamps. Collier and Matthew were ordered by Clinton to return to New York, and there the commodore boasted that damage inflicted in Virginia amounted to "upward of a Million Sterling."

On May 27 Governor Henry notified the Continental Congress of the British raid and added:

> After their departure from Portsmouth, they drew up their whole fleet before Hampton, and by a parade of their flat-bottomed boats, threatened a descent on that place; but a considerable body of troops, under Colonel Marshal, were so well prepared to receive them, and maintained so firm a countenance, that they did not choose to hazard the experiment, and yesterday, about noon, they hoisted sail and proceeded to sea.

Collier and Matthew set the stage for the 1780 Chesapeake Bay expedition of General Alexander Leslie and the 1781 invasions of Virginia by turncoat Benedict Arnold and General Cornwallis. What the Collier-Matthew invasion proved (and Cornwallis would fail to heed) was that military success in Virginia depended upon control of the bay and access to the sea.

To bypass the British blockade at the Virginia Capes, main supply lines between France and the Chesapeake went through Accomack and Northampton Counties on Virginia's Eastern Shore. Such vital supplies as medicine and munitions were shipped into Chincoteague and Metompkin Creeks, transported over land to small vessels in the upper Chesapeake, and then slipped past the enemy ships stationed in the bay. A fort was built on Parramores Beach to protect the incoming supply ships and to intercept the British raiding barges entering Metompkin Creek.

Nearby, on Hog Island, the British established an operating base under the command of loyalist Captain John Kidd, whose tenders and barges plundered the Shore communities for food and livestock to supply British warships in the area.

The year 1779 saw Samuel Chase accused of forming partnerships to corner the flour market and shipping the flour in violation of the congressional embargo. Chase countered by charging Charles Carroll, Matthew Tilghman, Samuel Wilson, and other members of the Maryland Senate with carrying on secret peace negotiations with the British. There are "traitors in the Senate!" cried Chase. The charges were dismissed for lack of evidence, but the Senate agreed to conduct an investigation to remove any suspicions. When Sam Adams heard the charge of treason against Carroll and Tilghman, he said that "Chase must have been mad." Back in Annapolis Samuel Wilson, influenced by Chase's role in the flour scandal, supported "An Act to Restrict Delegates of this State from Engaging in any Trade either Foreign or Domestic." The act passed both houses.

Thomas Jefferson, having succeeded Patrick Henry as Virginia governor, endorsed a proposal to establish at William and Mary the first chair of law in an American college. Its first occupant was George Wythe, who used the post to give direction to the American legal system. At William and Mary, Wythe had taught law to two of the nation's future presidents, Jefferson and James Monroe, and to John Marshall, a future chief justice.

Wythe had freed his slaves and was not one of those southern aristocrats opposed to the campaign to enlist blacks into the Continental Army. Slaveowners, horrified at the idea, did not yield until thousands of slaves escaped to the British. After that, an estimated five thousands slaves fought and died for the American cause of liberty. Some were drafted; others, under false promises of freedom, volunteered. Most were cooks, waiters, drummers, or laborers. Some were spies. A few, like Cesar Tarrant of Wythe's native county on the Chesapeake, ran away from their masters and and joined the Virginia Navy. Tarrant became a ship's pilot because of navigational skills and knowledge of the state's treacherous and poorly charted waterways; he was wounded during the war and later emancipated by the Virginia Assembly for meritorious services.

The Virginia Navy had commissioned more than thirty vessels by 1779, but they were so poorly armed and manned they were almost useless in defending Chesapeake waterways from enemy privateering raids. The Navy was all but wiped out in 1779 (and again in 1781) when the British burned Virginia's shipyards and port towns and captured or sank many of its vessels, some while afloat, others under construction or repair.

The poor condition of the Virginia Navy was worsened in 1779 by the fraudulent behavior of a man who had been commissioned in February to build a vessel of war. Although Mark Talbot, the builder, had been paid a substantial amount of money during the period of construction, the vessel was never delivered. Talbot claimed the vessel had been destroyed by the enemy, but the Virginia Board of War believed that he had used public money to build other vessels which he sold to privateers. Talbot was prosecuted by the state Attorney General for breach of contract.

The shortage of vessels was only part of the problems facing Governor Jefferson, who eventually admitted that lack of military knowledge and experience made him the wrong man for the job. The state's manpower needs were so critical that the Virginia Assembly ordered county courts to apprentice at least half the orphans in their care to navy duty. Recruiting efforts were hampered further when the Assembly reduced the ration of whiskey allotted per man in order to preserve grain. In Maryland when every white male over the age of eighteen had to swear an oath of fidelity to the state, the impact on military enlistments was insignificant.

But there were a few good moments that spring. Virginia's seagoing brigs *Mosquito* and *Liberty* took the British ships *Noble* and *Jane*, both transporting valuable cargoes. The *Liberty*, under Richard Barron, captured the *Fortunatus*, a large 120-gun British schooner which the Virginia crew (lacking cannons) peppered with musket balls. Several weeks later the *Liberty* saved a merchant ship from sinking after it had capsized off Newport News in the James River. The *Liberty* would continue to taunt the enemy throughout the war and remain on duty until late 1787, seeing longer service than any other American vessel.

In addition to the 22-gun *Defence* (which would be sold to a Baltimore merchant), most of the twenty-two vessels in Maryland's Navy were galleys or barges designed to protect shallow waters. The Maryland commodore Thomas Grason, while in command of the *Conqueror* and the *Chester*, would drive Tory privateers away from the Virginia Capes a week after British raiders destroyed the Maryland privateer *Lady Washington* and Virginia galley *Protector* in the Wicomico River.

Other Virginia galleys bore such names as *Washington, Norfolk Revenge, Safeguard, Dragon, Hero, Henry* and the *Gloucester* which became a prison ship. All had been requisitioned by Congress to guard Chesapeake troop convoys and merchantmen.

Some bay security was provided by the Continental Navy, which was told that, "as often as circumstances and the safety of your ships will admit it, you are to enter the mouths of Delaware and Chesapeake for the purpose of destroying the small armed vessels from New York that lurk about the Capes to the certain destruction of almost every Merchantman that sails."

By 1779 the Continental fleet had added thirteen frigates: *Effingham, Providence, Queen of France, Confederacy, Baltimore, Virginia, Delaware, Hampden, Boston, Raleigh, Congress, Randolph*, and *Montgomery*. The *Virginia* had been taken in 1778 while trying to run the blockade off the Virginia Capes, but none would survive long enough to see service at the Battle of Yorktown in 1781. Three would be destroyed to avoid capture, seven would be surrendered to the British, one would be blown up at sea, two would be burned.

Trumbull, last of the Continental frigates, was launched in August and placed in command of James Nicholson, but it would take until May 1780 before the ship could assemble a crew. Within the month, in close action with the British privateer *Watt* north of Bermuda, the *Trumbull* was "cut to pieces," wrote the captain of the ship's marines. After losing two masts, the *Trumbull* returned to Baltimore for repairs. It would remain inactive until August 1781 when, damaged by heavy winds, it would not be able to withstand an attack by two British warships, *Iris* and *General Monk*. The career of James Nicholson was scuttled along with the *Trumbull*.

Between 1777 and 1783, some two hundred Maryland privateers would successfully evade the British fleet in Chesapeake Bay to harass enemy vessels as far away as the West Indies. The owners of these vessels got rich off the war and also supplied America with desperately needed military supplies captured from the British. It has been estimated that American privateers captured nearly seven thousand British merchant vessels and cargoes valued at eight million dollars.

America's great naval hero in the Revolutionary War was John Paul Jones. In September 1779, aboard his flagship *Bon Homme Richard* in command of a fleet of several small vessels, including the *Alliance* and the *Pallas*, Jones came upon a fleet of forty merchant vessels convoyed by the 40-gun British frigate *Serapis* and the *Countess of Scarborough*. While *Pallas* was capturing the *Countess*, the *Richard* engaged the more superior *Serapis* in close combat that lasted for more than three hours. Finally, Jones's ship was so badly damaged that the British captain asked if Jones was ready to surrender, to which Jones by tradition replied, "I have not yet begun to fight." But, according to Quaife, the famous boast was not uttered by Jones in heat of battle but invented forty years later by a subordinate who worshipped him. Jones, in his report of the battle to Benjamin Franklin, said he merely replied "in the most determined negative." In the end—with the rigging of both ships entangled and both crews assailing each other in hand-to-hand fighting until the mast of the *Serapis* crashed to the deck—it was the British captain who struck his colors. Jones transferred his crew from the sinking *Bon Homme Richard* to the *Serapis* and led his fleet to the Netherlands, the *Richard* sinking en route, two days after the battle.

One version of the battle has the *Alliance* disappearing at the beginning of the fight, only to return toward the end and fire its guns at Jones instead of the British. According to Jones's account, when most of the *Bon Homme Richard's* aged guns were of no use about midway in the battle, his gunnery officer and others tried to surrender the ship. Jones said that the sinking of the *Richard* was not so much from gun damage caused by the *Serapis* but from the guns of the *Alliance*, commanded by Pierre Landais, a Frenchman commissioned in the Continental Navy.

John Paul Jones was born John Paul in Scotland in 1747. He was a gardener's son who spent his spare time on the beach or fishing, dreaming of a life of adventure on the sea. Lacking the money or influence to pursue a career in the Royal Navy, he joined the merchant marine at age thirteen and was apprenticed aboard the brig *Friendship* to load cargo transported between Barbados and Virginia. In 1760 John Paul was learning the slave trade as third mate on the *King George*, and two years later as chief mate on the *Two Friends* out of Kingston. By age twenty-two he had given up the slave trade and become master of the brig *John*, proving himself a good navigator and a man skilled in cargo transactions. He taught himself to read and write and adopted the manners of an English gentleman.

In 1772, after he had obtained command of the *Betsy*, a large square-rigger out of London, John Paul was attacked by a mutinous seaman while in port at Tobago. John Paul killed the seaman with his sword and then, on foolish advice, abandoned his command and caught a ship that was about to go to sea. It was then that he took the name John Paul Jones.

Nothing was heard of Jones until he arrived at Philadelphia in 1775 and introduced himself to the newly formed Continental Navy. He was immediately appointed a first lieutenant, and received his captain's commission in August 1776. Jones displayed his daring by capturing several merchant ships as he eluded a convoy of British frigates. But Jones's tour of duty with the American Navy was frustrating, one in which he was frequently overlooked for promotion because of his unwillingness to get along with either superiors or subordinates. "There were few officers who sailed with him who did not feel the lash of his tongue," wrote Coggins, "and occasionally the toe of his boot."

It was not until June 1777 that Jones was given command of the sloop *Ranger*, which would be the first ship to fly the Stars and Stripes flag recently adopted by Congress. But the command that earned him his fame as perhaps the nation's greatest naval hero was the *Bon Homme Richard*, a converted East India trading vessel *Duc de Duras*, which had been purchased for Jones by the French and renamed in honor of Franklin. Jones's squadron consisted of both American and French naval vessels, accompanied by privateers. Many nations were represented in his crews.

Jones was responsible for the only military operation of the Revolutionary War on English soil. In April 1778 he led a raiding party into Whitehaven, a northern port town located on Solway Firth where Jones had begun his seaman apprenticeship.

The highlight of his naval career was the defeat of the far superior frigate *Serapis* in September 1779. After the war Jones settled in France, dying in Paris in 1792. His body was shipped to America in 1905 and buried with honors in the chapel at the United States Naval Academy in Annapolis. John Paul Jones is remembered today as the Father of the American Navy.

By late 1779 the British had evacuated all their northern military strongholds, except New York City, and accelerated their southern campaign in the Carolinas and Georgia. That maneuver would shift the focus of the war away from the Chesapeake until the arrival of Britain's Commodore George Gayton and General Alexander Leslie with fifty-four vessels and 2,500 troops in October 1780.

Meanwhile, the Board of War recommended "that a fast sailing Boat be kept as a look out at Smith's Island [near the southern tip of the Eastern Shore] to give the alarm in Maggoty [Magothy] Bay on the approach of an Enemy; from thence an Express to be sent across the Country to Northampton Courthouse; the Boat then to proceed to York with the alarm. The [Eastern Shore] Battery at Cheriton to be repaired and the Guns there remounted immediately for the defence of that Inlet; That the Brass piece of Ordnance be brought to the Western Shore, and that the Iron four pounders and the two pounders, with two Swivels be left with Colonel Corbin. That two Gallies be stationed [on the Atlantic Ocean] between the South end of Hog Island and Chincoteague. That the Continental Soldiers on the Eastern Shore, which amount...to a complete Company, be ordered to rendezvous at Bridge Town, and that a Captain &c. be ordered over to command them."

Though the guns were quiet, the icy winter of 1779-80 was said to be the worst in memory for bay region residents. Huge ice drifts immobilized Chesapeake traffic, and it was possible to walk across the bay as far south as the Virginia Capes, within cannon range of the British blockade.

Seat of War

1780-1781

Great Britain's fate in America was decided on March 1, 1780, when Jean Baptiste Donatien de Vimeur, Comte de Rochambeau was appointed by the French king to command twelve infantry battalions to assist "his allies, the United States." In May, Lafayette, now a division commander in the Continental Army and a close friend of Washington, told the general that a French fleet of six ships and six thousand troops was en route to Rhode Island to support the American attack on General Clinton's army in New York. (The Marquis also announced the birth of his son, George Washington Lafayette.)

Patriots in Rhode Island celebrated the arrival on July 11 of the French Navy under command of Chevalier de Ternay. The fleet was transporting Rochambeau's army, which the general offered to put under Washington's command. The presence of the French was key to Washington's anticipated siege of the British position in New York. Washington believed that the capture of the main British army would be a difficult but devastating blow that would shorten the war. The arrival of Rochambeau would give the allies a combined strength of ten thousand men, to confront the seventeen thousand under Clinton in New York. But the allied troops would see no action until the Yorktown battle in September.

On July 23 British Rear Admiral Thomas Graves arrived at New York with a force that was supposed to ensure Great Britain's naval superiority in America. He joined with Admiral

Marriot Arbuthnot to block Newport and restrain the French squadron commanded by Admiral Louis, Comte de Barras.

After France had entered the war on the American side, Maryland and Virginia cut back on their navies, leaving the Chesapeake and its rivers "much infested with the Privateers and Cruisers of the Enemy," according to official reports. As the victims of depleted navies and with too many waterways to protect, some Chesapeake Bay areas had to rally to their own defense. A Maryland militia officer in St. Mary's County declared:

> It is really distressing to know the resources, and credit, of our State, will not furnish us with means of protection against the Enemys Barges that are now in our Bay & Rivers, plundering the Inhabitants, on the Shores, and keeping the whole of them in constant alarm and dread.

Finally, the Maryland General Assembly reacted to the raids with more acts for defense of the bay—enlarging, outfitting, and manning the fleet of barges. On August 28 Maryland Governor Thomas Sim Lee informed Jefferson:

> The alarming State of the Trade of Virginia and Maryland in the Chesapeake and above all, the extreme Difficulty and Hazard of supplying the Northern Army with Provisions from Virginia and the Southern Parts of this State, occasioned by the continued and increasing Depredations of the Enemy have rendered the immediate Expulsion of them from the Bay, an Object of Magnitude.

The governor said that again Baltimore merchants had undertaken to furnish two Brigs and three large Barges, with men, arms, and ammunition, "accompanied by two fast sailing State Boats to act as Tenders." He solicited support from the

Virginia governor who acknowledged the Chesapeake as "the unavoidable channel of all our commerce" and would instruct the Virginia Navy to clear the bay "of the hostile vessels which infested it."

Signals of Recognition were devised for Maryland and Virginia vessels meeting in the Chesapeake: *He who first makes the signal is to take in his foretop-gallant sail and hoist the Continental ensign at the foretop-gallant mast head. The other to answer by letting fly his maintop-gallant sheets, and hoisting a Continental Jack at the maintop-gallant mast head.*

The new force resulted in the capture of two Tory barges, owned by privateers Joseph Wheland and Joseph Shoemaker, at the mouth of the Patuxent River, but Wheland escaped to continue to raid the bay communities and plunder food supplies intended for the Continental Army. To make the raids less profitable for the Tories, patriots stripped the homes along the shore of the Potomac and on the St. Mary's islands of their valuables.

In the lower Chesapeake, the Virginia brig *Jefferson* teamed with the pilot boats *Liberty* and *Patriot* to capture five British privateers.

James Barron was appointed Commodore of the Virginia Navy and would operate out of the state's naval headquarters in Hampton. The son of Samuel Barron, James had been the commander of Fort George (today's Fort Monroe) at Old Point Comfort. Before the Revolution, he and his brother Richard gained their seagoing experience as masters of British merchant vessels. James would become "the most famous officer" in the Virginia Navy. His son, also named James Barron, would rise to the rank Senior Officer in the United States Navy and go down in history as the man who killed the American hero Stephen Decatur in a duel following the War of 1812.

Virginia's defense needs also forced Jefferson to plead with Congress "in the most earneste manner to send all the aid in small arms which can be spared." Should an enemy fleet attempt to take control of the Chesapeake, said Jefferson, "they would find us in a condition incapable of resistance for want of small arms. Our militia have been long ago defurnished of their arms for the use of the regulars."

The manpower needs of Maryland's military in 1780 led to the enlistment of slaves and to legislation which subjected free black males to the draft. Blacks also served as pilots for the Maryland Navy. Some slaves were rewarded with their freedom; free black volunteers were given land.

Elsewhere, Washington ordered fifteen hundred troops to reinforce General Lincoln in South Carolina; Congress sent Commodore Abraham Whipple with four Continental frigates to Charleston; but before a Virginia artillery regiment could join up with the American forces at Charleston, the city had surrendered to General Clinton in what history has recorded as "the worst American disaster of the war"; Clinton returned to New York and left the southern command to Lord Cornwallis who defeated troops commanded by the incompetent General Horatio Gates at Camden, South Carolina; Washington replaced Gates with General Nathanael Greene as the southern campaign turned to America's favor with a victory at King's Mountain, North Carolina; the Dutch declared war on Great Britain over the right to search ships at sea; and a "league of armed neutrality" was formed by Russia and other nations with the warning they would side with America unless British privateers stopped plundering their merchant vessels.

The Royal Navy returned to Chesapeake Bay in October 1780, transporting more than two thousand troops under the command of Major General Alexander Leslie. The fleet consisted of the *Romulus*, the 44-gun flagship of Commodore George Gayton, the 32-gun *Blonde*, and the 16-gun *Delight*, along with one of the Goodrich privateers and several smaller craft. On October 21, Gayton began preparations to establish a naval base at Portsmouth. Britain's military adviser Richard

Oswald had described the town's strategic importance in controlling Virginia and Maryland, noting particularly "the Naval Excursions that could be issued from thence into their great Rivers ...where the Estates and property of many of their leaders might be surprised & laid hold of." Oswald's appraisal:

THE TOWN OR VILLAGE OF PORTSMOUTH, ON NORFOLK RIVER OR CREEK, which falls into James River is a Place of great Importance. It is only 7 leagues from the Capes, or Ocean.

There is Water up to Portsmouth for a 40 Gun Ship, all standing. Portsmouth is only 8 Miles from the mouth, where the Creek falls into James River.

Hampton Road is only 2 Miles below the mouth of that Creek & is a fine safe Road, & has Water for the greatest ship in the Navy.

Portsmouth stands on the River—but has a large Swamp or morass behind it, & is all around secured by an Impracticable Country.

A ship riding in Hampton Road, if alarmed by an Enemy gets into Portsmouth or Norfolk River. She has only about 10 Miles to go up to the Town.

An Enemy from the Sea cannot get to Hampton Road before nottice is had of his approach, & the Ship gets away.

Running into Norfolk River, she cannot be followed, there being Batteries on both Sides the River.

Nor can an Enemy remain long in Hampton Road for fear of being surprised by our Ships from New York.

Portsmouth has a short Communication with N. Carolina so there is no want of Provisions. It is to be made a Place d'Armes. I think it is of the next Consequence to New York as a Seaport.

The Object of this Settlement is to shutt up the Navigation of Virginia & Maryland by 6 or 8 Armed

Vessels for cruising Cross the Chesapeak Bay—to rendezvous at Hampton Road & running up occasionally to Portsmouth for Victualling & refitting. If attended to it will do more for recovering those two Colonies than all the Armies we could send thither.

As a young man, Oswald had lived in Virginia and engaged in trade in the area around Norfolk, Portsmouth, and the Elizabeth River. He concluded that the Portsmouth base, "if well taken care of would besides become the most convenient Rendevous for all W. India & other Cruisers & Privateers besides those allotted for the Chesapeak."

On October 23 Leslie occupied Newport News and Hampton, where the galley *Henry* was burned while undergoing repairs. Meanwhile, Jefferson had called up militia to defend Portsmouth and asked Congress to assign Light-Horse Harry Lee's Continental horsemen to the state. One militia division was assembled at the James River near Smithfield under Generals Muhlenberg and Weedon, and another under General Thomas Nelson on the lower peninsula.

By October 30 Leslie had abandoned Hampton and Newport News and moved his troops across the James to Suffolk. It appeared that the British planned to remain in the bay region, but an American victory at King's Mountain, North Carolina, caused Cornwallis to order Leslie's expedition to Charleston. Virginians believed that their hastily established defenses had forced the British to leave in such haste that they left several undamaged vessels in Gosport shipyard. Hampton residents cheered the departing fleet and toasted a small band of militiamen who had defeated the last foraging raid by one hundred Royal Marines. Twenty marines were killed, wounded, or captured; there was one militia casualty. But the worst was yet to come for Virginia.

In December when Clinton learned that Chesapeake Bay had been abandoned, he sent sixteen hundred troops to Virginia under newly commissioned Brigadier General

Benedict Arnold. This was the man whom Washington had once praised as one of fortune's favorites who "will do everything that his prudence and valor shall suggest to add success to our arms." But later he would say that Arnold was "hackneyed in villainy [and] lost to all sense of honor and shame."

Now the villain was determined to lay Washington's beloved Virginia to waste by burning its main source of income—tobacco. Arnold's objective was property, not people. He would attempt to avoid military encounters and exercise a policy based on the belief that Virginia's ruin would demoralize Congress and shorten the war.

Arnold would take advantage of Thomas Jefferson's weakness as a governor. Unable to come to grips with the need to build a strong Virginia defense, Jefferson had confined his military activities to supplying men and supplies to Washington's army. As a result, his state was unprepared for the ruinous invasions in 1781 by Arnold, Lord Charles Cornwallis, and Major General William Phillips. He had hoped that Arnold would make Norfolk his headquarters and focus his activities in the lower Chesapeake region, but burned-out Norfolk held no appeal for Arnold. His primary interest in the bay was as an anchorage for his fleet, which included the 44-gun *Charon*, the *Fowey*, four frigates, three sloops, two brigs, and sixteen other vessels. Within hours of his arrival, Arnold had captured several local vessels for use in transporting his army up the James as far as Richmond. Along the way, Virginia's great plantations and supply depots would be plundered and destroyed with little opposition.

On New Year's Eve, however, when British regulars landed on the lower peninsula and marched into Hampton seeking river pilots familiar with Virginia waterways, they were forced to return to their boats by a company of Virginia militia. It would be one of the few times that Arnold's raiders were driven off.

Benedict Arnold, born in 1741 in Norwich, Connecticut, rose to the rank of captain in the militia before joining the Continental Army as a colonel in April 1775. After an unsuccessful raid on Quebec, he distinguished himself during the naval battle on Lake Champlain. Passed over for promotions and seeing others given credit for his victories—and heavily in debt for his extravagant living—Arnold brooded over his country's lack of gratitude and respect. In 1780, while in command of West Point, he offered General Clinton a plan to surrender the fort to the British. Late one night on the banks of the Hudson, he met with Major John Andre to arrange final details of his defection to the British. Andre was captured on his return to British lines, in disguise and carrying information on the West Point defenses. He was hanged as a spy.

Arnold escaped to the British ship *Vulture* and demanded twenty thousand pounds sterling for his treachery. He received only about a third of that amount, was named Brigadier General in the British Army, and for the first three months of 1781 became the scourge of Virginia.

From the Hampton Roads anchorage, Arnold's army was transported by an amphibious force up the James River to Burwell's Ferry. Arnold then proceeded to Westover and plundered Benjamin Harrison's plantation, Berkeley Hundred, releasing about forty slaves. Harrison was in Philadelphia at the time, pleading with Congress for troops to defend Virginia.

From Westover Arnold went to Petersburg, fought off a small group of Continental troops, and marched his army into Richmond. There, after robbing the capital city of its stores and treasure in the first week of 1781, Arnold sent a message to Governor Jefferson offering not to burn Richmond if the British were allowed to remove the city's tobacco. Jefferson rejected the offer and Arnold ordered the destruction of government buildings, a powder magazine, and the state cannon factory nearby.

Arnold also confiscated large quantities of salt, so critical to the preservation of food. Earlier, Maryland's Council of Safety had sent this plea to the West Indies: "For God's sake, send us all the salt you possibly can. Our people are in greatest distress for Want of it." Salt was so scarce that the Hampton saltworks had been placed under the guard of local militia. John Page wrote:

> If we had but Salt enough to satisfy our Country, Men who begin to complain for want of it, and Arms and Ammunition, we should be able to make a very good Stand against all the Forces that can be sent to Virginia.

With Richmond in near ruin, the British returned to Westover, where they boarded their vessels and proceeded down the river. At Charles City Courthouse a detachment of forty British rangers under Colonel John G. Simcoe surprised and defeated about 150 militiamen. About two weeks later, after meeting no significant opposition at Smithfield and other points on the lower James, Arnold arrived at Portsmouth and set about establishing a permanent post. During the expedition Arnold had lost seventeen men killed and twenty-three wounded; most of the loss occurred in a militia ambush near Hood's Point, commanded by Colonel George Clarke. One of the participants was John Marshall, who wrote:

> ...near Hoods, Colonel Clarke drew a party of them into an ambuscade, and gave them one fire with some effect; but on its being partially returned, the Americans broke and fled in the utmost confusion.

It may have been the news of this encounter which motivated James Madison to write facetiously to Edmund Pendleton: "I am glad to hear that Arnold has been at last fired at."

The pessimism concerning Virginia's poor defense situation was described as "gloomy, humiliating, apparently almost desperate" by Charles Campbell. From his 1860 history:

> Thus it happened, that while the regular troops of Virginia were serving at a distance in other States, the militia, after five years' war, was still so unarmed and undisciplined that no effective resistance was made to this daring invasion [by Arnold's army].... Virginia had entered upon the war when she was already loaded with debt, and exhausted by her Indian war, and by her non-importation policy, before the war began. Intersected by rivers, she was everywhere exposed to the inroads of the enemy; and a dense slave population obstructed the prompt movement of the militia....The bulk of the people were staunch whigs and well affected to the French alliance but they were growing despondent, and some were even beginning to fear that France was prolonging the war so as to weaken America as well as Great Britain and to render the new confederation dependent upon its allies. With the aid of a superior French fleet there could be no doubt of the successful issue of the war; without that aid, there was too much reason to fear that the people would not be kept much longer firm, in so unequal a contest.

A letter complained of money "squandered away no one knows how, or wherefore... neither man, horse, musket, cannon, wagon, boat, or any one thing in the world that could be found for our defence. In this situation it need not surprise you that Arnold, with a handful of bad troops, should march about the country, take and destroy what he pleased [and] feast with his tory friends."

Across the harbor from Portsmouth, Hampton townspeople were deploring the lack of security that permitted hundreds of redcoats to raid local farms and seize livestock and poultry and then overwhelm a militia company at nearby Big Bethel Bridge. Miles King, a Hampton official, informed Governor Jefferson that their only protection was now "a Guard of six men below Old Point Comfort, and a guard of twelve men at Newport News, which suffered 17 Boats full of Troops to land and make about fifty Fires." He continued: "The number of the Enemy don't discourage us, but what we want is men to stand by us. The late unfortunate affair in this County will I hope sufficiently prove the Courage of our County men. In that Action many guns were lost, and what Small quantity of Ammunition the men had, was nearly Expended. We are now in want of about sixty stand of arms, flints, powder & Ball, and some men to assist us, and then our County here will turn out as much cheerfulness as ever." King concluded:

> Light Horses are very necessary for this part of the Country tho' we have only three. I was just now informed that forty five sail of vessels were counted in the Bay this morning, including the Line of Battle Ships.

Jefferson also received a letter from Washington. The general was worried that the progress the British were making in Virginia was "very alarming" but held out hope for the "Naval superiority" promised by Lafayette.

On January 20 Lafayette had written to Count de Vergennes:

> With a naval inferiority it is impossible to make war in America. It is that which prevents us from attacking any point that might be carried with two or three thousand men. It is that which reduces us to defensive operations, as dangerous as they are humiliating. The English are conscious of this truth, and all their movements prove how much they desire to retain the empire of the sea. The harbours, the country and all the resources it offers appear to invite us to send thither a naval force.

France had an obvious interest in America's success in the Revolutionary War. Lafayette noted: "the advantage of the United States being the object of the war, and the progress of the enemy on that continent being the true means of prolonging it, and of rendering it, perhaps, even injurious to us, it becomes, in a political and military point of view, necessary to give us, both by vessels sent from France and by a great movement in the fleet in the islands, a decided naval superiority for the next campaign." Washington's army was praised: "The Continental troops have as much courage and real discipline as those that are opposed to them. They are more inured to privation, more patient than Europeans....They have several officers of great merit."

With Virginia's small navy helpless against Arnold's raids, Virginians had looked for the French fleet to arrive in the bay to block Arnold's escape. But when a French squadron did appear on February 15, it remained only four days and Arnold's raiders were free to continue their pillage of tobacco and military stores.

Washington had requested the support of the entire French fleet in the Chesapeake, but the fleet was still blocked by the British at Newport. It was only because a storm had damaged some of the British ships that French Admiral Sochet Destouches was able to gain a temporary superiority over the British Admiral Arbuthnot, permitting him to detach Le Bardeur de Tilly with a small squadron consisting of the 64-gun *Eveille* and two frigates. The squadron commander was instructed to control the Chesapeake, protect allied land and sea forces, cut off any British reinforcements, and leave Arnold without naval support in Virginia. But Arnold was advised of the approach of the French squadron and withdrew his vessels to the Elizabeth River. There, in addition to the British artillery on the shore, he had the safety of waters too shallow for heavier ships to pursue. The French put to sea, failing to block the Elizabeth or to deliver the support expected by Lafayette—but Tilly did destroy six Tory privateers and at the Capes captured the *Romulus*, a 50-gun British Navy ship coming to the Chesapeake from Charleston.

Washington dispatched Lafayette to Virginia in February with twelve hundred men: three regiments of light infantry drawn from the New England and New Jersey regiments of the Continental Army. His orders were to capture Arnold and "execute the punishment due his treason and desertion in the most summary way." Washington said it would be "an event particularly agreeable to this country." He hoped to trap Arnold between Lafayette's army and the French fleet that was supposed to be waiting in Hampton Roads.

When Lafayette arrived at the Head of Elk landing in upper Chesapeake Bay, he transported his troops and supplies to Annapolis in small craft converted to gunboats. The expedition was convoyed by James Nicholson, whose squadron contained his privateer flagship *Nesbit* and two other armed vessels. Lafayette learned at Annapolis that the French support he expected in Virginia would not be there. Lafayette's arrival in the state capital was fortuitous, however. According to Maryland historian John M. Hemphill II, he "took to the water as commander of a hastily improvised warship to drive off two British naval vessels." The British had tried to burn Maryland ships under construction at Stephen Seward's boatyard.

Lafayette's presence in Annapolis was noted by Margaret Ogle (the wife of Maryland's future governor Benjamin Ogle): "The divine Marquis de la Fayette is in town, and is quite the thing."

Away from the battlegrounds, a government was being shaped by the Continental Congress. The Articles of Confederation, ratified on March 1, was a "league of friendship" which reserved sovereignty to the individual states. It would loosely govern the thirteen states until independence was won. Under the Articles, as governing body of the new nation, Congress assumed a new title: "The United States in Congress Assembled."

A major obstacle to obtaining adoption of the Articles of Confederation was overcome when Virginia offered to relinquish to the United States all claims to the Northwest Territory won for the state in 1778 by George Rogers Clark. A condition to the Virginia offer was that the purchase of Indian lands by speculators in other states be declared void. Background to the dispute was summarized by John Marshall:

> Within the chartered limits of several states were immense tracts of vacant territory, which, it was supposed, would constitute a large fund of future wealth; and the states not possessing that advantage insisted on considering this territory a joint acquisition.

A proposal by Jefferson in 1776 had attempted to dictate the future of the West by relinquishing Virginia's western territories on the basis that they "shall be established on the same fundamental laws" as those which governed Virginia and "shall be free and independant of this colony and of all the world."

Maryland was one of the states not possessing large tracts of vacant territory; it had been denied opportunities for territorial expansion by Lord Baltimore's proprietary charter. A shortage of available land jeopardized the Maryland economy. The state needed, and demanded, an interest in the vacant territories that were to be ceded to the United States. The Maryland Declaration read in part:

> We declare that we will accede to the Confederation, provided an Article or Articles be added thereto, giving full power to the united States in Congress assembled to ascertain and fix the Western Limits of the States claiming to extend to the Mississippi or South Sea, and expressly reserving and securing to the united States a Right in Common in, and to all the Lands lying to the Westward of the Frontiers as aforesaid, not granted to,

surveyed for, or purchased by Individuals at the Commencement of the present War, in such Manner that the said Lands be sold out, or otherwise disposed of for the Common Benefit of all the States.

Maryland hesitated to ratify the Articles of Confederation even after Virginia gave up its western claims. But when Maryland applied to the French minister for military aid in defending the Chesapeake against the British Navy, he refused until the state agreed to adopt the Articles.

Congress pledged to use the ceded lands for the common good of all the states, the first step in the expansionism which ultimately settled the entire continent under the American flag. Virginia's western territory would form the states of Illinois, Indiana, Ohio, Michigan, Wisconsin, and part of Minnesota.

In March 1781, after Tilly returned to Newport, Rochambeau and Destouches decided to execute Washington's original strategy and send the entire French fleet to the Chesapeake. Destouches would command a force of eight warships and three frigates, transporting an additional twelve hundred troops to support Lafayette in his campaign against Arnold. In Annapolis, Lafayette was informed that help was coming and to continue his journey to Hampton Roads.

On March 16 the Destouches expedition was overtaken off the Virginia Capes by a British fleet of the same size, commanded by Arbuthnot. Hindered by strong winds, the two fleets were severely damaged in the exchange of gunfire. When the French line broke, and Destouches was unable to consolidate his command, he maneuvered his fleet past the disabled British ships and out to sea. The French returned to the base at Newport, leaving control of Chesapeake Bay to the Royal Navy and leaving Lafayette again without the promised support. The return of the French fleet to Rhode Island may have saved Benedict Arnold "from the fate which his treason merited," wrote John Marshall.

James Madison and Theodorick Bland sent the following dispatch to the Continental Congress:

> The unfortunate circumstances which have attended the Naval engagement of Chesapeake on the 16th ultimo, we feel with unspeakable regret, as they [the British] have snatched from us the pleasing prospects we had cherished for some time past, of frustrating the Sanguine project of the Enemy (of subjugating most of the Southern States in this Campaign) and thrown our Country into a Situation which must require her utmost executions....

Americans were the victims of their own humiliating blunder on March 19 when Captain William Buckner of the Virginia Navy escorted the wrong fleet into Chesapeake Bay. It was only after he boarded one of the ships did Buckner realize that he was guiding a British not a French fleet. "Buckner would remain a prisoner for one year," wrote Goldenberg and Stoer, "and the ships he led in brought reinforcements to Arnold."

Lafayette tried to return to Head of Elk on March 13 but Annapolis was blockaded by two British ships, the sloops *Hope* and *General Monk*. He camped his troops outside the town and traveled alone to Williamsburg in order to observe Virginia's military strength and to meet General Frederich Wilhelm Augustus von Steuben. The baron had been given command of the newly established Virginia Continentals. Lafayette left Virginia on March 28 to rejoin his troops in Maryland.

A day earlier, after occupying Petersburg, Arnold's army had been reinforced by Major General William Phillips with twenty-six hundred fresh troops. Phillips assumed control of the Virginia campaign and Arnold remained as second in command.

Meanwhile, in a letter to Lafayette, Washington mentioned a planned attack on the British headquarters in New York and granted the young Frenchman permission to participate if he wished. Then he changed his mind. On April 6, concerned that Phillips was going to support Cornwallis in the south, Washington told Lafayette to place his troops under General Greene's command in North Carolina.

Nicholson used two small vessels to convoy Lafayette's troops across the upper bay to Head of Elk. From there Lafayette informed Washington that he would try to avoid capture by the British ships by leading his troops to the south by land. He also wrote that the troops were "Very Uneasy at the idea of joining the Southern Army," and that he himself preferred to participate in Washington's attack on New York.

While British marines and loyalist privateers under Arnold and Phillips were pillaging plantations and supply depots up and down the James River, worried officials in Maryland observed that "after they have accomplished their Business in Virginia, it is more than probable they will visit us." As expected, British raiders sailed up the bay and, near St. Michael's River in Talbot County, robbed Wye House of many of its paintings and other treasures. They also threatened Mount Vernon, keeping "the Inhabitants on the waters of Potomack in constant alarm," looting and burning the warehouse on Port Tobacco Creek. In a state handicapped by the lack of guns, munitions, and trained men to use them, nothing was safe from the "plundering Banditts."

On April 8 the Maryland authorities contacted Lafayette at Head of Elk and urged him to delay his march to the south. They asked for his help in defending their state against anticipated British raids on the military stores and provisions at Annapolis and Baltimore. Lafayette replied:

> I...Most sincerely Lament the depredations Committed By the Ennemy. This cruel and Savage way of Making war is the More Exasperating as it is out of our power to punish or prevent these

devastations. Every town laying in the Bay or the Rivers is so defenseless and exposed that each of them Requires a force to defend it superior to what the ennemy will send for its Reduction. So far as Relates to armed Vessels and privateers, I should think that Militia Could be Collected to oppose the landing of a few sailors. As to the Movements of the British troops, they are so Rapid, and it is so impossible to defend Both shores of every River that with the Least judgement they may elude their opposition.

Lafayette then advised the Governor's Council that he would interrupt his march south and comply with the governor's request, "However inadequate I am to the defense of Annapolis, Baltimore, and Alexandria..."

To the Chevalier de La Luzerne, he wrote: "The governor of Maryland informs me that the ennemy ships are sailing back up the Potowmack and intend to burn Alexandria. He fears for Baltimore and Annapolis. I shall march hard in that direction tomorrow, but defending these rivers is about as easy as defending the rivers on the moon."

Lafayette left Head of Elk on April 13 and three days later was in Baltimore, where he confiscated "a Large Number of Waggons to Carry the troops as far as Potowmack." When he received reports that Phillips had reached the lower bay with British troops and was widening the destructive raids in Virginia, Lafayette was forced to give up his defense of Maryland and accelerate preparations for the march south—a march that would never reach the Carolinas.

Desertion had become a major problem among Lafayette's troops, who complained about the southern campaign. Lafayette put down a threatened mutiny by hanging one of his men and then borrowing on his private credit to purchase clothing and provisions for the troops. In a letter to Washington he wrote:

The Merchants of Baltimore Lend me a sum of about 2000 pounds which will procure some shirts, Linnen over alls Shoes, and a few Hatts. The ladies will make up the Shirts and the over alls will Be made By the detachment So that our Soldiers Have a chance of Being a Little more Comfortable. The Money is Lent upon My Credit, and I Become a Security for the payment in two year's time, when by the french Laws I may better dispose of my Estate.

Washington praised Lafayette's generosity as "an everlasting monument of your ardent zeal & attachment to [America's] Cause & the Establishment of its Independence."

After two days of travel by "waggons and horses," Lafayette and his men arrived at Washington's home at Mount Vernon, overlooking the Potomac. While there he informed Washington that the enemy had been at his home and freed many of his slaves. He said that what affected him most, however, was news that

Mr. Lund Washington [a cousin] went on board the enemy's vessels and consented to give them provisions. This being done by the gentleman who in some measure represents you at your house will certainly have a bad effect, and contrasts with spirited answers from some neighbors that had their houses burnt accordingly.

Washington admonished his cousin:

I am very sorry to hear of your loss; I am a little sorry to hear of my own; but that which gives me most concern is, that you should go on board the enemy's vessels and furnish them with refreshments. It would have been a less painful circumstance of your noncompliance with their request, they had burnt my house and laid the Plantation in ruins.

On April 21 Lafayette reached Alexandria and took command of all American troops in Virginia. His force was too small to take the offensive against a foe which now combined the armies of Arnold and Phillips. He had only the support of von Steuben's newly enlisted Virginia Continentals and a few untrained militia companies. From now on, Lafayette's real effectiveness would be in sniping at the enemy rear and forcing the enemy to turn away from the destruction of Virginia to pursue him "from river to river." In the long wait until the French fleet arrived, Lafayette's "snipe and run" tactic probably saved Virginia from conquest.

On April 29 Phillips sent Arnold from Portsmouth with some two thousand men to march on Petersburg. Arnold burned tobacco and military stores intended for Washington's army and easily resisted the militia charge led by General Peter Gabriel Muhlenberg, second in command to von Steuben in Virginia. The British then proceeded to Osborne's Wharf on the James fifteen miles below Richmond, where von Steuben had stationed a militia company with orders to intercept the enemy. After a three-hour skirmish, Arnold's guns drove the Virginians across the Appomattox River over a bridge which they dismantled to discourage pursuit. The militia suffered about seventy casualties and the enemy took most of the Virginia flotilla which had been assembled on the James for an assault on the British at Portsmouth. In an effort to scuttle the vessels before escaping to shore, the Virginians were able to sink or burn four ships, five brigantines, and a number of smaller vessels. Two ships, three brigantines, five sloops, and two schooners laden with two thousand hogsheads of tobacco plus flour and other supplies were captured by the British.

After the long march from Baltimore—through Alexandria, Fredericksburg, and Bowling Green—Lafayette's three regiments of light infantry reached Richmond just in time to break up a raid by Phillips's army. It surprised Lafayette when Phillips left the city without a fight and proceeded down the James toward Hampton Roads, stopping at Warwick to burn several mills and warehouses, and seize five hundred barrels of flour and five vessels. Lafayette, fearing he might be trapped between the armies of Phillips and Arnold, sent a request for immediate support to Major General Anthony Wayne in Pennsylvania. He asked Jefferson for men but men were not available. What he did receive from Jefferson was "a small map of the vicinity of Williamsburg, York, Hampton, and Portsmouth done on a scale of 5 miles to the inch which may serve for Pocket Purposes, and a larger one of the vicinities of Portsmouth on a scale of a mile to the inch which may be resorted to where greater accuracy is requisite."

Maryland Governor Thomas Sim Lee notified Jefferson in May that the Maryland Line had embarked at Head of Elk, en route to the southern campaign. He urged that Virginians take every precaution to prevent their capture by the British fleet. Already, he said, lookout boats had sighted "several small Privateers in the Bay and one or two as high up as Wiccomico in Virginia." The spirit and courage of the Maryland Line won praise and admiration from the men they fought with and those they fought against. No Continental troops had "won greater glory than the Maryland Line," wrote James McSherry in his *History of Maryland* (published 1904). They were the first Americans to use the bayonet in battle, and they were the troops "most often called to lead with that bloody weapon into the ranks of the foe. They seldom shrank from the encounter." They had repelled repeated charges by British regulars in the battles of Long Island and White Plains, saving Washington's army from disaster, and had routed the enemy at Harlem Heights. The Marylanders distinguished themselves in American successes at the battles of Trenton and Princeton, and held their own against overwhelming odds at Brandywine. Again, in the south, they used the bayonet "with terrible effect." Yet for more than two years, the battalion fought "without a shilling of pay," wrote Brigadier General Otho Holland Williams.

The Maryland Line defeated Tarleton's legion in 1781 at the battle of Cowpens, near the boundary separating North and South Carolina. The British had just annihilated a force of Virginia Continentals en route to Charleston, many of whom were massacred after surrendering. The Continentals were replaced by fourteen hundred poorly trained Virginia militia.

To take advantage of the Chesapeake's many tributaries, Lafayette had William Frazier's shipyard on the Mattaponi River build flatboats large enough to carry forty men each but light enough to be drawn on carriages by only two horses. Lafayette learned from Virginia Commodore James Barron that his lookout boat had sighted British ships sailing north on the Chesapeake, guided by loyalist pilots familiar with the bay and its rivers. The commodore reported that "40 Sail in number with several large Barges ful of Troops" seemed bound for Baltimore, leaving behind in the Hampton Roads harbor two warships and eight other vessels. He estimated that the ships were transporting about three thousand men and two hundred horses; from the Hampton Roads harbor to Maryland on a good wind was at least a day's voyage. Lafayette replied: "Should they move up the Potomack, I will move there with the greatest rapidity." It was an empty promise. After the enemy's repeated threats on the Potomac, nearly capturing George Mason's plantation Gunston Hall, Lafayette could only warn Maryland officials that without immediate reinforcements in Virginia, or naval support on the Chesapeake, he did not see how an invasion of the state could be prevented. Yet in a surprising turnaround, in a letter to Washington reporting on enemy strength in lower Chesapeake Bay, Lafayette was brash enough to write: "Should a french fleet Now Come in Hampton Road the British Army would, I think, Be ours."

Maryland officials, worried about their defense, ordered that troops requested by Lafayette "be stopt."

Jefferson was told by General George Weedon that the British "have committed Considerable Depradations" in Maryland. He reported intelligence he had received concerning enemy ships on the Potomac proceeding "to Hollis's marsh where a body of militia were drawn together under the command of Colo. Richard Henry Lee." He said the fleet "consisted of Three Ships, Three Brigs, and Seven others of different sizes." On the Virginia side of the Potomac, the British tried to land "at Stradford near the Marsh and were beat off by the Militia." The fleet sailed up river as far as "Genl. Washington's seat, and some of their small Vessells went to Alexandria, cut out a Tobacco Vessell which however was by the Vigilence of the Inhabitants recovered and part of the pirats taken. On their return, the British "took off several of Mr. Washington's Negroes and did him other damage," before sailing down the bay. Weedon reasoned that the purpose of the British raid was "to distract us from succouring Genl. Green" in Carolina.

Cornwallis, failing to notify Clinton in New York, abandoned the Carolinas in April to take part in the Virginia campaign. With the pressure off, General Greene urged Lafayette to remain in Virginia. He was told to "conduct the Military operations as circumstances should dictate to be proper." Greene included this personal note:

> I have only one word of advice to give you (having entire confidence in your ability zeal and good conduct), that is not to let the love of fame get the better of your prudence and plunge you into a misfortune, in too eager a pursuit after glory. This is the voice of a friend, and not the caution of a General.

Greene had gone to Maryland during the previous winter to recruit soldiers for his southern army. A successful draft "would dampen the hopes of the enemy more than ten Victories," he said, and stop "the spread of desolation and horror throughout the Carolinas." When this mission failed, Greene warned Maryland of the dangers to come should the south be lost. But at the time, Marylanders were more concerned about the presence of the British Navy in the Chesapeake.

A message from Cornwallis in Wilmington had ordered Phillips to meet him at Petersburg. Lafayette, trailing the British, also marched to Petersburg on the opposite side of the James, there to sit and wait. On May 10 Phillips joined Arnold for the rendezvous with Cornwallis, but he was suddenly taken ill and died four days later. Arnold would regain command of British forces in Virginia until Cornwallis arrived on May 20.

Lafayette's letter to Washington on May 15 was not unexpected:

> With the handful of men I have, there is no chance of resisting the combined armies unless I am speedily and powerfully reinforced.

Clinton opposed the decision by Cornwallis to go to Virginia and told him he considered the plan "likely to be dangerous to our interest in the southern colonies." Events over the next five months would prove him right. Nevertheless, Cornwallis wrote to Clinton:

> I cannot help expressing my wishes that the Chesapeake may become the seat of war.

He felt that the Virginia rivers were "advantageous to an invading army" and believed the British should concentrate on this "center of insurrection" even if it meant evacuating New York. In fact, on May 10 he had assured Phillips

> that I am quite tired of marching about the country in quest of adventure. If we man an offensive war in America we must abandon New York and bring our force into Virginia, then we have a state to fight for, and a successful battle may give us America.

The irony was that while Cornwallis was eyeing Virginia from Carolina, Washington was watchful of New York, convinced that it was the center of Clinton's strategy for victory over America; and Clinton was determined to defend New York from an expected attack by Washington.

Another reason Cornwallis wanted to go to Virginia was to improve the health of his army, which in past months had nearly been ruined by sickness incurred in the Carolinas. But Clinton called Virginia "the graveyard of armies." Washington too was concerned about the ill effects that a hot, humid summer in his native state would have on his troops, particularly the French.

Clinton had already devised a strategy for Virginia. From North Carolina, General Horatio Gates advised Jefferson that Lord Cornwallis planned "to take immediate possession of Portsmouth in Your State." Cornwallis's plan was to try again to post a naval station there, so that the British could launch a northward drive against Pennsylvania or the peninsula between the Chesapeake and Delaware bays. He believed that a Chesapeake base, supported from the sea, would interrupt America's north-south communications and destroy Washington's food supply line. He was warned, however, not to move his troops into Virginia until Clinton could afford to send sufficient reinforcements from New York. Cornwallis ignored Clinton and obtained the king's approval. In the rush to execute his plan, Cornwallis had reduced his campaign effectiveness at the battle of Guilford Court House in North Carolina and entered Virginia with a weakened army of fifteen hundred men. In deserting the Carolinas he had sworn to secure for the crown, he endangered the southern loyalists left behind.

When forced to yield, Clinton took a different stance on the value of a Virginia campaign. He now declared: "Virginia has been looked upon as universally hostile, Maryland less so, but has not been tried; but in Pennsylvania, on both sides of the

Susquehanna, and between the Chesapeake and Delaware, friends of the king's interests are said to be numerous." Having now agreed that the key was to subdue Virginia, he instructed Arnold to cooperate with Cornwallis in the destruction of the Virginia warehouses which had supplied Greene's army in the Carolinas. Cornwallis, who had been second in command to Clinton since 1778, would take control of all British forces in Virginia, which ultimately would number between eight and nine thousand men.

In a letter to Chevalier de La Luzerne, the French minister to America, Lafayette expressed concern over the odds he would have to face against Cornwallis's infantry and cavalry. After reporting on the transport ships which had arrived in the bay and were sailing up the James, he added: "I would really like to know, Monsieur le Chevalier, if people expect to see me *give this madman Cornwallis a good thrashing*." His appraisal of the local situation was simple: "There is no fighting here unless you have naval superiority, or an army mounted on race horses." Complaining about the late arrival of General Wayne and his Pennsylvanians, Lafayette suggested that "if we had remained en route as long as they have, the British would be in possession of all of Virginia."

Below is an excerpt from Lafayette's letter to Washington on May 24, the day the Virginia General Assembly left Richmond to regather in Charlottesville:

> Public stores and private property being removed from Richmond, this place is a less important object. I don't believe it would be prudent to expose the troops for the sake of a few houses most of which are empty. But I am wavering between two inconveniences. Was I to fight a battle, I'll be cut to pieces, the militia dispersed, and the arms lost. Was I to decline fighting, the country would think herself given up. I am therefore determined to scarmish, but not to engage too far, and particularly to take care against their

immense and excellent body of horse whom the militia fears like they would so many wild beasts.

Was I any way equal to the ennemy, I would be extremely happy in my present command. But I am not strong enough even to get beaten.

On May 27, Cornwallis outflanked Lafayette at Richmond and forced him to evacuate the city. Lafayette's three light infantry regiments were simply no match for the reinforced British army. He maneuvered for time, careful to avoid direct confrontation—racing back and forth across the state with Cornwallis in pursuit. Lafayette took his troops north to the Rapidan River, twenty miles above Fredericksburg, and hoped to meet General Wayne and his Pennsylvanian reinforcements. Cornwallis followed for a short distance, then stopped to focus his raids on the American supplies stored along the North Anna River.

Cornwallis strengthened his cavalry by appropriating the fine horses he found in the stables of the Virginia gentry. The fresh horses made him so confident of overtaking Lafayette that he wrote in a letter that was intercepted, "the boy can not escape me." But after many miles of chasing "the boy" from river to river, he gave up the chase and camped west of Elk Hill on the James. From there Cornwallis made preparations to attack von Steuben's Continentals until he learned that Wayne had joined Lafayette on June 10. Lafayette's strength had increased to two thousand Continentals and more than three thousand militia.

In early June Governor Jefferson and the Virginia legislature had barely escaped capture by a British force of 250 mounted men led by Colonel Banastre Tarleton. The government, after being driven from Richmond, had reassembled in Charlottesville. Then, notified that Tarleton was coming, Jefferson and most of the legislators fled to Staunton on the other side of the Blue Ridge Mountains. Seven of the legislators were captured.

So rapid were Tarleton's movements, wrote Marshall, "that a mere accident prevented his entering the town before any notice of his approach was given. A private gentleman [Jack Jouette] who was acquainted with a nearer route than the great road, hastened to Charlottesville on a fleet horse with the interesting intelligence, and entered the town about two hours before the British cavalry."

Jack Jouette, a captain in the Virginia militia, had seen the British at the Cuckoo Tavern in Louisa County the night of June 3 and overheard Tarleton's plan to capture the legislature and the governor. The distance from the tavern to Charlottesville was about forty miles, and Jouette raced his horse over dark mountain roads to reach Jefferson's home at Monticello at 4:30 a.m., a few hours before the British arrived. Jefferson made immediate plans to send his wife, daughters, and house guests to safety. But only when he sighted the approach of Tarleton's cavalry did he mount his horse and ride into the woods. Others who eluded the secret raid were Patrick Henry, Richard Henry Lee, Benjamin Harrison, John Tyler, and Thomas Nelson, Jr. Their capture, along with Jefferson, would have meant disaster for Virginia and the American cause. Later, in gratitude to Jack Jouette for frustrating enemy designs, the state Assembly presented him "an elegant sword and a pair of pistols."

Though Tarleton had been instructed to destroy all supplies and tobacco during his raid, Jefferson's only loss at Monticello was wine, which was confiscated by Tarleton's troops without his permission.

Jefferson was accused of cowardice by his political foes, but the "closet heroes" never explained how he was expected to stand single-handedly "against a legion of armed enemies." Light-Horse Harry Lee wrote that the British chased "our governor from hill to hill and our legislature from town to town."

The Tarleton raid was a topic in Jefferson's journal: "The nonsense which has been uttered on the *coup de main* of Tarleton on Charlottesville is really so ridiculous... to notice it." He then described what happened when the British nearly captured him:

> Learning that the legislature was in session at Charlottesville, they detached Colo. Tarleton with his legion of horse to surprise them. As he was passing through Louisa on the evening of the 3rd of June, he was observed by a Mr. Jouett, who suspecting the object, set out immediately...and knowing the by-ways of the neighborhood, passed the enemy's encampment, rode all night, and before sun-rise of the 4th called at Monticello with notice of what he had seen, and passed on to Charlottesville to notify the members of the legislature. The Speaker of the two houses, and some other members were lodging with us. I ordered a carriage to be ready to carry off my family; we breakfasted at leisure with our guests, and after breakfast they had gone to Charlottesville; when a neighbor rode up full speed to inform me that a troop of horse was then ascending the hill to the house. I instantly sent off my family, and, after a short delay for some pressing arrangements, I mounted my horse, and knowing that in the public road I should be liable to fall in with the enemy, I went thro' the woods, and joined my family at the house of a friend where we dined. Would it be believed, were it not known, that this flight from a troop of horse, whose whole legion was within a supporting distance, has been the subject, with party writers, of volumes of reproach on me, serious or sarcastic? That it has been sung in verse, and said in humble prose that, forgetting the noble example of the hero of La Mancha, and his windmills, I declined a combat, singly against a troop, in which victory would have been so glorious?

Forgetting, themselves, at the same time, that I was not provided with the enchanted arms of the knight, nor even with his helmet of Mambrino. These closet heroes forsooth would have disdained the shelter of a wood, even singly and unarmed, against a legion of armed enemies.

Sir Banastre Tarleton was an outstanding British cavalry officer when he volunteered to serve in America with Cornwallis, who appointed him a lieutenant colonel of the British Legion. The reputation Tarleton had earned during the successful early southern campaigns with Clinton and Cornwallis was tarnished when he and his rowdy, undisciplined troops (mostly loyalists) were defeated by General Daniel Morgan at the Battle of Cowpens in North Carolina. In 1781 Tarleton's raiders were feared and Tarleton himself was despised for the "barbaric cruelty" associated with his name from the Charlottesville mountains to Chesapeake Bay.

Following the Tarleton raid, Simcoe's rangers destroyed a supply station near the Chickahominy River. On the way to Williamsburg, the rangers were surprised at Spencer's Tavern by a Lafayette detachment of Pennsylvania infantry, Virginia rifles, and 120 mounted troops. Though the British held the numerical advantage, Simcoe claimed himself the victor and withdrew his rangers, fearing an ambush by Lafayette's entire army. The Americans had twenty-three casualties and fourteen men missing. Cornwallis reported thirty-three casualties, but Lafayette counted sixty British lost and one hundred wounded.

On June 25 Clinton urged Cornwallis to "take a defensive post" at Yorktown and send three thousand men to help defend New York from the anticipated attack by Washington. But first, Cornwallis sent four hundred men to destroy a supply depot at Point of Fork where the Fluvanna and Rivanna Rivers join to form the James, forty-five miles above Richmond.

Von Steuben's Continentals, guarding the depot, lost the supplies but escaped across the Fluvanna when the British were unable to pursue for lack of boats.

At the time of Clinton's troop request, Cornwallis had an army of five thousand redcoats and eighteen hundred Hessians—more than enough men to raid the new state capital of Richmond and also take over Virginia's original colonial capital of Williamsburg. But he was worried that once he had given up the troops to Clinton, he would not be able to defend a post on the peninsula. Nevertheless, he and his advisors went to Yorktown to appraise its possibilities as a base. Fired at from Gloucester Point just across the York, the party quickly returned to Williamsburg and Cornwallis decided that Portsmouth might better serve as a base because of its access to the bay.

Cornwallis left Williamsburg on July 6. As his army was about to cross the James at Green Springs, he had his first encounter with Lafayette and almost lured an advance party led by Wayne into a trap. But a bold bayonet charge enabled Wayne's troops to escape, although during the heat of combat Lafayette lost his horse.

Lafayette was permitted to rest his troops at Malvern Hill, midway between Williamsburg and Richmond, and Cornwallis proceeded to Suffolk, then on to Portsmouth.

At Portsmouth the British general was preparing to send three thousand men to New York when a message from Clinton instructed him to send the troops to Philadelphia instead. Then on July 20 he was told to keep the troops and evacuate Portsmouth. Clinton wanted him to establish a naval base at Old Point Comfort on the site of the Fort George ruins, a base that would allow him to protect the bay and its entrance to the sea. Amid this confusion of directives, Cornwallis and a group of engineers visited Old Point Comfort and decided that the site was too low to defend from attacking ships. Military historian Richard P. Weinert, Jr. listed other factors that made the site unsuitable: shortage of construction materials in the area, lack of drinking water, and difficulty of maintaining a safe anchorage for British ships in Hampton Roads. Cornwallis informed Clinton that he would erect his command headquarters at Yorktown:

> At present I am inclined to think well of York. The objections to Portsmouth are that it cannot be made strong without an army to defend it, that it is remarkably unhealthy, and can give no protection to a ship of the line.

Cornwallis concluded:

> I shall take the liberty of repeating that if offensive war is intended, Virginia appears to me to be the only Province in which it can be carried on, and in which there is a stake. But to reduce the Province and keep possession of this country, a considerable army would be necessary.

With reservations, Clinton accepted Yorktown as the Virginia base of operations, though he still wanted a naval station at Old Point Comfort. From there, he said, Cornwallis could monitor traffic in and out of the Chesapeake and maintain an easy escape route, either by sea or up the bay to Delaware. Cornwallis should have listened.

Washington's attack on New York would never happen, although he and Rochambeau had come to a tentative agreement that would require not only Rochambeau's army but also the French fleet stationed in the West Indies under the command of Admiral Francois Joseph Paul de Grasse.

At the end of May, in the first of a series of letters he sent to de Grasse, Rochambeau described a "very grave crisis" in the states, especially in the south, and the American need for ships, troops, and money. The depleted Continental Army had been widely dispersed. Slightly more than three thousand troops remained with Washington; others were holding the line in

New Jersey or on the western frontier, a few had joined Lafayette in Virginia, and the battleworn Continentals with General Greene were struggling in what appeared to be a losing cause in the south.

On the other side, Lord Cornwallis had more than five thousand regulars plus nearly three thousand Hessians and Tories in Virginia alone, and Clinton's New York army numbered about fifteen thousand.

Yet Washington and Rochambeau, with a combined allied force of less than eight thousand men, had been discussing an impending move against Clinton's stronghold. That the invasion would be foolhardy without a strong fleet was the point stressed by Rochambeau when he told de Grasse that "all the means at hand can do nothing without the assistance and naval superiority which you can bring us."

Rochambeau also expressed concern about Washington's plan to win the war at New York, declaring his own preference for an attack against Yorktown. But he would leave the choice to de Grasse.

In a follow-up letter on June 11, he wrote:

> I must not conceal from you, Monsieur, that the Americans are at the end of their resources, that Washington will not have half of the troops he is reckoned to have, and that I believe ...at present he does not have six thousand men; that M. de Lafayette does not have a thousand regulars with militia to defend Virginia, and nearly as many on the march to join him...that it is therefore of the greatest consequence that you will take on board as many troops as possible; that four or five thousand men will not be too many, whether you aid us to destroy the works at Portsmouth, Virginia, near Hampton Roads, where up to now they have always kept fifteen hundred men while the others operated in the country, and all their flotillas with which they have tormented the poor Marquis de Lafayette on the rivers in a very

evil manner [or] to aid us afterwards to lay siege to Brooklyn...I am quite persuaded that you will bring us naval superiority, but I cannot too often repeat to you to bring also the troops and money.

Rochambeau had already raided his own war chest to pay the disgruntled American troops.

On July 28 the reply to Rochambeau from Admiral de Grasse named the Chesapeake his choice of attack, "the one from which the advantage you propose may be most certainly attained." De Grasse said he would sail on August 13 from Santo Domingo directly to Chesapeake Bay, where he would remain until October 15 and then return with his troops to the West Indies. He offered to bring his entire fleet of twenty-eight ships, artillery and equipment, plus three thousand troops under the command of the Marquis de Saint-Simon to reinforce Rochambeau's French regulars and Washington's depleted Continentals. And to replenish the allied war chest he would bring 1,200,000 *livres* borrowed from Spanish officials in Havana. Later, the admiral would request Washington to supply soldiers to help build a naval battery at Old Point Comfort (the site rejected by Cornwallis) and would ask that a hospital be established in the town of Hampton for the men in his fleet who needed medical care. The Virginia Board of War had already established military hospitals in Hampton, Williamsburg, York, and Portsmouth.

For security reasons, Rochambeau was vague in his letters to Washington regarding the French proposal to blockade the Chesapeake Bay entrance and invade Virginia instead of New York. Washington had no code for communications with his commanders, and in May had written openly to Lafayette that French and American troops would launch a joint attack against New York. The letter was intercepted by a British patrol and delivered to Clinton.

Later, when Washington learned of Admiral de Grasse's decision to sail to Virginia instead of supporting his campaign against the British stronghold in New York, he had no choice but to change his strategy and redirect the allied forces against the Cornwallis base at Yorktown. Fortunately, the intercepted letter to Lafayette would work in Washington's favor when his August troop movements appeared to Clinton to be preparations for an assault on the British forts on Manhattan Island. To complete the deception, false reports were circulated that Admiral de Grasse was bringing his fleet north.

Now that he had a new destination and timetable to guide his strategy, Washington was convinced that he could mount a superior force to capture Cornwallis's army while the French fleet blocked attempts by Clinton to send relief.

A year earlier, a Virginia member of Congress, Joseph Jones, had written to Jefferson of his concern about America's dependence upon the French: "I have been much and still am depressed to think that America should do so little for herself while France is preparing to do so much. That we should, contending for every thing dear and valuable to her, look on with folded arms and suffer other Powers almost unassisted by us, to work out our solution and Independence. The Idea is humiliating. The Fact must be dishonorable and our Posterity will blush to read It in future story."

Benedict Arnold had been recalled to New York in June, leaving a trail of plunder and destruction in the lower Chesapeake and along the James River banks. Though able to elude Washington's vengeance, he could not escape the wrath of Philip Freneau's pen:

> With evil omens from the harbor sails
>   The ill-fated ship that worthless Arnold bears,
> God of the southern winds, call up thy gales,
>   And whistle in rude fury round his ears.
> With horrid waves insult his vessel's sides,
>   And may the east wind on a leeward shore

> Her cables snap, while she in tumult rides,
> And shatter into shivers every oar...
>
> But if, at last, upon some winding shore
> A prey to hungry cormorants you lie,
> A wanton goat to every stormy power,
> And a fat lamb, in sacrifice, shall die.

In mid-August Washington informed Admiral de Grasse that he and Rochambeau would meet him at Chesapeake Bay with an allied army, and asked de Grasse to send frigates and transports to the Head of Elk landing to carry the troops down the bay to Virginia. He then instructed Lafayette to position his troops in a manner that would prevent a Cornwallis retreat to North Carolina.

By now Lafayette's army had increased to forty-five hundred officers and men. His original light infantry had been reinforced by Wayne's Pennsylvanians, von Steuben's Continentals now commanded by Colonel Christian Febiger, three Virginia militia brigades, two artillery regiments, and a few regular cavalrymen and volunteer dragoons. Still, he lacked the strength or discipline to engage Cornwallis. Desertions had continued to frustrate Lafayette and inhibit troop movements as harvest time approached and enlistments expired. He wrote to the commander of the Virginia state forces, "You may as well Stop the flood tide as to Stop Militia whose times are out."

A joint attack by Lafayette and Wayne against Cornwallis near Jamestown had underestimated British troop strength in that region and cost Lafayette's small army nearly two hundred casualties plus several cannons. General Wayne, in one of those reckless maneuvers which had earned him his "Mad Anthony" nickname, was almost captured; and probably the only thing that saved Lafayette was Cornwallis's failure to pursue.

That experience and similar setbacks increased the need for subterfuge. Thus Lafayette scattered his forces in separate camps which were not too distant from each other to concentrate rapidly. It was supposed to mislead Cornwallis into thinking the American army was larger than it actually was.

Yet Cornwallis seemed almost indifferent to Lafayette and his evasive schemes. Under the Cornwallis command, redcoats continued to overrun Virginia while British ships continued to sail up the Chesapeake as far as the Maryland waterways, where royal marines torched the fine homes, pillaged farms and supply depots, and gave sanctuary to runaway slaves.

Richard Henry Lee wrote to his brother Arthur: "The enemies design seems to be by great distress and much delusion to bring over the minds of the people." He complained that Virginians "find themselves abandoned, and they are exposed to the infinite acts and fraud of our enemies and of our internal Tories....The enemy affect to leave harmless the poor, and they take everything from those they call the rich. Tis said that 2 or 3000 Negroes march in their train, that every kind of stock which they cannot remove they destroy—eating up the green wheat and by destroying of the fences expose to destruction the other growing grains. They have burnt a great number of warehouses, full of tobacco and they are now pressing on to the large ones on Rappahannock and Potomac Rivers." Lee concluded: "Cornwallis is the scourge."

Lafayette wrote in his memoirs: Cornwallis "flattered himself" that once he had secured Virginia, it would be a simple task "to take possession of Baltimore and march towards Philadelphia."

The Cornwallis arrogance would be countered by Lafayette joy on hearing that the French fleet under de Grasse was on its way to the Chesapeake and would be joined by de Barras's squadron from Rhode Island, and that soon Washington and Rochambeau would arrive in Virginia with a large allied army. Until then, Lafayette would try to carry out Washington's directive and prevent Cornwallis from retreating to the south—a possibility that still haunted him as late as August 30 when he told Governor Nelson (who had replaced Jefferson): "I expect every minute that our prey is escaping."

But Lafayette continued to snipe at Cornwallis from a safe distance and hoped to keep him within the fort being constructed on the York River. He had followed Cornwallis to the lower peninsula and taken a position not far from Yorktown where the Mattaponi and Pamunkey Rivers meet. There he could watch until the French fleet arrived to block the general's escape to the sea. General Clinton, of course, believed that Cornwallis was safe, having accepted the ruse that the allied move on New York would occur at any moment.

Although Lafayette had hoped to distinguish himself in the New York campaign, he wrote to Washington from Yorktown:

> I heartily thank you for having ordered me to remain in Virginia; it is to your goodness that I am indebted for the most beautiful prospect which I may ever behold.

Despite the evasion tactics Lafayette was forced to adopt, many accounts of the period agree that the 1781 Virginia campaign enhanced his military reputation. John Marshall wrote of Lafayette:

> That with so decided an inferiority of effective force, and especially of cavalry, he had been able to keep the field in an open country, and to preserve a considerable proportion of his military stores, as well as his army, was believed to furnish unequivocal evidence of the prudence and vigour of his conduct.

If "prudence" were a term to describe Lafayette it was because the size and quality of his army made it essential that he display some degree of caution. By nature he was daring, often reckless. Ever the seeker of glory on the battlefield, Lafayette would record in his *Commentaries* that it was his plan to drive Cornwallis to Yorktown and "force him between the rivers [York and James] in such a way that he would have no means of retreat." To subtract nothing from Lafayette's skill and courage, that was not the way he saw the situation at the time—when he had neither manpower nor directive to entrap Cornwallis's large army at Yorktown. What Washington had urged was that Lafayette *delay* any retreat by the British general until the French fleet arrived in the Chesapeake. To the Virginia governor, Lafayette complained that his troops were in such need of arms and medical aid that "should it be known to Lord Cornwallis, he may ruin us at one stroke." Nevertheless, Lafayette continued to creep up on Yorktown, where the British general waited quietly for the navy that would never come.

Battle of the Capes

1781

Lord Cornwallis occupied Yorktown and Gloucester Point on opposite sides of the York River, utilizing all of his troops to construct fortifications. It was not a wise move. By situating his base on what he termed "nearly impassable swamps," Cornwallis lost control of Chesapeake Bay, leaving himself no route of escape except over land—a factor that would prove fatal when the route was blocked by an army stretching from the York to the James.

Lafayette sensed immediately the danger that faced Cornwallis at Yorktown. In a letter to Washington on August 6, 1781, he wrote:

> York is surrounded By the River and a Morass. The Entrance is But Narrow. There is However a Commanding Hill, at least I am So informed which if occupied By them would Much Extend their works. Glocester is a neck of land projected into the river and opposite to York. Their vessels the Biggest of whom is a 44 Are Between the two towns. Should a fleet Come in at this Moment our Affairs would take a very Happy turn.

Yorktown was a small port town situated on a thirty-five-foot bluff overlooking the York River. The main body of Lord Cornwallis's army was encamped in the fields around Yorktown, close to outer bastions which were positioned to impede enemy approach. A small detachment of seven hundred men—which would soon be reinforced by Tarleton's legion—was posted at Gloucester, connected to Yorktown by ferry where the river narrowed.

High on the list of military theorists and British historians who condemned Cornwallis's decision to take his stand at Yorktown was Winston Churchill, who wrote:

> Cornwallis held that Virginia was the heart and centre of the Patriot cause and that all efforts should be concentrated on its conquest and occupation. There is no doubt he was wrong. Charleston, not Virginia, was the military key to the South. It was the only Southern port of any consequence, and the only place from which he could receive supplies for himself and deny them to the rebels.

But how consequential would Charleston have been if blockaded by a French fleet with the same superiority that kept the British from entering Chesapeake Bay to support Cornwallis at Yorktown?

Washington had set his mind on winning the war in New York, opening with an assault on the British forts at the north end of Manhattan Island. That would force Clinton to order up troops from Virginia and thereby relieve the pressure on Lafayette. Yet, as revealed by the entry in his diary on August 1, he had complained about the shortage of manpower the operation would require. He said the New York plan would have been in "perfect readiness...if the States had furnished their quotas of men agreeably to my requisitions." He had received "not more than half the numbers" requested.

Rochambeau's alternative to move to the Chesapeake area had been resisted initially by Washington's concern about the southern climate. He worried that "the French soldiers would sicken in the summer heat of Virginia." He knew also that his own soldiers, particularly those from New England, loathed the "snakes, heat, and mosquitoes," and the "poisonous" swamps rife with malaria, yellow fever, typhus, and dysentery. Of equal concern to Washington was the knowledge that he would have to move his army to Virginia by a land march of more than four hundred miles, a march that might cost him a third of his troops.

Washington's decision to turn his attention to the south was made for him by Admiral de Grasse's communique that his fleet would arrive at the Chesapeake on August 30, before a reinforced British navy had the chance to block his entrance to the bay.

On August 15 Washington informed Lafayette:

> The Concorde Frigate is arrived at Newport from Count de Grasse. He was to leave St. Domingo the 3rd of this month with a Fleet of between 25 and 29 sail of the line and a considerable Body of land forces. His destination is immediately for the Chesapeake. So that he will either be there by the time this reaches you, or you may look for him every moment. Under these circumstances—whether the enemy remain in full force, or whether they have only a detachment left, you will immediately take such a position as will best enable you to prevent their sudden retreat thro' North Carolina, which I presume they will attempt the instant they perceive so formidable an Armament.

After maneuvers contrived to convince General Clinton that he was still pursuing his original New York strategy, Washington left the Hudson and quietly headed south without detection. He notified Admiral de Grasse: "We have determined to remove the whole of the French army, and as large a detachment of the American as can be spared, to the Chesapeake, to meet your Excellency there."

Excerpts from the journal of Dr. James Thacher, attached to the Continental Army, indicated that Clinton was not the only one expecting the allied armies to march on New York:

General orders are now issued for the army to prepare for a movement at a moment's notice. The real object of the allied armies in the present campaign has become a subject of much speculation. Ostensibly an investment of the city of New York is in contemplation—preparations in all quarters for some months past indicate this to be the object of our combined operations. The capture of this place would be a decisive stroke....General Washington and Count Rochambeau have crossed at the North River, and it is supposed for the purpose of reconnoitering the enemy's posts from the Jersey shore. A field for an extensive engagement has been marked out on the Jersey side, and a number of ovens have been erected and fuel provided for the purpose of baking bread for the army. From these combined circumstances we are led to conclude that a part of our besieging force is to occupy this ground....But New York is well fortified both by land and water and garrisoned by the best troops of Great Britain.

Dr. Thacher noted that the British in New York had been reinforced by "three thousand Germans from Europe." On August 21 he discovered that his army was "increasing rapidly toward Philadelphia [and] our destination can no longer be a secret. The British army under Lord Cornwallis is unquestionably the object of our present expedition." He now saw that Washington and Rochambeau had devised

> a judiciously concerted stratagem, calculated to menace and alarm Sir Henry Clinton for the safety of the garrison of New York and induce him to recall a part of his troops from Virginia for his own defence....The deception has proved completely successful....General Washington, having succeeded in a masterly piece of generalship, has now the satisfaction of leaving his adversary to ruminate on his

own mortifying situation, and to anticipate the perilous fate which awaits his friend Lord Cornwallis in a different quarter. Major General Heath is left commander-in-chief of our army in the vicinity of New York and the highlands, and the menacing aspect of an attack on New York will be continued till time and circumstances shall remove the delusive veil from the eyes of Sir Henry Clinton, when it will probably be too late to afford succour to Lord Cornwallis.

He concluded that the British "might, without risking a great deal, harass our army on its march and subject us to irreparable injury; but the royalists are more dexterous in availing themselves of treachery and insurrection than in effecting valourous achievements."

On the day that Rochambeau's army departed from Rhode Island to join Washington in New Jersey, Admiral de Barras sailed for the Chesapeake with siege artillery for the attack on Yorktown.

Faulty communications failed to alert British Admiral George Rodney in time to obstruct the French fleet's passage to Virginia. Rear Admiral Samuel Hood, with fourteen ships, had inspected the Chesapeake on August 23, and finding no enemy ships in the bay he sailed to the British base at Sandy Hook, New Jersey. It was not until early September that Rodney would send a ship to New York with orders that Admiral Graves sail immediately for Chesapeake Bay; the directive would not arrive until after the French and British navies had engaged at the Virginia Capes.

Summer's heat was taking its toll on Lafayette's army. On August 24 he wrote:

> The hot weather in this country is so excessive that one can scarcely operate in the month of August. It has another draw-back, and that is illness. Almost all of my men just now are sick with fever.

In addition, he had learned from Wayne that his Pennsylvanians were "totally bare foot."

A recent letter from Washington was filled with impatience and anxiety:

> But my dear Marquis, I am distressed beyond expression, to know what is become of the Count de Grasse, and for fear the English Fleet, by occupying the Chesapeake (towards which my last accounts say they were steering) should frustrate all our flattering prospects in that quarter. I am also not a little solicitous for the Count de Barras, who was to have sailed from Rhode Island...and from whom I have heard nothing since that time.

Washington again urged Lafayette to keep an eye on Cornwallis in event his retreat by water should be cut off by the arrival of the French fleet: "I am persuaded you will do all in your power to prevent his escape by land. May that great felicity be reserved for you!"

In the meantime, Cornwallis had removed the remainder of the troops from Portsmouth to consolidate his forces at Yorktown, where he believed he would be protected by the river and the marshy lands of Yorktown Creek. Colonel Josiah Parker of the Virginia militia wrote that Portsmouth was now "a mere heap of rubbish." He noted: "A number of Negroes are left dead & dying with the Small Pox."

Cornwallis had neglected to hold a Chesapeake Bay port for the British fleet.

A French fleet of twenty-six warships, plus frigates and troop transports, entered Chesapeake Bay on August 30, guided by thirty American pilots who had been waiting for Admiral de Grasse at Cap-Francais, the port of Haiti-Santo Domingo. The fleet anchored in Lynnhaven roadstead near today's Virginia Beach. Its pride was the admiral's flagship, the 110-gun *Ville de Paris*, said to be the greatest warship afloat. In ten days de

Grasse would be joined by de Barras, who had left Newport with a squadron of eight ships.

The 26-gun British frigate *Loyalist* pursued the French into the bay and was captured by the 74-gun *Glorieux*. The 28-gun British frigate *Guadaloupe* escaped and rendezvoused with the 44-gun *Charon*, two smaller frigates, and six armed sloops stationed at Yorktown. The French cruisers *Valiant* and *Triton*, guided by John Sinclair of Gloucester, were dispatched to the York River to assist the *Glorieux* in containing the enemy ships. Admiral de Grasse dispatched the 50-gun *Experiment* and the frigates *Andromaque* and *Diligente* to the James River to stop any escape attempt by Cornwallis to North Carolina.

As soon as Cornwallis heard that the French Fleet had appeared at the Virginia Capes, he sent a coded message to Clinton: "There are between thirty and forty sail within the capes, mostly ships of war and some of them very large." It was not until September 2 that Clinton realized the allied army was moving south.

Two days earlier, Corporal Stephan Popp, one of the Hessians at Yorktown, recorded in his diary: "The French ships now showed clearly in the harbor. They drew up in a line on the sea, occupied the straits, and placed troops ashore at Hampton." He observed that "a great number of rebels and French approached from Williamsburg. Therefore we had to look forward to an attack by the foe daily by land and sea."

Five thousand French troops, commanded by Saint-Simon, were put ashore at Jamestown. This increased the allied strength under Lafayette to nearly ten thousand—against eight to ten thousand British regulars and hired Hessians under Cornwallis. A Virginia lieutenant was impressed by the striking appearance of the French troops in their splendid uniforms. Lafayette, embarrassed by the ragged display of his militia, remarked: "I shall endeavor to keep it a little out of sight."

The French fleet was accompanied by fifteen merchant vessels which unloaded artillery and military supplies paid for by Admiral de Grasse from his personal fortune.

Cornwallis remained in his York River fortifications and made no attempt to engage the enemy. Failing to frustrate the landing of Saint-Simon's troops at Jamestown, he allowed himself to be hemmed in at Yorktown with no exit to the sea and no realistic prospect of support from New York. To block any escape to the south Lafayette stationed his main force between Williamsburg and the Hampton Road south of Yorktown, posted Wayne's Pennsylvanians on the James, and ordered the Weedon's militia to surround Gloucester.

Cornwallis's dilemma led Weedon to write "that we have got him handsomely in the bag." He rhapsodized:

> I am all on fire. By the Great God of War, I think we may all hand up our swords by the last of the year in perfect peace and security.

Once the French troops were ashore, they were shocked by the aftermath of the British raids on the lower peninsula. Lieutenant Karl Gustaf Tornquist described atrocities he found on "a beautiful estate two miles from Hampton." There he saw a pregnant woman who had been "murdered in her bed through several bayonet stabs." He said "the barbarians had opened both her breasts and written above the bed canopy: *Thou shalt never give birth to a rebel!*" Elsewhere he found "five heads cut off [and] arranged on a cupboard in place of plaster-cast figures, which lay broken to pieces on the floor." Animals had also been butchered: "The pastures were in many places covered with dead horses, oxen and cows. A storehouse of tobacco, which had been collected from Virginia, Maryland, and the Carolinas during many years, containing ten thousand hogsheads of tobacco, was laid in ashes." Tornquist concluded: "We did not find a single trace of inhabitants, for those who had been unable to flee lay on the ground, as a token of the godless behavior of their enemies." (From Tornquist's account of *The Naval Campaigns of Count de Grasse During the American Revolution, 1781-1783*, translated by A. Johnson of Philadelphia, 1942.)

About the same time, a memorandum written by Britain's war adviser Richard Oswald cited American abuses against loyalists in the Carolinas:

> The Inferior people patrol the Country & sometimes murdering Innocent, though suspected, persons. They seem to like this way of life better than staying at their Farms & labouring in an Industrious way as usual.

American women were frequently called upon to prove themselves patriots. Swepson Earle told of the day on Virginia's Eastern Shore when two British soldiers threatened to murder the infant child of Mrs. Thomas Teackle unless she revealed the whereabouts of her husband, a lieutenant in the Continental Army. Mrs. Teackle replied, "You have the power and can abuse it. I would not tell you, not even to save the life of both my child and myself." The child was unharmed and the mother was told that "if all the colonists were as brave as you are, they could never be conquered."

Admiral Graves sailed from New York on September 1, showing no great alarm over rumors that Admiral de Grasse was moving his fleet to Chesapeake Bay. When his latest report indicated the bay was still quiet, he had written to Hood at Sandy Hook: "No intelligence yet of De Grasse." Still expecting an allied assault on New York, the two admirals had set out to intercept the main French fleet from the West Indies as well as the de Barras squadron coming from Newport. The joint British fleet, under Graves's command, contained nineteen heavily armed warships and seven frigates. Not only had Graves miscalculated the strength of the French naval force, but by the time he realized he was wrong about the destination, the French had entered the Chesapeake.

The British fleet, delayed by repairs, arrived in sight of the Virginia Capes on September 5. Graves planned to wait a day before he contacted Cornwallis at Yorktown, but then a lookout frigate saw the masts of the French ships anchored in the bay twelve miles away (although at first the British believed the masts to be trunks of charred pine trees, a familiar sight along the Virginia coast).

At the same time, French scouts thought the approaching ships were Admiral de Barras's squadron. The British fleet was unexpected and de Grasse was not prepared for battle; nearly two thousand of his officers and men had gone ashore to gather water and supplies and six of his ships had been detached for other duty.

The American army passed through Philadelphia in early September, closely followed by the French army. Aware that Clinton was not in pursuit, both Washington and Rochambeau now abandoned deception and marched openly for Virginia. Just south of Chester, Pennsylvania, news reached Washington that the French had entered Chesapeake Bay. The general was so excited to know at last the whereabouts of the French admiral that he rode back to Chester to tell Rochambeau.

The allies marched south until they arrived at Head of Elk in the upper Chesapeake. From there, Rochambeau and most of the French troops traveled south by land to Annapolis, where they would board the waiting French ships. En route to Baltimore, they had to make a treacherous crossing of the Susquehanna north of where the river emptied into the bay. At the point of crossing, the Susquehanna was very rapid but extremely shallow and the horses stumbled over large stones at every step until they reached the other side.

Washington raced to Baltimore by horse.

The remaining troops (French and American) crowded aboard a makeshift fleet of Maryland barges and galleys, overloaded with artillery and Duc de Lauzun's Legion of infantry. From Head of Elk the boats sailed down the bay until a storm forced them into port at Annapolis.

For a while it had looked as though Washington would be missing much of his army. The Continental troops of Pennsylvania, New York, and New Jersey refused to march until they received their back pay. "It is a common maxim, that, without severe discipline, 'tis impossible to govern the licentious rabble of soldiery," wrote Franklin in his *Autobiography*. Once again the French came through. Rochambeau made a gift to Washington of fifty thousand *livres*. It was a third of all the cash he had.

The Battle of the Virginia Capes began unexpectedly on September 5. It took hours before the two fleets were ready to face each other, and then the fight started in a state of confusion because of the unreadiness of the French and a mixup in the British signal flags. Admiral de Grasse moved his fleet out of the bay so that his ships would have room to maneuver. During that time, Graves gained the wind but did not use it to his advantage. In this clumsily managed encounter between two great powers—which may have been the most important battle of the war—the fleets were so positioned that only the lead ships or vanguard would see close action. British ships approached the French at an angle. When guns did explode with deadly aim, the worst damage was inflicted on the British, although many of the ships in both fleets did not engage at all. By sunset, the firing ceased and the fleets withdrew within the cover of smoke to a safe distance to tend their wounded. In just over six hours, each had suffered more than two hundred men killed or wounded.

For the next few days, the fleets drifted nearly a hundred miles south of the bay and lost sight of each other around Cape Hatteras. Admiral de Grasse, fearing the British might take control of the Chesapeake, returned on the night of September 9. Two days passed before the British fleet showed up to discover there was no way to enter the Virginia Capes. The de Barras ships had arrived and overwhelming odds now forced Graves to sail to New York to make repairs and assemble a larger fleet for another try at the French. Though the battle was indecisive, it denied Cornwallis the support he desperately needed. Graves would write: "The enemy have so great a naval force in the Chesapeake that they are absolute masters of its navigation."

On the day of the battle, Virginia Colonel St. George Tucker sent this encouraging news along to his wife Fanny:

> About the middle of last week twenty-nine ships of line and four frigates arrived in our bay, with four thousand land forces sent to our assistance by Louis the Great. Besides these there are three thousand marines to be landed in case of emergency. Of the fleet there are ten sixty-fours; eighteen seventy-fours, and one ship of an hundred and ten guns! A fleet of twelve sail of the line has arrived in the West Indies to keep the enemy still employed in that quarter. Of the troops, three thousand five hundred landed at James Town three days ago and are now on their march to this city. Five hundred are left on board to land at York river. The fleet lies from Lynnhaven bay to the mouth of the York river, and some, we are informed, have proceeded within two or three miles of the town. The British fleet still lies at York, and their land forces are now in the town....
>
> Our troops lie from four miles beyond this town to near James Town; so that Cornwallis is as effectually hemmed in as our troops were in Charlestown. Our force may now be reckoned to be eight thousand men—of which six thousand are regulars, exclusive of the marines whom I mentioned above.
>
> Nor is this all, for, to my great surprise and pleasure, I was this morning informed from undoubted authority that General Washington is at the Head of Elk with five thousand troops, which are to be embarked from thence in transports.
>
> I have not yet done. The French fleet of ten line-of-battle ships, which lay at Rhode Island, are now actually on the way hither, and are daily expected. Whether the Count de Rochambeau, with his troops,

is on board, I know not, nor, indeed, is it very material, I conceive.

If after such a torrent of good news I could wish to add another article, it would be that Lord Cornwallis, with his whole army, were in our possession. But this I hope, in that providence to which I prostrate myself with grateful adoration for the present happy aspect of our affairs, will be the subject of some future letter; or that I may, to the happiness of seeing you again, add that of being able to give you the first notice of so important and so happy an event.

My paper would blush to contain matters of lesser moment after what I have written.

After the Battle of the Capes, a French observer reported the French fleet "formed in very bad order," while the British fleet was "in the best possible order, bowsprit to stern, bearing down on us." But the overly cautious Graves failed to use his advantage and permitted Admiral de Grasse "a full hour and a half" to organize his scattered fleet. Graves's second in command, Rear Admiral Samuel Hood, said the lack of decisive action caused Graves to lose "a rich and most delightful harvest of glory." Hood told a friend in the British Admiralty that Graves was "clearly unequal to the conducting of a great squadron." A member of the House of Lords had this to say about Graves: "He had lost no engagement, no ships...He had merely lost America."

Hood's letter, written from Sandy Hook aboard the *Barfleur*, showed no restraint in discussing the "improper actions" of Graves at the Capes:

> It would, in my humble opinion, have been a most fortunate event had Mr. Graves gone off to Jamaica upon Mr. Digby's arrival as commander-in-chief by commission, and I am persuaded you will think so too, when I relate one circumstance only. On the 7th I received a letter from Mr. Graves, desiring I would

meet the flag officers and some captains upon a consultation on board the London at ten o'clock the next morning, and acquaint Lord Cornwallis and Captain Reynolds that their company was desired also. Soon after we were assembled, Mr. Graves proposed, and wished to reduce to writing, the following question: "Whether it was practicable to relieve Lord Cornwallis in the Chesapeake?" This astonished me exceedingly, as it seemed plainly to indicate a design of having difficulties started against attempting what the generals and admirals had most unanimously agreed to and given under their hands on the 24th of last month, and occasioned my replying immediately that it appeared to me a very unnecessary and improper question, as it had been already maturely discussed and determined upon to be attempted with all the expedition possible; that my opinion had been very strong and pointed (which I was ready to give in writing with my name to it); that an attempt under every risk should be made to force a junction with the troops the commander-in-chief [Graves] embarks in his Majesty's fleet with the army under General Earl Cornwallis at York; and admitting that junction to be made without much loss, and the provisions landed, I was also of opinion the first favorable opportunity should be embraced of attacking the French fleet, though I own to you I think very meanly of the ability of the present commanding officer. I know he is a cunning man, he may be a good theoretical man, but he is certainly a bad practical one, and most clearly proved himself on the 5th of last month to be unequal to the conducting of a great squadron.

A more detailed look at the battle shows that Admiral Graves was too slow to act and made too many mistakes. The British fleet, though outnumbered, was able to approach the entrance to the bay on a strong tide to catch the French unprepared. "They came down upon us with a following wind," said the Chevalier de Vaugirard, "with an assurance which made us think they did not know our strength." Still, at about noon, the disorganized French fleet was able to straggle out to sea. But in its haste, the van took a wide lead and left the support ships far behind in a confused line of battle.

Thus it would appear that the British had the advantage, but the hesitant Graves overextended his battle line and approached the Capes at an angle, taking the same tack as the French, losing the opportunity to destroy the French van before it could be joined by the ships in the center and rear. Now with nineteen ships stretched over a distance of five miles to cover the twenty-four enemy ships, Graves traded strength for weakness. The oblique approach prevented the British from forming a tight line, and they were unable to fire in unison on the French ships. That the French fleet had 1,788 guns to 1,402 guns for the British was not a deciding factor. Much more significant were the questionable tactics which removed nine French ships and more than half the British fleet from the action.

After four hours, the vanguard of both fleets closed in on each other at broadside. Guns opened fire. In a fierce exchange, the French van somehow managed to inflict much more damage than it suffered, pounding the British van into near submission. When the wind changed, the fleets pulled away from each other. According to Graves, the French had taken flight. The French saw it differently. The British, said the captain of the *Citoyen*, "hauled their wind at the moment that they fired their broadsides." He accused Graves of fearing to fully engage. "The enemy, although master of the wind," said the French captain, "only engaged far off and simply in order to be able to say that they had fought."

Another French officer made this report:

> The two vans having come so close as to be almost within pistol-shot, the fire was long well sustained,

and the affair seemed to be decisive, when Admiral Hood made a signal to the English rear division, which he commanded, to bear down upon the French rear. [Admiral de Grasse] witnessed this movement with pleasure and prepared to tack his whole fleet together, bearing NNW, which would inevitably have thrown the English line into confusion; but Admiral Graves anticipated him and signalled his whole fleet to keep to the wind. The heads of the two fleets gradually fell off in consequence of this new order of the English admiral.

Gunfire ceased at 6:30 p.m. For the next five days, the two fleets drifted to the south until they lost contact. Rear Admiral Hood, aboard the *Barfleur*, sent this communique to Graves:

I flatter myself you will forgive me the liberty I take in asking whether you have any knowledge where the French fleet is, as we see nothing of it from the Barfleur. By the press of sail de Grasse carried yesterday (and he must have done the same the preceding night by being where he was at day-light), I am inclined to think his aim is the Chesapeake. In order to be strengthened by the ships there, either by adding them to his present force, or by exchanging his disabled ships for them. Admitting that to be his plan, will he not cut off the frigates you have sent to reconnoitre, as well as ships you expect from New York? And if he should enter the bay, which is by no means improbable, will he not succeed in giving most effectual succor to the rebels?

The British returned to the Capes to find that de Grasse's fleet had indeed been strengthened by the arrival of de Barras's ships. Graves asked Hood's advice and received this reply:

Sir Samuel Hood presents his compliments to Rear Admiral Graves...but he really knows not what to say in the truly lamentable state we have brought ourself."

When Graves met in council with his two commanders, Hood and Rear Admiral Francis Samuel Drake, aboard the flagship *London*, he informed them the damaged *Terrible*, a 74-gun ship, would be burned, leaving the British with eighteen ships of line. Hood shook his head in despair. "We should have barred the entrance [of the bay] to de Grasse," he said, "now he has barred it to us."

Graves estimated that the French fleet had suffered much less damage than his fleet, which no longer had the maneuverability and speed to carry on the fight. He decided to sail immediately to New York and "use every possible means for putting the squadron into the best state for service."

Admiral de Grasse was ready to resume the battle:

> If the wind continues and the English do not escape tonight, we shall meet them at closer range tomorrow morning, and I hope the day will be a happier one, which will permit us to go back and take those Johnnies in the Chesapeake. What a joy it will be to have the ships of de Barras united with ours!

British losses in the Battle of the Capes were the topic of a report in the *New Jersey Gazette* on September 16:

> British lost the Terrible and Vengeance...one sunk and the other burnt; the Fortunate...taken in the bay; the Princess, of seventy guns, lost all her masts, had ninety men killed, and fifty that lost either their legs or arms, and was obliged to throw all her guns overboard...as she made nine feet of water in her hold in one hour.

The Battle of the Capes has received less attention and space from American historians than many less critical land battles in the Revolutionary War, yet it may have been the war's determining engagement. "Strategically, it was the most important battle of the war," wrote Dupuy. And in *The History of the British Navy*, Michael Lewis called it "one of the most decisive battles of the world." A British correspondent would write to London's *Political Journal*:

> ...the fate of Lord Cornwallis and of America may be said to rest upon the merits and demerits of the action of the 5th of September, and not upon those of any circumstances, either previous or subsequent.

But the battle was fought unseen and unrecorded by land observers; its only eyewitnesses were participants—and they were men of the French and British navies. Though Washington initially referred to the Battle of the Capes as "a partial engagement," he later said it seemed to have been "of much greater importance than was at first estimated." This generally downplayed naval clash, which isolated Cornwallis and in effect ended the war, did not include a single American. It was France's gift to America's independence.

Cornwallis learned the true strength of the French fleet in Chesapeake Bay on September 17. He immediately told Clinton that he saw no hope of rescue by sea, now that the de Barras squadron had joined de Grasse, giving the French thirty-six heavily armed ships. "This place is in no state of defense," he warned. "If you cannot relieve me very soon, you must be prepared to hear the worst."

On September 24, 1781, Lafayette celebrated his twenty-fourth birthday among his troops camped on the Pamunkey River. From there, he could observe the Yorktown operation at close range.

- 10 -

Surrender

1781

Without France, Americans might still be British. A French army officer described the impact of the Battle of the Capes: "If the French had been defeated in this action, it would have left the British in possession of Chesapeake Bay, and would have thwarted the plans of General Washington for the capture of Yorktown, and of the British army."

Prior to the siege at Yorktown, General Clinton summed up the situation from afar:

> I was so confident of our naval strength and Lord Cornwallis' capacity for retaining his post, at least as long as his provisions lasted, that I kept 5000 select troops ready in transports for joining him the instant I should hear that Admiral Graves had cleared the Chesapeake of the enemy's ships and a safe passage was opened for their going thither. For several experienced, sensible officers of rank who had lately left his Lordship at Yorktown were clearly of the opinion, which they delivered in council, *that the position he was in might be defended with the troops he then had against twenty thousand assailants for at least three weeks after opened trenches....*

But when I received the admiral's letter of the 9th of September favouring me with an account of his action on the 5th, I confess my faith in our naval superiority began to waver.

This very unpleasant state of doubt, indecision and hope continued until the 23rd when the arrival of Lord Cornwallis' letter of the 16th and 17th of September informed us that Barras' squadron had not been in the action of the 5th, and that his junction with the Count de Grasse augmented the French fleet to thirty-six sail of the line. So unexpected a naval superiority on the side of the enemy—which far exceeded everything we had in prospect—was not a little alarming, and seemed to call for more than common exertion to evade the impending ruin. I consequently solicited an immediate conference in full council with the flag officers of the fleet... when it was unanimously resolved that above 5000 troops should be embarked in the king's ships as soon as they could be refitted, and every possible effort made to form a junction with the army at Yorktown. A letter was consequently dispatched to Earl Cornwallis, with the approbation of the council, to inform him of their resolution and *that there was every reason to hope we should start from New York about the 5th of October*, to which I had an opportunity of adding that Admiral Digby was just arrived with three ships of line.

But I must confess that, after I was thus fully apprised of the enemy's strength and informed by the admiral of the crippled condition of his fleet, I should not have been greatly displeased to have heard that Lord Cornwallis had made his escape to Carolina with everything he could take with him.

Though Admiral Robert Digby "was hourly expected" to assist Cornwallis, Clinton had felt all along that Yorktown's fate would depend upon Admiral Graves' success against de Grasse. "But," wrote Clinton, "the admiral's efforts having failed, and it appearing from His Lordship's postscript of the 17th that he knew the French ships of line then investing his post were at least one-third in number more than we had any probability of even after Admiral Digby should join us, it was manifest His Lordship could have no hopes of relief."

It was not until Yorktown was lost that the indecisive Clinton sent a fleet to help Cornwallis.

While Washington and the Franco-American army were still on the way to Virginia, Admiral de Grasse urged Lafayette to attack Yorktown. He offered to reinforce Lafayette's troops "not only with all the marines of the fleet, but with as many seamen as he should require." According to John Marshall's account:

> The Marquis de St. Simon...united himself with the admiral in pressing this measure. He stated that the works of Cornwallis being incomplete, Yorktown and Gloucester might, in all probability, be carried by storm if attacked by superior numbers. The temptation was great for a young general scarcely twenty-four years old. A full excuse for the attempt was found in the declaration by De Grasse, that he could not wait for the arrival of the troops from the north. Success would have given unrivaled brilliancy to the reputation of Lafayette, but would necessarily have cost much blood. Lafayette refused to sacrifice the soldiers which were confined to him, to his personal glory, and persuaded De Grasse to await the arrival of Washington and Rochambeau, when the capture of Cornwallis would be certainly made without the waste of human life.

And without loss of honor.

The allied army had assembled in Baltimore and Annapolis, and on September 16 a messenger from Washington instructed the troops to depart aboard five frigates and nine transports supplied by Admiral de Grasse. But there had been no news about the battle between the French and British navies, and the tranports were delayed until it could be ascertained there was no immediate danger from a British attack. In two days, the troops would be transported down the bay to be disembarked at Jamestown.

A week earlier, Washington and Rochambeau were in northern Virginia, the first time in six years that Washington had been in his native state. At Mount Vernon, he entertained Rochambeau and the senior officers of the French fleet. He also wrote to Lafayette: "We are thus far, My Dear Marquis, on our way to you." Washington added this postscript: "I hope you will keep Lord Cornwallis safe, without Provisions or Forage untill we arrive."

By September 18 Washington and Rochambeau had joined Lafayette in Williamsburg and learned about the French "victory" at the Capes. Prior to his visit to Admiral de Grasse on his flagship, Washington urged him by letter to keep his fleet in Hampton Roads:

> Give me leave in the first place to repeat to Your Excellency that the enterprise against York under the protection of your Ships is as certain as any military operation can be rendered by a decisive superiority of strength and means; that it is in fact reducible to calculation, and that the surrender of the british Garrison will be so important in itself and its consequences, that it must necessarily go a great way towards terminating the war, and securing the invaluable objects of it to the Allies....
>
> Your Excellency's departure from the Chesapeake by affording an opening for the succour of York, which the enemy would instantly avail himself of, would frustrate these brilliant prospects, and the consequence would be not only the disgrace and loss of renouncing an enterprise, upon which the fairest expectations of the Allies have been founded, after the most expensive preparations and uncommon exertions

and fatigues, but the disbanding perhaps the whole Army for want of provisions....

I most earnestly entreat Your Excellency farther to consider that if the present opportunity should be missed; that if you should withdraw your maritime force from the position agreed upon, that no future day can restore us a similar occasion for striking a decisive blow; that the british will be indefatigable in strengthening their most important maritime points, and that the epoch of an honorable peace will be more remote than ever.

The confidence with which I feel myself inspired by the energy of character and the naval talents which so eminently distinguish Your Excellency leaves me no doubt that upon a consideration of the consequences which must follow your departure from the Chesapeake, that Your Excellency will determine upon the possible measure which the dearest interests of the common cause would dictate....

Upon the whole, I should esteem myself deficient in my duty to the common cause of France and America, if I did not persevere in entreating Your Excellency to resume the plans that have been so happily arranged... rendering the Chesapeake inaccessible to any Enemys Vessel....

Let me add Sir that even a momentary absence of the French fleet may expose us to the loss of the British Garrison at York as in the present state of affairs Lord Cornwallis might effect the evacuation with the loss of his Artillery and baggage and such a sacrifice of men as his object would evidently justify.

When the two met aboard the *Ville de Paris*, Admiral de Grasse embraced Washington and saluted him as "My dear little General!" As Washington's eyes slowly scanned Hampton Roads, observing the large fleet, he called it "an impressive and reassuring sight." De Grasse said he would anchor the French fleet off Cape Henry where it could guard both the James and the York Rivers. He asked that Hampton set up a hospital to care for his squadron's sick, numbering more than fifteen hundred men.

In Virginia, Washington found what he had hoped for from the very beginning of the war—control of the sea and a land force far superior in number to that of the British. For the Yorktown battle, he would command an allied army of twenty thousand men—about twice the size of the Cornwallis army. Included in the American force were two Maryland regiments and three brigades of Virginia militia.

Washington could now see that his decision to side with the French in changing the point of attack from New York to Virginia was not only the correct decision but (as Larrabee noted) was in line with his strategy "to strike the enemy in the most vulnerable quarter."

Washington established his headquarters at Williamsburg. From there Colonel St. George Tucker wrote to his wife:

> Cornwallis may now tremble for his fate, for nothing but some extraordinary interposition of his guardian angels seems capable of saving him and his whole army from captivity.

The last transports of allied troops and equipment arrived at Jamestown on September 26. Assured that they would be supplied by the governors of Maryland and Virginia, the troops marched toward Yorktown with Washington out in front on his light sorrel horse.

An important supply line to the allied troops at Yorktown was organized by Virginia Commodore James Barron, who commanded a fleet of small craft convoyed by the only two Virginia Navy vessels to survive the British cannons.

The siege began on September 28, with Americans camped to the right of Yorktown, and the French on the left, forming a semicircle around the British defenses. Across the York River, at Gloucester, Colonel Tarleton was encircled by six hundred of Lauzon's infantry and eight hundred French marines.

The Yorktown battle resolved one of the problems which had confronted the Continental Army command from the outset of the war: the ill feeling and distrust that sometimes resulted from regional differences, especially among troops in the north and those in the middle and southern states. At one stage, a New England officer had this to say about the contempt existing between regions:

> It has risen to such a height that the Pennsylvania and New England troops would as soon fight each other as the enemy.

Washington urged his officers to "exert themselves, that these animosities and disorders will in a great measure subside." By the time they arrived at Yorktown, the troops had fought together long enough that resentments had gradually disappeared.

Fully expecting naval support from New York, Cornwallis knew that his army alone was not enough to defend Yorktown under siege. He counted on the marshland of Yorktown Creek to defend the west and southwest boundaries. To the south he located his headquarters at Wormeley Creek, which flowed into the York River about two miles below the town. On the east the Yorktown-Hampton Road was straddled by the main fortification. Redoubts (or small outworks) covered the Williamsburg Road west of the town. Between the swampy conditions created by the two creeks there was a narrow plain known as Pigeon Quarter; it was the only accessible land approach to the Yorktown fortifications and within range of the British guns. Redoubts were built in Pigeon Quarter to impede an overland assault. A half-mile beyond that plain Cornwallis built an outer defense, spreading his troops in order to keep the enemy from occupying the ground between the two lines. The Gloucester Point defense consisted of trenches, with four redoubts and three batteries mounting nineteen guns.

When Cornwallis learned on September 29 that reinforcements had reached New York and that soon the British fleet would sail to Chesapeake Bay, he consolidated his troops within the inner defense line. The allies immediately moved into Pigeon Quarter and occupied the abandoned redoubts, placing them just seven hundred yards from Cornwallis's main fortification.

On October 3 a British foraging party under Colonel Tarleton was attacked by Lt. Colonel John Mercer's militia about four miles from Gloucester, in a skirmish that cost each side about two dozen casualties. Later the Virginia militiamen were joined by Lauzun's dragoons in an effort to confine the British within their defenses. Lauzun described the operation in his memoirs:

> Just as we reach the Gloucester plain some Virginia state dragoons came up in great fright and told us that they had seen the English dragoons out and that for fear of accident they had hurried to us at full speed without stopping to see anything more. I went forward to learn what I could. I saw a very pretty woman at the door of a little farmhouse on the high road; I went up to her and questioned her; she told me that Colonel Tarleton had left her house a moment before; that he was very eager to shake hands with the French Duke. I assured her that I had come on purpose to gratify him. She seemed very sorry for me, judging from experience, I suppose, that Tarleton was irresistible; the American troops seemed to be of the same opinion.
>
> I was not a hundred steps from the house when I heard pistol shots from my advance guard. I hurried forward at full speed to find a piece of ground where I could form a line of battle. As I arrived I saw the English cavalry in force three times my own; I

charged it without halting; we met hand to hand. Tarleton saw me and rode towards me with pistol raised. We were about to fight single-handed between the two troops when his horse was thrown by one of his own dragoons pursued by one of my lancers. I rode up to him to capture him; a troop of English dragoons rode in between us and covered his retreat; he left his horse with me. He charged me twice without breaking my line; I charged the third time, overthrew a part of his cavalry and drove him within the entrenchment of Gloucester. He lost an officer, some fifty men, and I took quite a number of prisoners.

On the same date, Colonel Richard Butler of Pennsylvania wrote in his journal: "I discover very plainly that we are young soldiers in a siege; one virtue we possess, that is perseverance." Next day he made this entry:

Two deserters from the enemy... report that Cornwallis' army is very sickly, to the amount of 2000 men in the hospital... that the troops had scarce ground to live on, their shipping in a very naked state and their cavalry very scarce of forage. 2000 French marines landed on Gloster side from Count de Grasse at 9 o'clock P.M. A small firing of small arms, which brought a very heavy cannonade all night.

Sergeant James Sullivan Martin of Connecticut described seeing Washington in the field:

One third part of all the troops were put in requisition to be employed in opening the trenches. A third part of our sappers [trench diggers] and miners were ordered out this night to assist the engineers in laying out the works. It was a very dark and rainy night. However, we repaired to the place and began by following the engineers and laying laths of pine wood end to end upon the line marked out by the officers for the trenches. We had not proceeded far in the business before the engineers ordered us to desist and remain where we were, and be sure not to straggle a foot from the spot while they were absent from us.

In a few minutes after their departure, there came a man alone to us, having on a [overcoat], as we conjectured (it being exceedingly dark), and inquired for the engineers. We now began to be a little jealous for our safety, being alone and without arms, and within forty rods of the British trenches. The stranger inquired what troops we were; talked familiarly with us a few minutes, when, being informed which way the officers had gone, he went off in the same direction, after strictly charging us, in case we should be taken prisoners, not to discover to the enemy what troops we were. We were obliged to him for his kind advice, but we considered ourselves as standing in no great need of it; for we knew well as he did that sappers and miners were allowed no quarters, at least are entitled to none by the laws of warfare, and of course should take care, if taken and the enemy did not find us out, not to betray our own secret.

In a short time the engineers returned and the aforementioned stranger with them; they discoursed together sometime, when, by the officers often calling him 'Your Excellency,' we discovered that it was Gen. Washington. Had we dared, we might have cautioned him for exposing himself so carelessly to danger at such a time, and doubtless he would have taken it in good part if we had. But nothing ill happened to either him or ourselves...

The next night, which was the sixth of October, the same men were ordered to the lines that had been there the night before. We this night completed laying out the works. The troops of the line were there already with entrenching tools and began to entrench, after General Washington had struck a few blows with a pickaxe, a mere ceremony, that it might be said, "Gen. Washington with his own hands first broke ground at the siege of Yorktown."

The journal of James Duncan of Pennsylvania discussed the online training ordered by Colonel Alexander Hamilton on October 7:

> Our next maneuver was rather extraordinary. We were ordered to mount the bank, front the enemy, and there by word of command go through all the ceremony of soldiery, ordering and grounding our arms, and although the enemy had been firing a little before, they did not now give us a single shot. I suppose their astonishment at our conduct must have prevented them, for I can assign no other reason. Colonel Hamilton gave these orders, and although I esteem him one of the first officers in the American army, must beg leave in this instance to think he wantonly exposed the lives of his men.

By early morning of October 7 Americans had dug in so close to Cornwallis's battlements they could see the British flag over Yorktown. American artillery had brought up six 18-pounders, six 24-pounders, four mortars, and two howitzers. Two days later the French secured their position and Washington was ready to launch the siege. After French guns began the bombardment, Washington is said to have put a match to a cannon and fired the first American shot (although this is disputed by Dupuy). For twenty-four hours, wrote Langguth, "Yorktown and its harbor took more than thirty-six hundred shots. Shells flew across the night sky in bright arcs, trailing long streams of fire."

Sergeant Martin reported:

> I was in the trenches the day that the batteries were to be opened; all were upon the tiptoe of expectation and impatience to see the signal given to open the whole line of batteries, which was to be the hoisting of the American flag in the ten-gun battery. About noon the much-wished-for signal went up. I confess I felt a secret pride swell my heart when I saw the 'star-spangled banner' waving majestically in the very faces of our implacable adversaries; it appeared like an omen of success to our enterprize, and so it proved in reality. A simultaneous discharge of all the guns in the line followed, the French troops accompanying it with 'Huzza for the Americans!'
>
> It was said that the first shell sent from our batteries entered an elegant house, formerly owned or occupied by the Secretary of State under the British government, and burnt directly over a table surrounded by a large party of British officers at dinner, killing and wounding a number of them. [Was that the shot fired by George Washington?]

Casualties were not confined to the military. Under a white flag, inhabitants who had been trapped in Yorktown "fled with their belongings to the river and hid themselves on the hillside in the sand and rocks," wrote Stephan Popp, a Hessian corporal. "Still they did not entirely escape, for many of them were fatally injured through the ricocheting of the bombs."

Gunfire reached the York River. Washington had reported that "a hot shot from one of the French batteries set the frigate *Charon* ...on fire and in the morning two transports shared the same fate."

Dr. Thacher also described the cannonade:

> From the bank of the river I had a fine view of this splendid conflagration. The ships were enwrapped in a torrent of fire, which, spreading with vivid brightness among the combustible rigging, and running with

amazing rapidity to the tops of the several masts, while all around was thunder and lightning from our numerous cannon and mortars, and in the darkness of night, presented one of the most sublime and magnificent spectacles which can be imagined. Some of our shells, overreaching the town, are seen to fall in the river and, bursting, throw up columns of water like the spouting of the monsters of the deep.

We now made further approaches to the town by throwing up a second parallel line and batteries within about three hundred yards; this was effected in the night, and at day-light the enemy were roused to the greatest exertions; the engines of war have raged with redoubled fury and destruction on both sides, no cessation day or night. The French had two officers wounded and fifteen men killed and wounded, and among the Americans, two or three were wounded. I assisted in amputating a man's thigh.

The siege is daily becoming more and more formidable and alarming, and his lordship must view his situation as extremely critical, if not desperate. Being in the trenches every other night and day, I have a fine opportunity of witnessing the sublime and stupendous scene which is continually exhibiting. The bombshells from the besiegers and the besieged are incessantly crossing each others' path in the air. They are clearly visible in the form of a black ball in the day, but in the night they appear like a fiery meteor with a blazing tail, most beautifully brilliant, ascending majestically from the mortar to a certain altitude and gradually descending to the spot where they are destined to execute their work of destruction.

It is astonishing with what accuracy an experienced gunner will make his calculations, that a shell shall fall within a few feet of a given point, and burst at the precise time, though at a great distance. When a shell falls, it whirls around, burrows, and excavates the earth to a considerable extent and, bursting, makes dreadful havoc around. I have more than once witnessed fragments of the mangled bodies and limbs of the British soldiers thrown into the air by the bursting of our shells....

The allies "resolved to take possession" of two small British redoubts which impeded their approach, wrote Dr. Thacher. The one on the left of the British garrison, bordering on the banks of the river, was assigned to our brigade of light-infantry, under the command of the Marquis de la Fayette. The advanced corps was led by the intrepid Colonel Hamilton....

The assault commenced at eight o'clock in the evening, and the assailants bravely entered the fort with the point of the bayonet without firing a single gun. We suffered the loss of eight men killed and about thirty wounded....

During the assault, the British kept up an incessant firing of cannon and musketry from their whole line. His Excellency General Washington, Generals Lincoln and Knox, with their aids, having dismounted, were standing in an exposed situation waiting the result.

Colonel Cobb, one of General Washington's aids, solicitous for his safety, said to His Excellency, "Sir, you are too much exposed here. Had you not better step a little back?"

"Colonel Cobb," replied His Excellency, "if you are afraid, you have liberty to step back."

Anticipating that Cornwallis's surrender was likely to occur at any moment, Thacher concluded: "Our artillery-men, by the exactness of their aim, make every discharge take effect, so that many of the enemy's guns are entirely silenced, and their works almost in ruins."

The intensity of allied bombardment took its toll. Gradually, the British guns subsided. Cornwallis had estimated the allied strength at "forty cannon, mostly heavy, and sixteen mortars, from eight to sixteen inches." And each day he watched Washington's guns move closer to Yorktown, until on October 12 his allied troops were within three hundred yards of Cornwallis, who sought safety in an underground bunker.

A day earlier, Cornwallis had informed Clinton that American batteries "continued firing without intermission." He concluded:

> We have lost about seventy of our men and many of our works are considerably damaged; with such works on disadvantageous ground, against so powerful an attack we cannot hope to make a very long resistance.

Cornwallis had two remaining redoubts near the York River, but they were under constant attack as Yorktown blazed with shells and grenades and rifle fire. On the night of October 14 the one closer to the river was charged by Hamilton's men who had to wade through mud with unloaded muskets and fixed bayonets; in just ten minutes the redoubt was taken. The other was captured the same night by the French, shouting *"Vive le Roi"* as they advanced on their objective.

Popp captured the horror of war: Under "heavy cannonading by the enemy," the Hessian soldiers "began to desert in large numbers and left their command, watches, and posts. Why? Out of fear!" On the night of October 14 "the enemy crept unnoticed close to the barricade of the trench." The French grenadiers then

> gained the wall after a stubborn counterattack without firing a shot. There they captured the command of some hundred men. A part of them saved themselves by flight. Some were even shot by us with grapeshot, mostly English and Hessians. A Hessian was found in three pieces. Some who would not give up were

stabbed to death. The enemy was also supposed to have lost many dead and wounded in this attack. They occupied the fort at once and made themselves stronger and stuck out their flag. They made a dreadful cry and hurrah at doing this.

The allied artillery hammered British defenses without relief, leaving the fortification in total ruin without a gun that could be fired. The situation was so desperate that Lord Cornwallis admitted defeat in his letter to Clinton on October 15:

> My situation now becomes very critical....The safety of the place is, therefore, so precarious that I cannot recommend that the fleet and army should run the risque in endeavouring to save us.

Cornwallis's only chance was retreat. He decided to abandon Yorktown and transport the remainder of his army across the river in small boats. Then he would pick up Tarleton and the small force still defending Gloucester and proceed by land through Virginia and Maryland until he reached Pennsylvania and New Jersey, where there was no significant opposition to interrupt his march to Clinton's headquarters at New York.

The plan did not anticipate the violent storm that prevented his escape across the York. As the British boats were scattered by the storm and blown down river they were captured by the Americans. Some managed to turn back. At Gloucester Colonel Tarleton wrote: "Thus expired the last hope of the British army."

A flag of truce appeared above the British fortification on the morning of October 17. Cornwallis wrote to Washington:

> I propose a cessation of hostilities for twenty-four hours, and that two officers may be appointed by each side, to meet at Mr. Moore's home, to settle terms for the surrender of the ports of York and Gloucester.

In his "ardent desire to spare the further effusion of blood," Washington granted a cease-fire for a period of two hours. He asked Cornwallis to submit his conditions for surrender in writing. The outline of conditions was received by Washington at 4:40 P.M. On October 18 he informed Cornwallis that "the same honours will be granted to the Surrendering Army as was granted to the Garrison of Charlestown." The British army was to surrender to the Americans; the navy to the French. Officers could retain their side arms and private property; rank and file soldiers were to be kept in prison camps in Winchester, Virginia, and Frederick, Maryland. Cornwallis and some of his officers were allowed to sail to New York on parole, aboard the sloop-of-war *Bonetta*, the vessel to be returned. The surrender ceremony would take place on October 19.

Cornwallis discussed the last days at Yorktown in his letter to Clinton on October 20:

> I have the mortification to inform your Excellency that I have been forced to give up the posts of York and Gloucester, and to surrender the troops under my command, by capitulation on the 19th inst. as prisoners of war to the combined forces of America and France.

He described the escape attempt on the night of October 16:

> At this time we knew that there was no part of the whole front attacked on which we could show a single gun, and our shells were nearly expended; I therefore had only to chuse between preparing to surrender next day or endeavouring to get off with the greatest part of the troops, and I determined to attempt the latter, reflecting that though it should prove unsuccessful in its immediate object, it might at least delay the enemy in the prosecution of further enterprizes. Sixteen large boats were prepared, and upon other pretexts were ordered to be in readiness to

receive troops precisely at ten o'clock. With these I hoped to pass the infantry during the night, abandoning our baggage, and leaving a detachment to capitulate for the town's people and the sick and wounded; on which subject a letter was ready to be delivered to General Washington.

After making my arrangements with the utmost secrecy, the light infantry, greatest part of the Guards and part of the Twenty-Third Regiment landed at Gloucester; but at this critical moment the weather, from being moderate and calm, changed to a most violent storm of wind and rain and drove all the boats, some of which had troops on board, down the river. It was soon evident that the intended passage was impracticable, and the absence of the boats rendered it equally impossible to bring back the troops that had passed; which I had ordered about two in the morning. In this situation, with my little force divided, the enemy's batteries opened at daybreak. The passage between this place and Gloucester was much exposed, but the boats having now returned, they were ordered to bring back the troops that had passed during the night, and they joined us in the forenoon without much loss.

Our works in the mean time were going to ruin....We at that time could not fire a single gun. Only one eight-inch and little more than an hundred cohorn [small mortar] shells remained. A diversion by the French ships of war that lay at the mouth of York River was to be expected. Our numbers had been diminished by the enemy's fire, but particularly by sickness, and the strength and spirits of those in the works were much exhausted by the fatigue of constant watching and unremitting duty.

Under all these circumstances, I thought it would have been wanton and inhuman to the last degree to sacrifice the lives of this small body of gallant soldiers, who had ever behaved with so much fidelity and courage, by exposing them to an assault, which from the numbers and precautions of the enemy could not fail to succeed. I therefore proposed to capitulate.

The British blundered their way into the war, then blundered their way into defeat. Britain's adviser on the conduct of war, Richard Oswald, had been opposed to Cornwallis's invasion of Virginia for tactical reasons. He compared the vain Cornwallis to the general of an earlier expedition who, when warned that he was leading his army to ruin, responded: "No matter...it will make a very good newspaper paragraph at home."

To win the war, the British had to win control of Chesapeake Bay. That opportunity had been there when they had "twice taken possession of and evacuated" the bay, said Admiral Rodney who had failed to intercept the French fleet while on its way from the West Indies to the Chesapeake. The British failed again when their ships delayed a last-minute attempt to save Cornwallis.

As Graves departed from New York on October 19—with a fleet of twenty-five warships and more than seven thousand of Clinton's troops—Cornwallis had already surrendered at Yorktown. But Graves would not know of that development until October 24 when he was informed by three men who had put to sea in a small craft and were rescued by the flagship *London*. They were James Robinson, a black man who had served as pilot aboard the *Charon*; a white member of the Quartermaster General's Department; and another black man named James Rider. All escaped from Yorktown when they heard about the surrender. Their report was confirmed on the following day by a message from the frigate *Nymphe*, which was en route to New York with Cornwallis's final letter to Clinton.

When Graves reached the Capes, the French fleet had blocked the entrance to the Chesapeake. Admiral Hood recommended that the British remain at the Capes to confine the French ships to the bay. But Graves believed his fleet lacked the speed "in so mutilated a state to attack them, had it been prudent." On October 29, he rejected Hood's recommendation and announced that "nothing was so proper as to return with the fleet to New York."

Admiral de Grasse wanted to engage the British in the open sea, but appeals from Washington, Rochambeau, and Lafayette changed his mind. It would have been the largest naval encounter in the world to that time. But not a shot was fired. The French remained secure in the bay and the British sailed to New York.

After Graves's ships were gone, a French naval lieutenant said: "They were too late. The fowl had been eaten."

In London most of the blame for the Yorktown defeat was placed not on Cornwallis but on Clinton. He was faulted for permitting the allied army to travel secretly to Chesapeake Bay and for failing to reinforce Cornwallis in time.

The war was yet to be won, as far as Washington was concerned, but Britain's Prime Minister Lord Frederick North knew the meaning of Yorktown when he cried, "Oh, God! It is all over!"

At the surrender ceremony on the afternoon of October 19, French and American armies formed lines a mile long on opposite sides of the dusty road leading from Yorktown to Hampton. The Americans were on the right facing west, with Washington and Rochambeau fronting their respective lines.

"Every eye was prepared to gaze on Lord Cornwallis, the object of peculiar interest and solicitude," wrote Dr. Thacher, "but he disappointed our anxious expectations; pretending indisposition."

At two o'clock the British troops marched out with shouldered arms, led by Brigadier General Charles O'Hara. Pleading ill, Lord Cornwallis had turned the unhappy ritual over to his second in command. O'Hara offered Cornwallis's sword to Rochambeau. The French general directed O'Hara to Washington, who indicated that Major General Benjamin Lincoln would receive the sword. It was Lincoln who had surrendered Charleston to the British on May 11, 1780.

In commenting on Cornwallis's decision to shrink "from the inevitable misfortune of war," Dr. Thacher concluded:

> ...when it is considered that Lord Cornwallis has frequently appeared in splendid triumph at the head of his army, by which he is almost adored, we conceive it incumbent on him cheerfully to participate in their misfortunes and degradations, however humiliating.

As Lincoln accepted the Cornwallis sword, the British band played a popular song entitled *The World Turned Upside Down*:

> If buttercups buzzed after the bee,
> If boats were on land, churches on sea,
> If ponies rode men, and if grass ate the cows,
> And cats should be chased into holes by the mouse;
> If the mamas sold their babies to gypsies for half a crown,
> If summer were spring, and the other way 'round,
> Then all the world would be upside down.

The British troops then marched down the road between the two lines. When they stopped, some of the soldiers laid down their arms as instructed, the remainder slammed "their arms on the pile with violence, as if determined to render them useless," wrote Thacher. According to another American officer, "the British officers in general behaved like boys who had been whipped at school. Some bit their lips; some pouted; others cried."

Hessian Corporal Popp wrote: "We were treated with justice and military usage. We had no complaints." He said he was "staggered by the multitude of those who had besieged us.

We were just a guard-mounting in comparison with them, and they could have eaten us up with their power."

The allied victory was reflected in the Yorktown casualties. Total American and French casualties were 262–with more than two French deaths to every American. The British had 552 casualties and surrendered more than seven thousand soldiers and 840 seamen to Virginia and Maryland prison camps. There were about two thousand British sick or disabled in Virginia hospitals.

Lafayette wrote: "The play is over."

Washington retired to his Williamsburg quarters, the home of George Wythe, and wrote a report which began:

> I have the Honour to inform Congress, that a Reduction of the British Army under the Command of Lord Cornwallis, is most happily effected.

He praised "the chearfull and able assistance" of the French, and stressed his indebtedness to Count de Grasse. "Nothing could equal the zeal of our allies, but the emulating spirit of the American officers," he wrote.

Tom Paine was blunt in attributing the Yorktown victory to French support, writing that "it was by the aid of this money, and this fleet, and of Rochambeau's army, that Cornwallis was taken; the laurels of which have been unjustly given to Mr. Washington."

Washington's report was delivered to Congress in Philadelphia by his aide, Colonel Tench Tilghman, of the Maryland Eastern Shore. Tilghman was still suffering from malaria when he boarded a small sailboat to travel down the York River and up Chesapeake Bay. His boat ran aground at Tangier Island, which he blamed on "the stupidity of the skipper" in his report to Washington, and the feverish Tilghman had to waste a night waiting for the tide to free his boat. By the end of the next day when the wind died down, he was still thirty miles south of Annapolis. Finally, he landed at Rock Hall on the Eastern Shore, obtained a horse and raced to Philadelphia, alerting people along the way of the Yorktown surrender. Well before sunrise on October 24 Tilghman rode into the city and relayed his news to a watchman, who yelled through the streets: "Past three o'clock and Cornwallis is taken!" Ill with fever and penniless, thirty-eight-year-old Tilghman had to depend upon the largess of members of Congress to pay for his room and board so that he could get some rest.

To announce the surrender, Congress held an early morning session—and the news provoked angry cries for the execution of Cornwallis for British atrocities in the south. Congress declared a day of celebration, and the Philadelphia press ran the following item under the headline, ILLUMINATION:

> Colonel Tilghman, Aid de Camp to his Excellency General Washington, having brought official accounts of the SURRENDER of Lord Cornwallis, and the Garrisons of York and Gloucester, those citizens who chuse to ILLUMINATE on the Glorious Occasion, will do it this evening at Six, and distinguish their lights at Nine o'clock.
>
> Decorum and harmony are earnestly recommended to every Citizen, and a general discountenance to the least appearance of riot.

Despite the plea for law and order, Philadelphia mobs attacked houses where windows were not illuminated. Rocks and insults were hurled at the darkened houses of the Quakers for their opposition to the war. "Scarcely one Friend's house escaped," wrote Elizabeth Drinker, wife of a Quaker shipper. "Many women and children were frightened into fits."

In a tribute to Tench Tilghman, written on his death in 1785, Washington said:

> He was in every action in which the main army was concerned. A great part of the time he refused to receive pay. While living no man could be more esteemed, and since dead none more lamented. No

one had imbibed sentiments of greater friendship for him than I had done. He left as fair a reputation as ever belong to human character.

Historian James H. Fitzgerald added a footnote to Maryland's impact on the American Revolution. He noted that "the last man killed in the struggle for independence, Captain William Wilmot, was a Marylander who succumbed to enemy fire just before the fall of Charleston," and that Tilghman "informally closed it with his famous ride bearing the news of victory to Philadelphia."

Soon after Cornwallis's surrender, a French cartographer drew a map entitled "Plan of Hampton in order to serve the establishment of winter quarters for the Legion of Lauzon." The map, identifying billets for French troops stationed there, managed to find space within the town's fifty acres to quarter several hundred soldiers among a hundred or so homes, inns, stores, custom house, tobacco warehouse, naval headquarters, burned-out church, shipyard, make-shift hospitals, and such taverns as the King's Arms, where George Washington was entertained and which served as a gathering place for townsmen and Frenchmen alike to toast the victory at Yorktown.

Rochambeau also spent the winter in Virginia, with detachments from his army billeted in Yorktown, Gloucester, and the village of West Point at the head of the York River.

Washington anticipated another year of fighting. He tried to persuade Admiral de Grasse to keep his fleet in American waters to support the effort against those positions still controlled by the British: New York, Wilmington, Charleston, and Savannah. But the French admiral sailed for the West Indies on November 5, promising to return the following summer. He would fail to keep the promise and fail to repeat the success which the Battle of the Virginia Capes had supplied to an otherwise undistinguished career. Admiral de Grasse would suffer a humiliating defeat in the West Indies and be captured by the British.

On November 23, Congress resolved that Lafayette

> be informed that on a review of his conduct throughout the past campaign and particularly during the period in which he had the chief command in Virginia the many new proofs which present themselves of his zealous attachment to the cause he has espoused and of his judgment, vigilance, gallantry and address in its defense have greatly added to the high Opinion entertained by Congress of his merits & military talents.

Washington, en route to Philadelphia, had stopped at Annapolis two days earlier and sparked this account in the *Maryland Gazette:*

> When the citizens received the pleasing information of his Excellency's arrival, all business ceased, and every consideration gave way to their impatience to behold their benefactor, and the deliverer of his country. On his appearance in the streets, people of every rank and every age eagerly pressed forward to feed their eyes with gazing on the man, to whom, under Providence, and the generous aid of our great and good ally, they owed their security, and hopes of future liberty and peace. The courteous affability, with which he returned their salutes, lighted up ineffable joys in every countenance.

On December 13 Congress recognized the surrender at Yorktown as the decisive turn in the war. But it would be another seventeen months before the peace treaty was signed.

Ten days later Lafayette sailed to France aboard the American frigate *Alliance*, having invested $200,000 of his personal fortune in the Revolution. He would return to the United States in 1824, when invited by the Maryland governor to revisit Annapolis. During that visit, the Assembly resolved unanimously that "Lafayette and his male heirs forever be made citizens of the State of Maryland."

- 11 -

Peace

1782-1783

The Cornwallis surrender at Yorktown saved Maryland from the all-out invasion of an army described by Barbara Tuchman as "the more active and menacing enemy force in the war." Defence, the sole survivor of Maryland's navy, spent the closing months of the war as a cargo vessel carrying tobacco to Europe. Virginia, sensing the war's end, retained only Commodore James Barron and the schooners Liberty and Patriot. Both states planned to rebuild their navies. The plan never materialized and loyalist privateers continued to pillage bay country waterways and harrass Chesapeake commerce.

In the spring of 1782 Maryland Commodore Thomas Grason was killed in a battle against five enemy barges and other armed vessels. The General Assembly immediately passed the "Act for the Protection of the Bay Trade" with instructions to arm and man four barges for the purpose of "attacking and expelling the enemy from our Bay." The Assembly also appointed a naval emissary to consult with Virginia officials on measures to protect Chesapeake trade, but the mission failed because of a shortage of funds and vessels, complicated by the frustrations which existed in any attempt to develop a workable partnership between the two governments.

Privateering raids on Delaware Bay forced merchants to arm the cargo vessel *Hyder Ally* and hire a crew that included a company of marines made up of sharpshooting backwoods riflemen. The commander was Joshua Barney, a young

Continental navy officer from Baltimore. On April 7, while Barney was convoying a fleet of merchant vessels near Cape May, New Jersey, the fleet was seen by the captain of the *General Monk*, a British warship far superior to the *Hyder Ally* in gunpower. Barney, concerned that the *Monk* "would blow us to atoms," quickly maneuvered the *Hyder Ally* to a point where its guns could blast the enemy with an uninterrupted barrage. When the two vessels were abreast and British marines tried to board the *Hyder Ally*, the sharpshooters cleared the *Monk's* deck with intensive riflefire. In thirty minutes the *Monk* was heavily damaged and more than half its crew was killed or wounded. Barney lost four men killed and eleven wounded. The *General Monk*, which was formerly the captured American ship *General Washington*, was returned to the Continental Navy under its original name with Barney in command. (Joshua Barney would command the Baltimore privateer *Rossie* during the War of 1812, taking prizes valued at $1.5 million in a single cruise.)

Sir Guy Carleton relieved Clinton as Commander-in-Chief of British Forces in America, but Britain had lost all prospects of victory after Yorktown. That defeat, along with follow-up losses to the French in the West Indies, led to peace talks. By March the House of Commons had voted against prolonging the war and George III was authorized to make peace with his former colonies. Prime Minister Lord North was succeeded by Lord Rockingham, the minister who had secured repeal of the Stamp Act in 1766. Preliminary peace discussions opened on April 12 with Benjamin Franklin; but by the time the Franklin commission was joined by John Jay, John Adams, and Henry Laurens in September, Rockingham had died and was replaced by William Petty, the Earl of Shelburne. For Great Britain, the task was complicated by the need to deal with the interests of America, France, Spain, and Holland simultaneously. Congress had instructed the commission "to be guided by the wishes of the French court," but the four Americans decided on their own to enter into separate talks with the British negotiators, including Richard Oswald.

As peace was being negotiated in Paris, Great Britain's military presence in America was confined to New York. New England and New Jersey were wary but the battlefields in the south were silent. It also appeared that war on the Chesapeake was nearing an end when Maryland's new commodore, Zedekiah Whaley, hoped he had reduced the threat of privateering raids by recapturing four of the Maryland small craft. But it was just a lull in the hostilities. Life on the Chesapeake and along the banks of its many tributaries was still in jeopardy. Yet to come was the Battle of the Barges, which has been called "the bloodiest naval battle of the Revolutionary War to take place in Chesapeake Bay."

On November 14, Commodore Whaley's fleet of four barges—*Protector, Defence, Terrible, Fearnaught*—chased two Tory barges away from Gwynn's Island and took the *Jolly Tar*. Two weeks later, Whaley continued to enlarge his fleet with the capture of two more barges, *Victory* and *Langodoc*. Reinforced by Colonel John Cropper and twenty-five Virginia volunteers from the Accomack militia on the lower Eastern Shore, the Maryland fleet left Onancock for Tangier Sound to engage a flotilla of heavily armed barges manned by Tories and escaped convicts. Commanded by Captain John Kidd and operating out of Onancock Creek, the flotilla had been plundering Eastern Shore towns in both Virginia and Maryland.

On the morning of November 30 the enemy barges were gone when Whaley arrived at Tangier Sound, and he proceeded up the bay. At ten o'clock his barges faced Kidd's flotilla in Dredge's Strait in Maryland above Smith Island. In a frenzied exchange of cannon and musket fire at close range, the dead and wounded on both sides mounted rapidly. Whaley's flagship *Protector* was nearly ripped apart by explosions, and members of the crew jumped overboard with their clothes in flames. Burning and drifting helplessly, the barge was boarded by the enemy and engaged in deadly hand-to-hand combat. Whaley and many members of his crew were killed; Kidd was wounded.

Once the guns were quiet, it was apparent to the remainder of Whaley's barges that they were outgunned with no chance of rescuing the *Protector*. They withdrew from the conflict with the Tory barges in pursuit. It was not long before Whaley's entire fleet was taken, adding last-ditch encouragement to the unforgiving Tory marauders who continued their efforts to paralyze the Chesapeake even after a peace treaty was signed.

Maryland officials, still trying to rebuild their fleet, put a penalty of fifty pounds on any privateer that lured sailors away from the ruins that represented the Maryland Navy. But the action was too late; the war was over.

A provisional treaty was agreed to on November 30. Great Britain officially recognized America's independence and its boundaries. The geography of the United States was defined as that territory south of the Great Lakes, north of Florida, and westward to the Mississippi River. Britain retained Nova Scotia and rejected the demand by Adams that Canada be ceded to the United States. The Spanish held Florida and the French gained control of Louisiana.

Congress received a text of the Treaty of Paris on March 13, 1783, and joined Great Britain in proclaiming the cessation of war. On April 15 the treaty was ratified by Congress and returned to Paris to be signed.

Few outsiders expected the new nation to survive, and most probably agreed with this conclusion of a British economist:

> They never can be united into one compact empire under any species of government whatever.

George III was convinced that his former colonies would come crawling back to the security of the British empire. As it turned out, the American Revolution was a blessing for Britain.

"No one foresaw that free trade with the new Republic would be better for England than forced trade with the colonists," wrote Perkins, "or that the United States would add vastly more to English wealth than her American colonies had ever done."

Before the armistice reached the Chesapeake, the town of Benedict, Maryland, was sacked and partially burned by the British. A week after the Benedict incident, William Paca, Maryland's new governor, wrote an angry letter to Washington concerning the sincerity of Great Britain's order to cease all offensive actions in America: "We beg leave to inform your Excellency that if such orders were ever given, they have been most shamefully violated by the enemy's barges and armed vessels in the Bay of Chesapeake."

The end of hostilities did not save the seven Tories tried and convicted of treason in Frederick County. As reported in J. Thomas Sharf's *History of Western Maryland* (published 1882), three of the Tories were sentenced to hang and told that

> you shall be cut down to the earth alive, and your entrails shall be taken out and burned while you are yet alive, your head shall be cut off, your body shall be divided into four parts and your heads and quarters shall be placed where his Excellency the Governor shall appoint. So Lord have mercy on your poor Souls.

Such was the justice of America's English heritage.

The last of the one hundred thousand loyalists who chose not to live in the United States departed from New York in late April for Canada and Europe. Nine states had passed legislation exiling prominent Tories, five had disenfranchised all loyalists, and the loyalists in most states were denied government office, barred from the professions, and had to pay up to three times the taxes levied on other Americans. All thirteen states permitted the confiscation of loyalist property, and Maryland alone gained in excess of two million dollars from the sale of this property. In the fall of 1780 the Maryland legislature had passed a law declaring that "all property belonging to British citizens in the State [was to] be seized and confiscated to the use of the State."

Before the war ended, Maryland confiscated about 280,000 acres of proprietary lands in settled areas plus 125,000 acres of frontier land which was then allotted to officers and men of the Maryland Line or sold to tenants. Although land distributed by tenants did enable them to rise above the tenant class into a freeholder status with the right to vote, most acquisitions permitted men of wealth to increase their holdings. These confiscated properties, whether proprietary or loyalist, included not only land but buildings, slaves, livestock, tobacco, and other commodities. Among major speculators of confiscated property were such Maryland patriots as Samuel Chase, Charles Ridgely, and William Paca.

Patrick Henry, whose passionate speeches had influenced the move for independence, now used his eloquence to plead the cause of exiled loyalists who asked to return to their Virginia homes. He also championed the cause of Virginia planters who had been deeply in debt to British merchants since before the war and refused to respond to British recovery suits. It was considered to be a debt of extravagance exceeding one million pounds sterling.

To escape British debts was why many Americans supported the Revolution. The bondage which peppered early revolutionary speeches was not the cry of America's slaves nor the societal restrictions that denied the poor the right to participate in their own government. It was the financial bondage of planters and merchants to British creditors and Parliament tax and trade regulations. Though the Revolution relieved the gentry of their debts, it did not free the slaves nor broaden political participation.

Still, as Thomas Paine wrote, it probably "contributed more to enlighten the world, and diffuse a spirit of freedom and liberality among mankind, than any human event...that ever preceded it." In time, as the American system refined its principles and ideals, its influence would relegate the divine rule of kings and tyrants to the junkyard of world politics.

After the Revolutionary War, a French-American, J. Hector St. John de Crevecoeur, asked "What is an American?" His answer was:

> He is either an European, or the descendant of an European. I could point out to you a family whose grandfather was an Englishman, whose wife was Dutch, whose son married a French woman, and whose present four sons have four wives of different nations. *He* is an American, who, leaving behind him all his ancient prejudices and manners, receives new ones from the new abode of life he has embraced, the new government he obeys, and the new rank he holds.

He concluded on this prescient note:

> Here individuals of all nations are melted into a new race of men, whose labours and posterity will one day cause great changes in the world.

Signing of the final peace treaty was delayed until negotiations between Great Britain and France could be completed. The signing ceremony took place in Paris on September 3. The treaty asked that "the most serene and most potent Prince George the Third" and the newly created United States "forget all past misunderstandings and differences that have unhappily interrupted the good correspondence and friendship which they mutually wish restored; and to establish such a beneficial and satisfactory intercourse between the two countries, upon the ground of reciprocal advantages and mutual convenience, as may promote and secure to both perpetual peace and harmony."

In Article I of the treaty, George III acknowledged the former colonies "to be free, sovereign and independent States," and he relinquished "all claims to the Government, propriety and territorial rights of the same." Article IV dealt (unsuccessfully) with the repayment of debts: "It is agreed that creditors on either side, shall meet with no lawful impediment to the recovery of the full value in sterling money, of all bona fide debts heretofore contracted." Article VII released all prisoners and instructed Great Britain to withdraw all armies and fleets from the United States with all convenient speed.

The final treaty was ratified by Congress in January of the following year. Most of the revolutionaries (except those who were heavily in debt to British creditors) probably agreed with Edmund Pendleton that "the peace upon the whole [was] a very liberal one."

Meanwhile, as the British evacuated New York on November 25, they took along seven thousand loyalists and some three thousand former slaves who had been promised their freedom. The French army also, over the protests of Virginia officials, returned home with the many blacks it had captured from the British.

On the same day the British left America, Washington's troops marched victoriously into Manhattan. One week later, Washington bid farewell to his officers at Fraunces Tavern:

> With a heart full of love and gratitude I must now take my leave of you. I most devoutly wish that your latter days may be as prosperous and happy as your former ones have been glorious and honorable.

One of those officers, Colonel Lewis Nicola, would suggest that the Continental Army establish a monarchy with Washington as king, and Washington would order Nicola to banish the thought.

Two days before Christmas, after a jubilant tour to the new nation's temporary capital city of Annapolis, Washington appeared before Congress to resign his commission:

> Having now finished the work assigned to me, I retire from the great theater of action, bidding an affectional farewell to this august body, under whose order I have so long acted. I here offer my commission, and take my leave of all the employments of public life.

Congress had moved from Philadelphia to Princeton in June before assembling for a six-month period in the new Senate Chamber of the Maryland State House in Annapolis. Following Washington's address, Congress moved to New York City which became the nation's capital until the establishment of a federal town on a Potomac site ceded to the United States by Maryland.

In 1784, in a letter to Virginia's new governor Benjamin Harrison, Washington recommended a navigational system for the James and the Potomac rivers that would bring trade from the western territory to the Atlantic. He believed, wrote John Marshall, that these rivers "afforded a more convenient, and a more direct course than could be found elsewhere, for that rich and increasing commerce." Washington held that a cooperative effort by Virginia and Maryland could link the James and Potomac Rivers with "the navigable waters west of the Ohio, towards the great lakes."

To work out the navigation problems, four Virginia commissioners (including James Madison and George Mason) met with four Maryland commissioners (including Samuel Chase) in March 1785. At a subsequent conference at Mount Vernon the commissioners agreed on jurisdiction of the Potomac and apportioned expenses for marking a channel through the Chesapeake.

A bill sanctioned by both states was the first to connect the navigation of the eastern and western United States. Now that the guns were quiet, the Chesapeake and its major rivers would again be active avenues of trade.

- Bibliography -

Guns on the Chesapeake

Adams, James Truslow, *The Epic of America*; Triangle Books, 1931

Adams, Robert M., *The Land and Literature of England*; Norton, 1983

Adams, Willi Paul, *The First American Constitutions*; University of North Carolina Press, 1980

American Revolution: Opposing Viewpoints, American History Series; John C. Chalberg, Consulting Editor; Greenhaven Press, 1992

Bailey, Thomas A., *Voices of America: Nation's Story in Slogans, Sayings, and Songs*; The Free Press Division of Macmillian, 1976

Bailyn, Bernard, "Politics and Social Structure in Virginia," reprinted in *Conflict and Consensus in Early American History*, edited by Allen F. Davis and Harold D. Woodman; D.C. Heath and Company, 1968

Barker, Charles Albro, *The Background of the Revolution in Maryland*; Yale University Press, 1940

Beeman, Richard R., *Patrick Henry: A Biography*; McGraw-Hill, 1974

Boatner, Mark Mayo III, *Encyclopedia of the American Revolution*; David McKay Company, 1966

Bode, Carl, *Maryland, A History*, W.W. Norton & Company, 1978

Bridenbaugh, Carl, *The Spirit of '76: Growth of American Patriotism Before Independence, 1607-1776*, Oxford University Press, 1975

Brodie, Fawn M., *Thomas Jefferson, An Intimate History*; W.W. Norton & Company, 1974

Campbell, Charles, *History of the Colony and Ancient Dominion of Virginia*, Lippincott, 1860

Carrington, Henry B., *Battles of the American Revolution 1775-1781*; New York, 1881

Chesapeake Bay in the American Revolution, edited by Ernest McNeill Eller; Tidewater Publishers, 1981

Churchill, Winston, *History of the English Speaking People: The Age of Revolution*; Dodd, Mead, 1957

Coakley, Robert W. and Stetson Conn, *The War of the American Revolution*; Center of Military History, United States Army, Washington D.C., 1975

Coggins, Jack, *Ships and Seamen of the American Revolution*; Stackpole Books, 1969

Crowl, Philip A., *Maryland During and After the Revolution: A Political and Economic Study*; Johns Hopkins Press, 1943

Davis, Burke, *The Campaign that Won America: The Story of Yorktown*; Dial Press, 1970

Dowdey, Clifford, "The Harrisons of Berkeley Hundred," *American Heritage*, April 1957

Documentary Source Book of American History 1608-1898, edited by William MacDonald; MacMillan, 1908

Dupuy, R. Ernest and Trevor N. Dupuy, *The Compact History of the Revolutionary War*; Hawthorn Books, 1963

BIBLIOGRAPHY

Earle, Swepson, *The Chesapeake Bay Country*; Thomsen-Ellis, 1934

Eckenrode, H.J., *The Revolution in Virginia*; Archon Books, 1964 (first published in 1916)

Encyclopedia Americana; Grolier Inc., 1993

Encyclopedia of American History, edited by Richard B. Morris; Harper & Brothers, 1953

Everstine, Carl N., *The General Assembly of Maryland 1634-1776*; The Michie Company, 1980

Fowler, William M. Jr., *Rebels Under Sail: The American Navy During the Revolution*; Charles Scribner's Sons, 1976

Gayley, Charles Mills, *Shakespeare and the Founders of Liberty in America*; MacMillan, 1917.

Gelb, Norman, *Less Than Glory: A Revisionist's View of the American Revolution*; Putnam, 1984

Goldenberg, Joseph A. and Marion West Stoer, "The Virginia State Navy," from *Chesapeake Bay in the American Revolution*, edited by Ernest McNeill Eller; Tidewater Publishers, 1981

Gwathmey, John H., *Historical Register of Virginians in the Revolution*, Richmond, 1938

Hargreaves, Major Reginald, "The Man Who Didn't Shoot Washington," *American Heritage*, December 1955

Hawke, David, "The American Revolution: Was It a Real One?" from *American Vistas 1607-1877*, edited by Leonard Dinnerstein and Kenneth T. Jackson; Oxford University Press, 1971

Hoffman, Ronald, *A Spirit of Dissension: Economics, Politics, and the Revolution in Maryland*; Johns Hopkins University Press, 1973

Interpretations of American History, edited by Gerald N. Grob and George Athan Billias; The Free Press, MacMillian, 1967

Jameson, Edwin M., "Tory Operations on the Bay," from *Chesapeake Bay in the American Revolution*, edited by Ernest McNeill Eller; Tidewater Publishers, 1981

Johnson, Samuel A., *An Interpretation of American History*; Barron's Educational Series, 1968

Kitman, Marvin, *The Making of the President 1789*; Harper & Row, 1989

Lafayette in the Age of the American Revolution: Selected Letters and Papers, 1776-1790, Volume IV, April 1, 1781-December 23, 1781, edited by Stanley J. Idzerda; Cornell University Press, 1981

Land, Aubrey C., *Colonial Maryland: A History*; KTO Press, 1981

Landers, Colonel H.L. of Historical Section, Army War College, *The Virginia Campaign and the Blockade and Siege of Yorktown, 1781*; U.S. Government Printing Office, 1931

Langguth, A.J., Patriots: *The Men Who Started the American Revolution*; Simon and Shuster, 1988

Larrabee, Harold A., *Decision at the Chesapeake*; Potter, 1964

Larrabee, Harold A., "A Near Thing at Yorktown," *American Heritage*, October 1961

Lee, Jean B., *The Price of Nationhood*; W.W. Norton & Company, 1994

Loewen, James W., *Lies My Teacher Told Me*; The New Press, 1995

Lynd, Staughton, *Intellectual Origins of American Radicalism*, Vintage Books, 1969

Mapp, Alf J. Jr., "The 'Pirate' Peer: Lord Dunmore's Operation in the Chesapeake Bay," from *Chesapeake Bay in the American Revolution*, edited by Ernest McNeill Eller; Tidewater Publishers, 1981

Marshall, John, *Life of Washington*, Vols. 1, 2 & 3; 1804-07.

"Maryland Constitutional Convention of 1776;" Maryland State Archives; Internet, 1996

Mayo, Bernard, *Myths and Men*, University of Georgia Press, 1959, and Harper & Row, 1963

McDonald, Forrest, *Formation of the American Republic 1776-1790*; Penguin Books, 1965

McDowell, Bart, *Revolutionary War*; National Geographic Society, 1967

McWilliams, Jane and Morris L. Radoff, "Annapolis Meets the Crisis," from *Chesapeake Bay in the American Revolution*, edited by Ernest McNeill Eller; Tidewater Publishers, 1891

Meister, Charles W., *The Founding Fathers*; McFarland, 1987

Merriam, Charles Edward, *A History of American Political Theories*; Russell & Russell, 1903

Middleton, Arthur Pierce, "Ships and Shipbuilding in the Chesapeake and Tributaries," from *Chesapeake Bay in the American Revolution*, edited by Ernest McNeill Eller; Tidewater Publishers, 1981

Miers, Earl Schenck, *Crossroads of Freedom*; Rutgers University Press, 1971

Morison, Samuel Eliot, *The Oxford History of the American People*; Oxford University Press, 1965

Naval Documents of the American Revolution, Vol. 2, edited by William Bell Clark; U.S. Government Printing Office, 1966

Neuenschwander, John A., *The Middle Colonies and the Coming of the American Revolution*; Kennikat Press, 1973

Perkins, James Breck, *France in the American Revolution*; Corner House, 1970

Plumb, J.H., *England in the Eighteenth Century (1714-1815)*, Penguin Books, 1951

Quaife, Milo M., Melvin J. Weig, and Roy E. Appleman, *The History of the United States Flag*; Harper & Brothers, 1961

Oswald, Richard, *Richard Oswald's Memorandum On the Folly of Invading Virginia (1781)*; University of Virginia Press, 1953

Russell, T. Triplett and John K. Gott, *Fauquier County in the Revolution;* Fauquier County American Bicentennial Commission, Warrenton, Virginia, 1976

Sarles, Frank B., Jr. and Charles E. Shedd, *Colonials and Patriots: Historic Places Commemorating Our Forebears 1700-1783*; United States Department of the Interior, National Park Service, 1964

Scheer, George F. and Hugh F. Rankin, *Rebels and Redcoats*; World Publishing, 1957

Schlesinger, Arthur, *The Colonial Merchants and the American Revolution, 1763-1776*; 1939

Selby, John E., *The Revolution in Virginia 1775-1783*; The Colonial Williamsburg Foundation, 1988

Shenkman, Richard, *I Love Paul Revere, Whether He Rode or Not*; Harper Perennial, 1995

Skaggs, David C., *Roots of Maryland Democracy, 1753-1776*; Greenwood Press, 1973

Stebbens, G.B., *Facts and Opinions Touching the Real Origin, Character, and Influence of the American Colonization Society*; John P. Jewett & Co., 1853; reprinted by Negro Universities Press, 1969

Stember, Sol, *The Bicentennial Guide to the American Revolution, Vol. 3*; Saturday Review Press, E.P. Dutton, 1974

Tazewell, William L., *Norfolk's Waters: An Illustrated Maritime History of Hampton Roads*; Windsor Publications, 1982

The American Reader, edited by Diane Ravitch; HarperCollins, 1990

The Old Line State, A History of Maryland, edited by Morris L. Radoff; Hall of Records Commission, 1971

The Papers of George Washington: Revolutionary War Series, Vol. 2, September-December 1775, edited by Philander D. Chase; University Press of Virginia, 1987

The Papers of Thomas Jefferson, Vols. 1-5, edited by Julian P. Boyd; Princeton University Press, 1950

The Readers Companion to American History, edited by Eric Foner and John A. Garraty; Houghton Mifflin, 1991

The Spirit of 'Seventy-Six: The Story of the American Revolution as Told by Participants, edited by Henry Steel Commager and Richard B. Morris; Bonanza Books, 1958

Times-Herald of Newport News-Hampton, Virginia, October 2, 1975 and November 14, 1975

Tuchman, Barbara W., *The First Salute: A View of the American Revolution*; Knopf, 1988

Turman, Nora Miller, *The Eastern Shore of Virginia, 1603-1964*; Eastern Shore News, Inc., 1964; Heritage Books, 1988

Wallace, Willard M., *Appeal to Arms: A Military History of the American Revolution*; Harper & Brothers, 1951

Ward, Christopher, *The War of Revolution, Vol. 1*; MacMillan, 1952

Wertenbaker, Thomas J., "Causes of Bacon's Rebellion," reprinted in *Conflict or Consensus in Early American History*, edited by Allen F. Davis and Harold D. Woodman; D.C. Heath and Company, 1968

Wirt, William, *The Life of Patrick Henry*; A.L. Burt Company, 1903; published originally in 1805

- Index -

1773 TEA ACT, 30 32
ACCOMACK COUNTY, 175
ADAMS, *xxvi* 40 60 132 138-139
  141 James Truslow *xx* 31 John
  xiv 25 39 86 126 129 131 137
  268 Robert M 4 Sam *xiv* 16 19
  25-26 30-31 170 176 Feared
  And Distrusted Radical *xx*
ALAMANCE CREEK, 25
ALEXANDRIA, 110 160 200 202
  205 Shipbuilding Center 112
ALLEN, Ethan 57 98 Seth 98
AMERICAN VICTORIES, *xxiv*
AN ANCIENT PROPHECY, (Poem)
  15
ANDRE, Maj John 190
ANGLICAN CHURCH, Dominant
  In Maryland And Virginia 154
ANNAPOLIS, 19 38 110 112 116
  130 134 148 160 163 165 170
  176 195 197-198 200 232 243
  262 265-266 274-275 Cultural
  Center Of Maryland *xix*
ANNE ARUNDEL COUNTY, 21
  48 128 149-150
APPOMATTOX RIVER, 202
ARBUTHNOT, Adm Marriot 183
  194 197 Blocks Newport 184
ARCHER, John 149
ARISTODEMOCRATIC, Form Of
  Government *xvi*
ARNOLD, Benedict 57 98 170 192
  198-199 202-203 206 208 217
  Burns Tobacco In Virginia 189
  Chesapeake Bay Invasion 175
  Confiscated Salt At Richmond
  191 Lake Champlain Defeat
  152 Life And Career 190 Raids
  In Virginia 194 Washington
  Orders His Capture 195

ARTICLES OF ASSOCIATION, To Form
  A New Provincial Government In
  Maryland 67
ARTICLES OF CONFEDERATION, 127
  141 168-169 195-197
ASSOCIATION OF FREEMEN, 67
WASHINGTON, 220
BACK RIVER, 72 83
BACON, Nathaniel *xviii*
BACON'S REBELLION, *xviii*
BAILEY, Thomas A 25
BAILYN, Bernard *xviii*
BALTIMORE, *xix* 20 74 87 97 110 112
  116-118 152 161 163 169 179 184
  200-202 204 219 232 243 268 Key
  Shipyard 112 Lord 17 44 60 196
  Lords 38 Lords-End Of 150-year
  Reign 129 Vigilante Society 152
BALTIMORE CLIPPER, 112
BALTIMORE COUNTY, Delegation To
  Maryland Convention 149
BALTIMORE INDEPENDENT
  CADETS, 103
BANKRUPTCY, Of Virginia Tobacco
  Planters 3
BARBADOS, John Paul Jones At 180
BARGES, Battle Of The 269
BARKER, Charles Albro 10
BARNES, Capt Thomas 115
BARNEY, Joshua 267 268 Commander
  Of The *Wasp* 87
BARRON, Capt Samuel 83 112 185
  Commodore James 103 112 133 185
  204 246 267 Killed Stephen Decatur
  In A Duel 185 Richard 103 112 119
  133 178
BEAR MOUNTAIN, New York 168
BEAUMARCHAIS, Pierre De 120
BEEMAN, Richard 50
BENEDICT, Maryland 271

BERKELEY, Norborne Baron De Botetourt 52 William Virginia Governor *xviii*
BERKELEY HUNDRED, Plantation Of Benjamin Harrison 190
BERMUDA, 179
BIG BETHEL BRIDGE, 193
BILL OF RIGHTS, 43
BLACKBEARD, 148
BLAIR, Baron Of (Lord Dunmore) 52
BLAND, 39 54 123 Richard 8 49 53 66 Theodorick 85 198
BLOCKADE, British 157
BLOODSHED, First-Between American Colonists And British Troops 24
BLUE RIDGE MOUNTAINS, 210
BOARD OF WAR, 182 Virginia 216
BODE, Carl 130
BODKIN POINT, 117
BOONE, Daniel 21 62 159
BOSTON, 56 Defense Of *ix* Occupied By British 52
BOSTON MASSACRE, 24-25
BOSTON PORT, Burgesses Express Sympathy For Shutdown Of 53
BOSTON PORT ACT, 34
BOSTON PORT BILL, 33 36-37
BOSTON TEA PARTY, 31-33
BOTETOURT, Gov-Dissolved Virginia House Of Burgesses 20
BOUCHER, John-Anglican Minister And Bay Region Loyalist 99
BOUND BROOK, 161
BOWIE, Walter 149
BOWLING GREEN, 141 202
BOYCOTT VIOLATORS, Names Published In Virginia 43
BOYLE, Thomas 87
BRANDYWINE, 203 Battle At *ix*
BRANDYWINE CREEK, 165 Washington's Defeat At 167
BRAXTON, Carter 56 66 141 Proposed Government Based On English System 136 137
BREED'S HILL, Battle At (Bunker Hill) 63
BRENT, William-His Plantation Burned By Dunmore's Raiders 145 146
BRIDGETOWN, 182
BRITISH ISLES, Chesapeake Warriors In *ix*
BROADSIDES, Posting Of 24
BROOKLYN HEIGHTS, 152
BUCKNER, Capt William 198
BUNKER HILL, 95 Battle Of 63
BURGOYNE, John Arrives In Boston 57 160
BURKE, Edmund 36
BURWELL'S FERRY, 53 190
BUTLER, Col Richard 249 Solomon 101
BYRD, William Virginia Loyalist 99
BYRON, Lord Praised Patrick Henry's Oratory 51
CABELL, William 66
CALVERT, Benedict 10 Cecil-Second Lord Baltimore *xii* George-First Lord Baltimore *xii*
CALVERT COUNTY, 149 151
CAMDEN, South Carolina 186
CAMM, Rev John-President Of William And Mary College And A Loyalist 99
CAMPBELL, 174 Charles 11 192 William 104
CANADA, 271 Attempt To Take By Force 58 Refusal To Take Side With Americans 58 Support Solicited 120
CAP-FRANCAIS, 228
CAPE HATTERAS, 233
CAPE HENRY, 157 169 173 246
CAPE MAY, New Jersey 268
CAPES, 259-260 Battle Of The 235-241 French Victory At The 244 Virginia *xxv*
CARLETON, Sir Guy 268
CARLSON, R 13
CAROLINA, 205 207 242
CAROLINA CAMPAIGN, *xxii* 171 182
CAROLINAS, 153 172 200 206 208

INDEX

CARRINGTON, Paul 66
CARROLL, Charles xiv 28-29 38 128-130 141 148-149 162 176 And B&O Railroad 131 Of Carrollton 9-10 Mission To Montreal 120
CARROLLTON, 38
CARROTMAN CREEK, Shipbuilding Center 112
CARY, Wilson Miles-Hampton's Militia Colonel 82
CATHOLICS, 23 Allowed To Vote In Maryland 150 Discriminated Against In Maryland 154 Find Sanctuary In Maryland xii
CAVALRY, Virginia-To Be Raised 120
CHADD'S FORD, 165
CHAES, Samuel 148
CHALBERG, 99 John C 29
CHALMERS, James-Maryland Tory 127 128 166 Plain Truth Pamphlet 155
CHARLES CITY COURTHOUSE, 191
CHARLES COUNTY, 21 99 128 145
CHARLES I, King Of England 2
CHARLES II, King Of England 1
CHARLESTON, 195 204 261 264 Fall Of x Not Virginia-The Military Key To The South 224 Surrender To Gen Clinton 186
CHARLESTOWN, 234 257
CHARLOTTESVILLE, 208-211
CHASE, 129 Samuel xiv 11 38 41 85 128 141 150 176 272 275 Samuel-Mission To Montreal 120
CHERITON, 182
CHESAPEAKE BAY, 86 103 115 116 153 157 160-161 166 169 172 178-179 182 184-186 188 195 197-198 204 207-208 212 214 216 218-219 224-225 227-228 231 236 238 240-241 244-245 248 259-260 262 269-271

CHESAPEAKE BAY (cont.) 275 Algonquin Indian Name x American Fear Of British Control 104 Avenue To A New Nation xxvi British Invasion-Failed 175 British Ships Stationed In-To Prevent Illegal Trade 59 Commerce Harrassed By Loyalists 267 Constant Threat Of British Control 111 Control Of - Essential To Victory xxiii 175 DeGrasse Returned To 233 Dunmore Calls For Blockade Of 104 Dunmore Calls For Warships In 56 French Control Of 234 French Fleet Arrives In 228 French Support Requested By Washington 194 Hostilities Against Dunmore 63 How Cornwallis Lost Control Of 223 Hurricane Causes Capt Squire To Abandon Ship 72 Large Part Played In Revolution xxvi Marylanders Concerned About British Presence In 206 Plantation Culture And Aristocracy xix Residents Alarmed At Blockade Of Boston 34 Rivers And Tributaries x Supply Lines From France 175 The "American Mediterranean" x War Continued 132
CHESAPEAKE REGION, Geography x
CHESTER, Pennsylvania 232 Americans Retreat To-After Brandywine Creek Battle 167
CHESTER RIVER, Key Shipyard 112
CHESTERTOWN, 113
CHICKAHOMINY RIVER, 212
CHINCOTEAGUE, 182
CHINCOTEAGUE CREEK, 175
CHOPTANK, Key Shipyard 112
CHURCHILL, Winston 98 224
CLAIBORNE, Thomas 20 108 William xii 20
CLARK, George Rogers 196 Raids Against British Outposts 159
CLARKE, Col George 191
CLINTON, Gen Henry 114 115 171 175 183 188 205-207 212-217 220 224 225 229 232 240-243 255-257 259-260 268

CLINTON (cont.)
And Surrender Of Charleston 186 Arrives In Boston 57 Benedict Arnold's Offer To Surrender West Point To 190 Replaced Howe 170 Sir Henry 226-227
COAKLEY, Robert W 34
COBB, Col 254
COERCIVE ACTS, 33 36 41 (Intolerable Acts) 33
COGGINS, 181 Jack 86 88
COLLIER, 173 175 Commodore 174 Commodore George 172
COLONISTS, In 1770 Many Had Nothing In Common With England 23
COLONIZATION, Motivated By Money And Expansionism *xii*
COLOSSAL BLUNDER, Britain's 31
COMMITTEE, Intercolonial- Established 27 Marine 169 Naval 111 116
COMMITTEE OF CORRESPONDENCE, 37
COMMITTEE OF SAFETY, 43 104 Virginia 66 67 81 119-120 Persecution Of Scottish Merchants 98
COMMITTEE OF WORCESTER COUNTY, Plan To Take Them Prisoners 101
COMMITTEES, Government By 44-45
COMMITTEES OF CORRESPONDENCE, County 42 Created In Virginia And Maryland 27
COMMITTEES OF SAFETY, Maryland 45
COMMON SENSE, Pamphlet By Thomas Paine 139
CONCORD, 52 Battle Of 52 55 Battle Of-Resistance Stage- Managed By Hancock And Adams? 51

CONNECTICUT, 127
CONSTELLATION, Ship 113
CONSTITUTION, Ship 113
CONSTITUTIONAL CONVENTION, Virginia 126
CONSTITUTIONS, State 127
CONTINENTAL ARMY, 118 158 173 183 190 195 225 231 274 Creation Of 60 Campaign To Enlist Blacks In 176 Depleted And Widely Dispersed 214 Deserters Banded With Tories 166 Distrust Among Troops From Different States 247 Necessity Of Maintaining In Colonies 6 Poorly Trained And Poorly Supplied *xxiv* Reinforcements For Washington 153 Required To Help On Eastern Shore 98
CONTINENTAL ASSOCIATION, 40
CONTINENTAL CONGRESS, 40 42-45 62 66 92 119 120 125 127-128 130- 131 136 141 152 157 161 167-168 170 175 195 198 First 39 41 Paper Currency Printed By 166 Required Enlistment In County Militia 67 Resolved To Destroy Dunmore's Fleet 103 Resolved To Use Force If Necessary 54 Second 57 Second Called For 53
CONTINENTAL TROOPS, Refused To March Without Back Pay 233
CONVENTION, Maryland 103 110 128 Virginia 56 96 103-101
COOCH'S BRIDGE, Delaware 166
CORBIN, Col 182
CORNSTALK, Chief 53
CORNWALLIS, Gen *xxiii* 161 188 199 205-207 209 212-214 216-221 224 228-231 234 243 246-249 251 254- 255 257 259-261 263-264 267 1781 Chesapeake Bay Invasion By 175 At Brandywine Creek 167 At Monmouth Courthouse 171 Denied Naval Support Due To Battle Of The Capes 233 152 Lord Charles 115 186 189 215 223 226-227 235-236 240-242 244-245 256 262 Thomas *xiv*

INDEX

COUNCIL OF SAFETY, Maryland 127 134 191 To Direct Activities Of Militiamen 67
COUNTRY PARTY, 17
COURT PARTY, 16-17
COWPENS, Battle Of 204 212 Bayonet Charge *x*
CRAIK, Dr James 99
CRESAP, Michael 62
CREVECOEUR, J Hector St John De 273
CROPPER, Col John 269
CROWL, Philip A 151
CUCKOO TAVERN, 210
CUMBERLAND, Shipbuilding Center 112
CURRENCY ACT, 3
CURRENCY BAN, 5
CURRENCY SHORTAGE, In Virginia 3
D'ESTAING, Comte 171
DARTMOUTH, Lord-Secretary Of State For The Colonies 56
DAWES, William Second Rider In Paul Revere's Midnight Ride 51
DEAN, Capt John 115
DEANE, Silas 152 161 163 Comments On Patrick Henry's Speech 51
DE BARRAS, Adm 219 229 232-233 238 240 242 Sails For Yorktown With Siege Artillery 227
DECATUR, Stephen-Killed In Duel 185
DECLARATION OF INDEPENDENCE, 125 Adopted 141 Jefferson's Wording Of 135 Signers Of 141
DECLARATORY ACT, 16
DEFENSE, Expenses Apportioned To Colonies According To Population 66
DE GRASSE, Adm Francois Joseph Paul 214-218 225 229 231 233 235 238-240 242-244 246 249 260 262 264 Count 228

DE KALB, Maj Gen Baron 172
DELAWARE, 153 166-167 214 Militia 165
DELAWARE BAY, 153 157 160 165 178 207-208 267
DELAWARE (RIVER), 115
DESERTIONS, 218
DESTOUCHES, Adm Sochet 194 197
DETROIT, Clark's Failed Attempt To Capture 159
DEYE, Thomas Cockey 149
DIGBY, Adm Robert 235 242 243
DIGGES, Dudley 66
DISARRAY, Cause Of British Failure *xxiii*
DISCONTENT, Popular 24
DISPUTES, Between Colonies Prior To Revolution *xiii*
DISTANCE, Contributed To Great Britain's Failure *xxiii*
DORCHESTER COUNTY, 38
DRAKE, Rear Adm Francis Samuel 239
DREDGE'S STRAIT, 269
DRINKER, Elizabeth 263
DULANY, 14 Daniel 12-13
DUNCAN, James 251
DUNMORE, Gov 70 Lord 37 52-57 67 69 77 79 81 82 84 91-93 95-99 101 106-108 113-115 117-118 125 132-133 145 146 Abandons Hampton Roads Harbor 132 Actions Lead To Resentment And Threats Of Violence 53 And Gunpowder Confiscation 54 Asked To Take Control Of Williamsburg 80 Attacked At St George's Island 147 Base At Gosport 69 Begins Raids On The Chesapeake 69 Bombards Norfolk 103 Commandeered Several Virginia Vessels In Hampton Roads Harbor 68 Delay Of Military Action Against His Raids 69 Departs From The Chesapeake 148 Descended From Royal Stuarts 52 Fled For Safety 58 Fled To Staten Island 147 Many Titles 52 Placed Virginia Under Martial Law 90-91

DUNMORE (cont.)
  Recruitment Of Blacks 91
  Sends Flag Of Truce From
    Gwynn's Island 143 Supported
    By Eden 134 Wanted To
    Destroy Mount Vernon 147
    Wounded 144
DUPUY, 251 Importance Of Battle
  Of The Capes 240
EARLE, Swepson 231
EASTERN SHORE, 38 110 113
  148 158 166 175 182 231 262
  269 Antagonism To Revolution
  127 Defenses To Be Improved
  And Livestock Destroyed 120
  Protestant Movements On 154
  Tory Rebellion Stopped By
  Smallwood 153 Virginia's-
  Subversive Loyalist Activities
  On 98
EAST INDIA COMPANY, 30-31
  33 And 1773 Tea Act 30
ECKENRODE, H J 16 43 57 108
EDDIS, William 29 35 42
EDEN, Sir Robert-Maryland's
  Proprietary Governor 34 60 117
  119 147 Attempt To Kidnap
  120 Discovered To Be
  Supporter Of Dunmore 134
EFFIGIES BURNED, Stamp Agent
  11
EFFINGHAM, Earl Of 55
ELIZABETH CITY COUNTY,
  Virginia-Supplied Men For
  Army Throughout War 63
ELIZABETH RIVER, 90 94 109-
  110 172-173 188 194
ELK HILL, 209
ELLEGON, John 166
ELLER, 111 Ernest McNeill 44 111
ELLIOT, Capt Thomas 115
ENLISTMENTS, Expired 218
  Military 178
EQUALITY, 138
ESSEX COUNTY, Virginia 36
ETHIOPIAN REGIMENT, 91
EUTAW SPRINGS, Struggle At x

EXPANSION, Restrictions On 5
FAIRFAX, Lord Thomas-Virginia
  Loyalist 99
FAIRFAX COUNTY, Virginia 33
FALMOUTH, 110
FEBIGER, Col Christian 218
FELLS POINT, 110 Battery Erected At
  117 Key Shipyard 112
FERGUSON, Patrick-Almost Shot
  Washington 167
FINCASTLE, Viscount (Lord Dunmore)
  52
FITZGERALD, James H 264
FITZHUGH, William 149
FLAG, First United States-Adopted By
  Congress 162 First Used In American
  Navy 88
FLEETS, French And Spanish 172
"FLOATING TERROR", Dunmore's
  Fleet 110
FLORIDA, 270
FLUVANNA RIVER, 212-213
FORT CLINTON, Taken By British 168
FORTESCUE, Sir John 143
FORT GEORGE, 185 213
FORT MCHENRY, 163
FORT MONROE, 185
FORT MONTGOMERY, Taken By
  British 168
FORT NASSAU, Bahamas 118
FORT NELSON, 172-173
FORT SACKVILLE, (Vincennes,
  Indiana) British Surrender At 159
FORT TICONDEROGA, Fall Of 163
  Retaken By Americans 165 *(See Also
  TICONDEROGA)*
FRANCE, 152 Alliance With 170
  Assistance From *xxv* Convinced To
  Support American Cause 160 Gives
  Support 120 Interested In America's
  Success 194 Recognizes American
  Independence 168 Supply Lines To
  Chesapeake Bay 175 Wished To
  Humiliate England 161
FRANKLIN, Benjamin *xiv xvii* 9 41 88
  111 132 141 152 170 180 181 233
  268

INDEX

FRANKLIN (cont.)
  Delegate To Second Continental Congress 57 -Mission To Montreal 120 Opposes Braxton's Proposal 137
FRAUNCES TAVERN, 274
FRAZIER, William 204
FREDERICK, Prison Camp 257
FREDERICK COUNTY, Maryland 12 38 130 149 271 Riflemen Supplied To Washington's Army 62
FREDERICKSBURG, 110 202 209
FREEDOM, English Roots Of American *xvi*
FRENCH, Immigrants 23
FRENCH AND INDIAN WAR, 6 87 161 Economic Impact Of *xix* End Of 1 4 Smuggling During 2 Veterans Illegally Given Land In Virginia 53 Washington's Skills Demonstrated In 60
FRENCH TROOPS, Land At Jamestown 229
FRENEAU, Philip (The Poet Of The American Revolution) 15 56 (Poem About Benedict Arnold) 217
GADSDEN, Christopher *xiv*
GAGE, Gen 49 57 Replaced By Howe 135 Thomas 33 43 51
GALLOWAY, Joseph 40
GASPEE, British Cutter Burned In Narragansett Bay 26
GATES, Gen Horatio 56 61 170 171 186 207
GAYLEY, Charles Mills *xvi-xvii-*
GAYTON, Commodore George 182 186
GELB, 120 Norman 5 142
GENERAL ASSEMBLY, Maryland 44 Virginia 208
GENTRY, Virginia *xix*
GEORGE III, King Of England 6 15 30 33 41 48-49 58 82 124 140 166 170 268 270 273-274

GEORGE III (cont.)
  Issues Proclamation Of Rebellion 70 Statue Pulled Down 141
GEORGIA, 172 British Campaign In 182 No Delegates At Continental Congress 39 Overrun By British Troops-Large Loyalist Population 171
GERMAINE, Lord George 160
GERMAN, Immigrants 23
GERMANS, Allowed To Vote In Maryland 150
GERMANTOWN, Americans Defeated At 168 Battle At *ix* Howe At 167
GERRY, Eldridge 136
GIRTY, Simon 159
GIST, Mordecai 103
GIVE ME LIBERTY OR GIVE ME DEATH!, Famous Speech By Patrick Henry 49-50
GLOUCESTER, 224 229-230 243 247-249 256-258 263-264
GLOUCESTER POINT, 213 223 248 Shipbuilding Center 112
GODDARD, William 152
GOLDENBERG, 198
GOLDEN HILL, Battle Of 24
GOLDSBOROUGH, Capt Greenbury 115 Robert 38 148
GOOD INTENT, Brig's Cargo Returned To England 26
GOODRICH, 186 John 109
GOSPORT, 89 99 109 119 144 172-173 188 Base For Dunmore 69
GOVERNMENT, New-Creation Of 137
GRASON, Thomas 112 178 267
GRAVES, Rear Admiral Thomas 227 231 233 235-239 241-242 259-260 Blocks Newport 183 Forced To Sail To New York 233
GREAT BRIDGE, First Battle Of 93-92 Second Battle Of 95-96
GREAT KANAWHA RIVER, 53
GREAT LAKES, 270
GREEN, Jonas 12 Gen 199
GREENE, Gen Nathanael 186 205 206 208 215

GREEN MOUNTAIN BOYS, Of
  Vermont 98
GREENSPRINGS, 213
GRENVILLE, George 5
GRIEVANCES, 9 35 40 Colonial 4
  Not The Only Reason For
  Revolution 142
GUILFORD COURTHOUSE,
  Battle Of 207
GUNSTON HALL, George
  Mason's Plantation 204
GWYNN'S ISLAND, 99 132-134
  143-144 269 Scene Of Misery
  As Dunmore Fled 144
HACKER, Lewis M 12
HAITI-SANTO DOMINGO, 228
HAMILTON, Alexander 251 254
HAMMOND, Capt Andrew Snape
  132-134 144 Blockade Of
  Chesapeake 115 116 Matthais
  11 149 Rezin *xiv* 11 135 149
HAMPDEN, Charles I 14 Squire
  John 14
HAMPTON, 90 101 109 119 132
  175 185 188-189 192-193 203
  216 229 246 264 Home Port Of
  Virginia Navy Througout The
  War 112 Saltworks Placed
  Under Guard 191
HAMPTON RIVER, 80-81
HAMPTON ROAD, 187
HAMPTON ROADS, *xi* 67 111 115
  116 134 147 188 195 197 202
  214-215 230 244 Arnold's
  Army At 190
HAMPTON ROADS HARBOR, 60
  74 109 173 204
HANCOCK, 32 Chided For
  Attempt To Subvert Maryland
  Government 120 John *xiv* 31
  43-44 58 61 80 111 John Built
  Fortune On Illicit Trade With
  France 2 John President Of
  Continental Congress 120
HANOVER COUNTY, Virginia 55
HANSON, Alexander Contee 30
  Judge 36

HARDWICK, Massachusetts 138
HARGREAVES, Reginald 167
HARLEM HEIGHTS, 203
HARRIS, Joseph 75
HARRISON, Benjamin 41 49 97 111 141
  190 210 275 Benjamin The Fifth 136
  Col 97 William 146
HARFORD COUNTY, 149
HAVANA, 216
HAWKE, David 130
HEAD OF ELK, (Elkton) Maryland 153
  165 166 195 198-200 203 218 232
  234
HEAT, A Problem For New England And
  French Soldiers 224
HEATH, Maj Gen 227
HEMPHILL, John M II 195
HENRY, Patrick *xiv xviii* 2 6 16 26-27 39
  41 96 103 118 123 158-159 170 176
  210 272 Feared And Distrusted
  Radical *xx* Calls For Military Action
  Against Dunmore 55 Calls For
  Virginia To Take A Defensive
  Posture 49 Careless About Preserving
  Personal Papers 50 Famous Speech
  By 49 First Governor Of Virginia
  Commonwealth 124 Gov 175 Named
  Ranking Officer Of Virginia Forces
  67 Resolution Resisted By
  Conservatives And Moderates 49
  Resolutions 6-7
HESSIANS, 167 213 215 255 As British
  Allies *xxiii*
HEWES, Joseph 88
HIGHLANDERS, Royal 173
HILLSBORO, (North Carolina) 25
HOBKIRK HILL, Struggle At *x*
HOFFMAN, Ronald 47
HOG ISLAND, 176 182 Base For
  Loyalist Privateers 60
HOLLAND, 268
HOLLIS'S MARSH, 205
HOLT, 77 John 69 72
HOOD, 231 238-239 259 260 Rear Adm
  Samuel 227 235 Zachariah 12 Stamp
  Agent For Maryland 11
HOOD'S POINT, 191

HOOKER, Richard *xv*
HOPKINS, Commodore 116 118
   Esek 88 John Burroughs Set
   Out To Destroy Dunmore's
   Flotilla 111 Stephen 88-84
HOPKINSON, Francis 162
HOTHAM, Commodore William
   157
HOUSE OF BURGESSES,
   Dissolved By Dunmore 37
HOWARD, John Eager 103
HOWE, Adm Lord Richard 108 152
   160-161 165-166 At
   Brandywine Creek 167 Col
   Robert 94 Gen 91 98 157 159
   169 Gen William-Replaced
   Gage 49 135 Maj Gen William
   xx 57 89 115 Replaced By
   Clinton 170
HUBBELL, Jay B Comments On
   Patrick Henry's Speech 49-50
HUDSON RIVER, 171 190 225
   Secured By British 168
ILLINOIS, 197
IMPRESSMENT, 161
INDEBTEDNESS, To British
   Creditors 5
INDEPENDENCE, As A People's
   Cause 24 Initially A
   Conservative Protest By The
   Elite 24 Movement In Virginia
   Led By Progressives 123 Never
   Before Suggested 28 Officially
   Recognized 270 Political And
   Economic Without Social
   Revolution 29 Supported By
   Only Thirty Percent Of The
   People *xx* Virginia Proposal
   That Colonies Unite For 58
INDIANA, 197
INDIANA COUNTRY, 159
INDIAN TRIBES, As British Allies
   xxiii Attacking Settlements In
   Kentucky 159
INNES, Maj James 73 75
INTOLERABLE ACTS, 33
IRISH, Immigrants 23

IRISH SEA, Raids In The 161
ISLE OF WIGHT COUNTY, Virginia
   109
JAMAICA, 235
JAMES I, King Of England *xv* 52
JAMES RIVER, 60 104 109-110 132 173
   178 187-188 190-191 199 202 206
   208-209 212-213 221 223 229-230
   246 275 Plantations And Depots
   Destroyed By Benedict Arnold 189
   217
JAMESTOWN, *xii* 103 218 229-230 234
   244 First Slaves Sold As Indentured
   Servants 139 Settlers-Unprepared For
   Wilderness *xiii*
JAY, John *xiv* 268
JEFFERSON, Thomas *xiv xvi xxv-xvi* 3 8
   16 17 19 23 26-28 39 49 51 60 65 88
   99 121 123-125 132-133 135-136 138
   141 145-147 152 154-156 158-159
   164 184-186 188 193 196 203 205
   207 209 217 220 Abolished Slave
   Trade But Did Not Free His Own
   Slaves 140 Calls For Reunion And
   Harmony With Britain 58 Comments
   About Dunmore's Attack On
   Hampton 82 Concerned About
   Runaway Slaves 92 Delegate To
   Second Continental Congress 57 Did
   Not Build A Strong Virginia Defense
   189 Gov of Virginia 176 177 Journal
   Entry Regarding Tarleton Planned
   Raid 211 Letter To Cousin John
   Randolph In England 85 Thought
   Norfolk Should Be Burned 107
   Warned Of Tarleton's Plan To
   Capture Him 210
JENIFER, Daniel 128
JENYNS, Soame 13
JEWS, 23 Refused Public Office In
   Maryland 154
JOHNSON, A 230 Samuel A *xxiv* 48 10
   Thomas 61 128 148 First Governor
   Of Maryland 151 162 Thomas Jr 38
JONES, John Paul 88 163 179 180 At
   Philadelphia 181 Born In Scotland
   180

294 GUNS ON THE CHESAPEAKE

JONES, John Paul (cont.)
  Buried At Naval Academy In Annapolis 182 Life And Career Of 180-182 Death In France 182 Joseph 217
JOUETTE, Jack 210 211
KEMP'S LANDING, 81 89-88 93 173
KENT COUNTY, 115
KENT ISLAND, 115 117
KENTUCKY, 21 Land Ceded To Virginia By Shawnee Nation 53
KEY, Francis Scott 163
KIDD, Capt John 60 176 269 270
KING, Henry 77 Miles 193
KING'S ARMS TAVERN, 264
KING'S MOUNTAIN, 188 North Carolina 186
KINGS MOUNTAIN, South Carolina 167
KINGSTON, John Paul Jones At 180
KING WILLIAM COUNTY, 20
KITMAN, Marvin *xxiv*
KNOX, Gen 254
LABORERS, 23
LAFAYETTE, Marquis De *xxv* 143 161 163 165 168 171 183 193-195 197-204 206 208-209 212-213 215-216 218-221 223-225 227-230 240 243-244 254 260 262 265 And Male Heirs Forever Citizens Of Maryland 266 Contributions To American Revolution 164 George Washington 183 Service Accepted By Congress 164 Wounded At Brandywine Creek 167
LAKE CHAMPLAIN, 57 Benedict Arnold At 190
LANCASTER, Pennsylvania 167-168
LANGGUTH, 251
LARRABEE, 246
LAURENS, Henry 268
LAUZON, 247 264
LAUZUN, 248 Duc De 232
LEADERSHIP, Consisted Of Men Of Privilege *xiv*
LEE, 39 95-96 119 170 Arthur 152 219 Francis Lightfoot 141 Gen 120 132 Gov Thomas Sim 184 203 Jean 146 Jean B *xxvi* 96 Light-Horse Harry 188 210 Maj Gen Charles 118 169 Maj Gen Charles-Captured 152 Maj Gen Charles-Prisoner In New York 159 Offers Scheme To Howe 160 Richard Henry 8 26-27 36 49 58 77 86 92 111 128 131 141 145 168 205 210 219 Richard Henry-Comments On Patrick Henry's Speech 51 Richard Henry Court-Martial Of 170 Richard Henry-Led Group To West Indies For Gunpowder 57 Richard Jr 102 Thomas Ludwell 66
LESLIE, 188 Capt Samuel 89 91 And Raids On The Lower Chesapeake 81 Gen Alexander 182 186 Chesapeake Bay Expedition 175
LEWIS, Gen 144 Gen Andrew 143 Michael-Importance Of The Battle Of The Capes 240
LEXINGTON, 52 Battle Of 51 55
LIBERTY TO SLAVES, Motto Of Dunmore's Ethiopian Regiment 91
LINCOLN, Maj Gen Benjamin 161 171 186 254 261
LIVINGSTON, Robert 132 William 65
LOCKE, John 136
LONDON, 236 John Paul Jones At 181
LONGFELLOW'S TALE, Of Paul Revere's Ride 51
LONG ISLAND, Battle Of *ix* 203
LOUISA COUNTY, 210
LOUISIANA, 270
LOUIS VI, King Of France 120
LOUIS THE GREAT, King Of France 234
LOYALISTS, 48 60 175 204 272 274 First Battalion Of Maryland 127 Fled To Great Britain Or Canada 143

LOYALISTS (cont.)
  Forced To Find Sanctuary 109
  Harsh Measures Against-
    Enforced In Maryland And
    Virginia 57 In Virginia 99
    Many On The Eastern Shore 68
    Maryland-Many Fled To Avoid
    Prison 57 Punished 271
    Virginia 78 Virginia-Stronger
    Measures To Be Taken 120
LUZERNE, Chevalier De La 200 208
LYNCH, Charles 154 Thomas 111
LYNCHING, Origin Of Term 154
LYNE, Capt George 78 80
LYNN, Staughton 138
LYNNHAVEN, 234 Roadstead 228
M'CLANAHAN, Col Alexander 144
MADISON, James 3 16 191 198 275
MAGGOTY (Magothy) BAY, 182
MAGNA CHARTA, *xviii*
MAIL, Seized And Read In Virginia 43
MALVERN HILL, 213
MANHATTAN, 274
MANHATTAN ISLAND, 217 224
MANNY, Margaret-Maker Of First American Navy Flag 88
MAPP, 80 104
MARINE CORPS, Established And Placed Under Washington's Command 88
MARINES, Royal 188
MARSHALL, John 51 94 175 176 191 196 198 220 275 Future Chief Justice 81 Thomas-Comments On Patrick Henry's Speech 51
MARTIN, Sgt James Sullivan 249 251
MARTINIQUE, Scene Of First Foreign Naval Engagement 135
MARYLAND, 166 198 Ceased To Be A Proprietary Colony In 1774 17

MARYLAND (cont.)
  Charter Granted To Lord Baltimore
    xii Declared Stamp Act Illegal 9 Did
    Not Possess Large Tracts Of Vacant
    Territory 196 Financial Depression 10
    First Taste Of War 116 Militia 165
    Minimum Connection With Britain
    38 Population At Time Of Revolution
    xi Proprietary Governor Forced To
    Resign 21 Shipping 110 Standstill On
    Independence 127 Troops Supplied
    By *xxv*
MARYLAND ASSEMBLY, 162
MARYLAND CONSTITUTION, 151
MARYLAND CONVENTION, 38 48 67 127 Radical Element 149 Whigs 148
MARYLAND DECLARATION, 196
MARYLAND DECLARATION OF RIGHTS, 150
MARYLANDERS, Protected By Charter From Taxes 2
MARYLAND GAZETTE, 10 12 25 44 48 116 149-150 265
MARYLAND JOURNAL, 152
MARYLAND LINE, 103 167 172 203-204 272 Highly Regarded 62
MARYLAND SENATE, 176
MASON, George 8 20 33 49 66 80 123-125 135-136 143 158 159 275 Spokesman For The Poor 125 His Plantation Almost Captured 204
MASSACHUSETTS, Large Supplier Of Troops 159 Raises Troops 52
MASSACHUSETTS CIRCULAR LETTER, 19-20
MASSACHUSETTS GAZETTE, 32
MASSACHUSETTS PROVINCIAL CONGRESS, Second 48
MATTAPONI RIVER, 204 220
MATTHEW, 175 Gen 173 Maj Gen Edward 172
MATTHEWS COUNTY, 132
MAYO, Bernard Comments On Patrick Henry's Speech 50
MCDONALD, Forrest *xxiv* 142
MCDOUGALL, Alexander 24
MCSHERRY, James 203

MERCER, George-Distributor Of Stamps For Virginia 11 James 66 Lt Col John 248
MERRIAM, 99
METOMPKIN CREEK, 175-176
MICHIGAN, 197
MIDDLETON, 112
MILITARY FORCE, Created In Virginia 67
MILITIA, *xxiv* 40 104 115 186 188 191 205 230 Accomack 269 Benedict Arnold In 190 Companies *xxv* Companies-Formation Of In Maryland And Virginia 47 Early Groups Were Badly Organized And Undisciplined 67 Maryland 45 60 116 145 184 Muhlenberg's-Easily Resisted By Arnold 202 NJ PA DE MD Called Out To Meet Howe 165 Recruits Deserting 127 Riflemen Drive Off British Forces At Hampton 82 Virginia 33 49 79 95 118 143 145 189 204 210 218 228 At Yorktown 246 Liberty Or Death Slogan 51 Sterner Discipline 120
MILITIAMEN, At First Battle Of Great Bridge 94
MINNESOTA, 197
MINUTEMEN, *xxiv* 43 52 103 From Culpeper County 81 92 Sent To Hampton From King And Queen County 80
MISSISSIPPI RIVER, 196 270
MONEY, Problems Plagued American Military Throughout Revolution 48
MONMOUTH COURTHOUSE, Battle At *x* American Assault Turned Back 171
MONROE, James 62 176
MONTAGU, George 134
MONTICELLO, Jefferson's Home 92 140 210 211
MONTREAL, 98 114 120

MOORE, Mr 256
MOORE'S CREEK BRIDGE, Battle At 114
MORGAN, Daniel 62 170 212
MORNING CHRONICLE AND LONDON ADVERTISER, 69
MORRIS, Robert *xiv* 48
MORRISTOWN, 161 172
MOULIN, Baron Of (Lord Dunmore) 52
MOUNT VERNON, 201 244 275 Threatened By British Raiders 199
MUHLENBERG, Col John Peter Gabriel 120 Gen 167 188 202
MUNITIONS, Confiscated By Royal Governors 53 Supplied From France And Spain 120
MURDOCK, William 9
MURRAY, John-Lord Dunmore 37 52
NANSEMOND RIVER, 110
NARRAGANSETT BAY, 86
NAVAL OPERATIONS, In Early 1776 114
NAVAL WARFARE, Early Incidents In 71
NAVIGATION ACTS, To Regulate Trade And Importation 2
NAVY, American-John Paul Jones And 181 British 104 197 Continental 111 133 161 169 178 268 Created 85-86 First Engagement In Foreign Waters 135 Maryland 112 114 178 186 270 Undermanned 166 Necessity For Bay Colonies To Build Their Own 111 Royal 180 186 197 Presence In Chesapeake Bay 166 Virginia 104 111 114 133 177 185 198 246 Orphans Apprenticed Due To Lack Of Manpower 177
NELLS, George 87
NELSON, Gen Thomas 188 Gov 220 Thomas Jr 141 210
NETHERLANDS, 180
NEW CASTLE, Virginia 55
NEW ENGLAND, 269 Attempt By British To Cut Off From Other Colonies *xxi* Not The Only Region Involved In The Revolution *ix*

INDEX

NEW JERSEY, 114-115 153-154 160-161 169-171 195 215 227 232 256 269 Militia 165
NEW JERSEY GAZETTE, 239
NEW ORLEANS, 114
NEWPORT, 169 194 197 225 229 231 Blocked By Graves And Arbuthnot 184 Rhode Island-British Naval Base Established At 152
NEWPORT NEWS, 178 188 193
NEW PROVIDENCE, Bahamas 118
NEWTOWN, 90
NEW YORK, 89 115 126 159 161 163 165-166 171 175 178 183 186 199 205-207 212 214 216-217 220 226-227 230-232 238-239 247-248 259 264 271 British Evacuation Of 274 British Victories In 168 Britain's Military Presence Confined To 269 Point Of Attack Changed From 246
NEW YORK CITY, 182 275
NEW YORK HARBOR, 84
NEW YORK JOURNAL, 69
NICHOLAS, Capt George 80 Col John 83 Robert Carter 49 92 102
NICHOLSON, Capt James 87 113 115 161 169 179 195 199 First Ranking Officer Of Continental Navy 86 Ridiculed In Baltimore Press 162 Samuel 113
NICOLA, Col Lewis 274
NINTH VIRGINIA REGIMENT, Of The Continental Army 115
NONIMPORTATION, 15
NONIMPORTATION AGREEMENT, 45 Economic Effect In Maryland And Virginia 34 35 Effects Of 47 Political Effect 35
NONIMPORTATION AGREEMENTS, Opposition 48

NORFOLK, 69 81-82 93-95 98 104 105 108 132 153-154 157 172-173 188-189 Anticipated Destruction Of 88-89 Burning Of 103-108 Virginia Troops Ordered To Sack 107
NORFOLK RIVER, 187
NORFOLK TORIES, 98
NORTH, Lord Frederick 30 58 77 British Prime Minister 260 268 Proposal For Reconciliation 59
NORTHAMPTON, 182
NORTHAMPTON COUNTY, 175
NORTH ANNA RIVER, 209
NORTH CAROLINA, 25 114 163 171 199 204 207 212 218 225 229 And Tobacco Embargo 30 Declared British Law Null And Void 57
NORTH RIVER, 226
NORTHWEST TERRITORY, 159 196
NORWICH, Connecticut-Birthplace Of Benedict Arnold 190
"NOT WORTH A CONTINENTAL", 166
O'HARA, 261 Brig Gen Charles 260
OCCOQUAN FALLS, 144
OGLE, Benjamin-Maryland Governor 195 Margaret 195
OHIO, 197
OHIO COUNTRY, 159
OHIO RIVER, 53 159 275
OLD LINE STATE, Origin Of Maryland's Nickname 103
OLD POINT COMFORT, 185 193 213 216
OLIVE BRANCH PETITION, 63
ONANCOCK, 269
ONANCOCK CREEK, 269
OSBORNE'S WHARF, 202
OSWALD, 188 Richard *xxii xxvi* 186-187 259 269 Cites American Abuses Against Loyalists 231
OXFORD, 110 Port Of Entry On Maryland's Eastern Shore *xix*
PACA, William 38 141 148 272 Maryland Governor 271
PAGE, John 17 19 66 82 88 102 121 134 147 191 Friend Of Jefferson 102

PAINE, Thomas 138 262 273 And Slavery 139 Disliked By Most Founders 139
PAMUNKEY RIVER, 220 240
PARIS, 163 Peace Treaty 269
PARKER, Col Josiah 228
PARRAMORES BEACH, 176
PATAPSCO RIVER, 112 117
PATERSON, John-Kent County Minister 100
PATTON, Gen George 118
PATUXENT RIVER, 100 114 185
PEACE TALKS, Failure Of 152
PENDLETON, Edmund 39 49 66 104 120 129 132-133 146-147 191 274
PENNSYLVANIA, 115 126 150 153 160 166-167 203 207 232 256 Militia 165 Population At Time Of Revolution *xi*
PENNSYLVANIA EVENING POST, 142
PENNSYLVANIA GAZETTE, 174
PENNSYLVANIANS, 228 230
PENSACOLA, Florida 161
PERKINS, 271 James Breck 160
PETERSBURG, 190 198 202 206
PETTY, William-Earl Of Whelburne-Prime Minister 268
PHILADELPHIA, 39 116 121 126 129 137 152-153 160-161 163 165 169-171 213 219 226 232 262-265 275 Clinton's Evacuation Of 171 Fall Of 168 Harrison At 190 Howe's March On 167 John Paul Jones At 181 Occupied By British 167
PHILLIPS, 199 202-203 206 Josiah-Privateer 100 Maj Gen William 189 Assumed Command Of Virginia Campaign 198
PIANKATANK RIVER, 132-133
PIGEON QUARTER, 247-248
PITT, William 13 15 36 41
PLAIN TRUTH, Tory Pamphlet By James Chalmers 128
PLATER, George 148
PLYMOUTH, 32
POCOMOKE RIVER, 101
POINT OF FORK, 212
POLISH, Immigrants 23
POPP, Stephan-Hessian Corporal 229 252 255 261
POPULATION, Of American Colonies In 1770 23
PORTSMOUTH, 93 109 119 132 154 157 172-173 175 186 188 192 202-203 207 213-216 228 Benedict Arnold At 191 Ordered Destroyed 120 Oswald's Appraisal Of 187 Virginia 69
PORT ROYAL, 119
PORT TOBACCO CREEK, 199
POTOMAC RIVER, 100 112 144-145 147 160 163 185 199-201 204-205 219 275 Actions Taken To Protect 96
POWER ELITE, 142
PRESCOTT, Gen Richard 169 Samuel-Third Rider In Paul Revere's Midnight Ride 51
PRICE, Dr Richard 155 Thomas 62
PRINCE GEORGE'S COUNTY, 21 149
PRINCESS ANNE, Virginia 153
PRINCESS ANNE COUNTY, 100
PRINCETON, 171 275 Battle At *x* Battle Of 203
PRIVATEERING, Impact On British And American Navies 87
PRIVATEERING RAIDS, 109
PRIVATEERS, 113-114 173-174 177-179 181 185-186 194 195 200 203 267 Devastated British Merchant Shipping 87
PROCLAMATION OF 1763, 4
PROCLAMATION OF REBELLION, Issued By George III 70
PROHIBITIONS, On Manufacturing 5
PROPERTY REQUIREMENTS, 151
PROPRIETARY GOVERNMENT, Of Maryland-Disintegration Of 38
PROSPERITY, During Revolutionary War *xiii*
PROTECTIONIST POLICY, Of Great Britain 2

PROTESTANT MOVEMENTS, 154
PROVIDENCE GAZETTE, 28 Definition Of Democratic Republic 137
PURDIE, Alexander 99
PURITANS, 23
PURVIANCE, Samuel 119 120
QUAIFE, Milo M 88
QUAIFRE, 180
QUAKERS, 23 154 263
QUARTERING ACTS, 6
QUEBEC, 114 Arnold's Unsuccessful Raid On 190
QUEBEC ACT, 4 41-42
QUEEN ANNE'S COUNTY, 115
QUIBERON BAY, France 163
RALEIGH, Sir Walter Failed Colonization Attempts *xii*
RALEIGH TAVERN, 20 37 53
RANDOLPH, 123 126 Edmund 125 Comments On Patrick Henry's Speech 51 John 82-83 Jefferson's Cousin A British Loyalist 99 Peyton 37 39 54-58
RAPIDAN RIVER, 209
RAPPAHANNOCK RIVER, 110 119 219
RECONCILIATION, Persistent Feeling In Most Colonies 48
REGIMENT, 23rd 258 Delaware 172 Eighth Virginia 120 First Virginia 62 Maryland Loyalist 166 Queen's Loyal Virginia 166 Third Virginia 62
RELIGIOUS FREEDOM, Promised To Canada's Catholics 120
REVERE, Paul 51 52 Paul And Boston Tea Party 31
REVOLUTION, A Blessing For Britain 271 A Struggle For Personal Power *xxvi* American-Beginning Of 1 Financial Reasons For 272 Founders Opinions Did Not Express Majority Views 142

REVOLUTION (cont.) Maryland's Impact On 264 Organization Up To Planters When Scottish Merchants Fled 99 Reluctance Of Virginia Conservatives To Join In 123
REVOLUTIONARY WAR, 19 38 42-43 First Day Of 51 Fought From Georgia To Maine *ix* Outstanding Maryland Military Leaders 103
REYNOLDS, Capt 236
RHODE ISLAND, 111 127 183 197 219 227-228 234 French Navy Arrives At 183 Militia 169
RICHMOND, *xi* 49 90 110 189 202 208-209 212-213 Becomes Capital Of Virginia 124 Benedict Arnold At 190 Duke Of 36
RIDER, James 259
RIDGELY, Charles 149 272
RINGGOLD, Thomas 9
RIVANNA RIVER, 212
ROBERTS, Thomas 73
ROBINSON, James 259
ROCHAMBEAU, 197 214-216 218-219 224 226-227 232 234 243-244 260-262 264 Gave Money To Pay Continental Troops 233 Jean Baptiste Donatien De Vimeur Comte De 183
ROCK HALL, 262
ROCKINGHAM, Lord-Prime Minister 268
RODNEY, Adm George 227
ROSS, Betsy 52 162
SAINT-SIMON, Marquis De 216 229-230 243
SAINT GEORGE'S ISLAND, 144-145
SAINT JOHN'S, Occupied By Arnold 57
SAINT JOHN'S CHURCH, 49 105 Hampton-Oldest Continuous Episcopal Parish 83 Richmond-Site Of Patrick Henry's Famous Speech 49
SAINT LAWRENCE RIVER, 98
SAINT MARY'S, 185
SAINT MARY'S COUNTY, 21 184
SAINT MARY'S RIVER, 100 144

SAINT MICHAEL'S RIVER, 199
SALT, Confiscated By Benedict Arnold 191 Scarcity Of 191
SANDY HOOK, 171 235 New Jersey 165 227 231
SANDYS, Sir Edwin *xv xvii* Espoused Constitutional Reform In 1614 *xiv*
SANTO DOMINGO, 216 225
SARATOGA, 170-171 American Victory At *xxiv* Burgoyne's Defeat At 160 Chesapeake Warriors At *ix*
SAVANNAH, 264 British Attack Turned Back 114 Fall Of 171 Georgia Gunpowder Seized From Royal Magazine 57 Siege At *x*
SCOTCH, Immigrants 23
SCOTTISH HIGHLANDERS, Captured By Barron Brothers 133-134
SCOTTISH MERCHANTS, 19 Opposed To American Independence *xiv* 99
SCOTTISH PATRIOTS, 99
SEABURG, Samuel 35
SELF-GOVERNMENT, By Early Colonists *xiv*
SELF-RELIANCE, American 6
SELF INTEREST, Realistic Reason For Revolution 142
SEPARATION FROM CROWN, Frightening And Inconceivable For Many Colonists 48
SERVANTS, Indentured 23
SEWARD, Stephen 195
SHAKESPEARE, *xvi-xvii*
SHARF, Thomas 271
SHAWNEE NATION, Battle With Virginia Over Land 53
SHEPHERD, Peter 149
SHERMAN, Roger 132
SHIP, Alfred 86 88 Alliance 179-180 265 Amelia 118 American Congress 147

SHIP (cont.)
Andrew Doria 86 133 Andromaque 229 Arundel 101 Baltimore 179 Barfleur 235 238 Betsy 181 Black Prince 86 Blonde 186 Bon Homme Richard 179-180 Bon Homme Richard Named In Honor Of Franklin 181 Boston 179 Cabot 86 111 Charon 189 229 252 259 Chasseur 87 Chester 178 Citoyen 237 Concorde 225 Confederacy 179 Congress 179 Conqueror 178 Constellation 113 Constitution 113 Countess Of Scarborough 180 Defence 87 113 116-118 147 178 267 269 Delaware 179 Delight 186 Diligente 229 Dolphin 161 Dragon 178 Drake 163 Duc De Duras 181 Dunmore 101 Edward 116-118 Effingham 179 Eilbeck 101 Emerald 157 Eveille 194 Experiment 229 Falcon 71 Fearnaught 269 Fly 86 Fortunate 239 Fortunatus 178 Fowey 53 58 63 133-134 189 Franklin 111 Friendship 118 180 Gaspee 26 Geddes 34 General Monk 179 198 268 General Washington 268 Glorieux 229 Gloucester 178 Good Intent 26 Guadaloupe 229 Hampden 179 Hannah 85 Harrison 111 Hawke 83 Hebe Johnson 118 Henry 178 188 Hero 178 Hope 198 Hornet 86 97 115-116 Hyder Ally 267-268 Iris 179 Jane 114 178 Jefferson 185 John 181 Jolly Tar 269 King George 180 King's Fisher 101 La Victorie 161 Lady Washington 178 Lafayette 113 Langodoc 269 Lee 85 Lexington 118 161 Liberty 111-114 178 185 267 Liverpool 101 London 239 259 Loyalist 229 Lynch 111 Magdalen 53 101 Margaretta 71 Mars 68 Mary and Jane 39 Mary and John 34 Mercury 63 68 101 Montgomery 179 Mosquito 178 Nesbit 195 Noble 178 Norfolk 161-162 Norfolk Revenge 178

INDEX 301

SHIP (cont.)
Nymphe 259 Otter 58 69 72-75
81 83 90 95 101 105 116-117
133 144-145 Otter Runs
Aground Off Bodkin Point 117
Oxford 133 Pallas 179-180
Patriot 111-113 185 267 Peggy
Stewart 44 68 Phoenix 157
Princess 239 Protector 178 269-
270 Providence 86 179 Queen
Of France 179 Rainbow 173
Raisonable 173 Raleigh 179
Randolph 179 Ranger 163 181
Reprisal 88 135 161 Roanoake
132 Roebuck 115 132 144-145
147 Romulus 186 195 Rossie
268 Safeguard 178 Samuel 116-
117 Serapis 180 182 Shark 135
Sidney 113 Terrible 239 269
Totness 68 Triton 229 Trumbull
87 179 Two Friends 180
Valiant 229 Vengeance 239
Victory 269 Ville De Paris 245
Ville De Paris-Said To Be The
Greatest Warship Afloat 228
Virginia 87 169 179 Vulture
190 Wasp 86-87 97 115-116
William 68 101
SHIPBUILDING CENTERS, 112
SHIPYARDS, 112 Virginia-Burned
By British 177
SHOEMAKER, Joseph 185
*SHOT HEARD ROUND THE
WORLD,* 52
SHULDHAM, Rear Admiral
Molyneaux 80
SIMCOE, 212 Col John C 191
SINCLAIR, John 229
SKAGGS, David C 35 68
SLAVERY, *xix* 139-140 And Slave
Trade 40
SLAVES, 23 141 149 175 177 272
274 As British Allies *xxiii*
Benjamin Harrison's-Freed By
Benedict Arnold 190
Dunmore's-Most Died Of
Smallpox 92

SLAVES (cont.)
Enlistment In Maryland 186 First
Brought To Virginia In 1619 139
Freed By Wythe 176 In Dunmore's
Army 93 In Maryland Prevented From
Going Over To The British 127
Liberated By Dunmore 147
Marylanders Agitated By Dunmore's
Threat To Free 110 Percentage Of
Population *xi*
SLAVE TRADE, John Paul Jones And
180
SMALLPOX, 228
SMALLWOOD, Col William 103 103
Gen William 153 Highest Ranking
Officer From Maryland 62
SMITH, John *xiii* 113
SMITH'S ISLAND, 182
SMITHFIELD, 81 188 191
SMITH ISLAND, 269
SMUGGLING, 2
SOLWAY FIRTH, John Paul Jones At
181
SOMERSET COUNTY, 158
SONS OF LIBERTY, 10-11 19 24-25 33
48 128 149
SOUTHAMPTON, Earl Of (Henry
Wriothesley) *xv*
SOUTH CAROLINA, 114 126 161 163
171-172 186 204 Slavery In 155
SOUTHERN DEPARTMENT, 171
SPAIN, 161 172 268
SPENCER'S TAVERN, 212
SPRIGG, Osborn 149
SPROULE, Andrew 69
SPROWLE, Andrew 144 Andrew Norfolk
Merchant And Loyalist 99
SQUIRE, Capt 67 72-77 82-84 103 116-
117 Seized Boats With Negroes In
Them 74 Matthew 59 76
STAFFORD, 146
STAMP ACT, 5-7 10-13 15-17 19 30 268
Declared Illegal By Maryland 9
Repeal 16 Victory 16
STAMP ACT CONGRESS, 9
STAR SPANGLED BANNER, 163

STATEN ISLAND, British Troops Encamped At 135 Failed Peace Talks On 152
STATUTE FOR RELIGIOUS FREEDOM, 154
STAUNTON, 209
STEPHEN, Adam 146 154
STEVENSON, John 149
STEWART, Anthony 44
STOER, 198
STONE, Thomas 141
STUARTS, Royal-Lord Dunmore Descended From 52
SUFFOLK, 110 173-174 188 213
SUGAR TAX, 1-2
SUSQUEHANNA RIVER, 165 208 232
SWEDISH, Immigrants 23
TABB, John 66
TALBOT, Mark-Shipbuilder Prosecuted For Breach Of Contract 177
TALBOT COUNTY, 21 199
TANGIER ISLAND, 100 262
TANGIER SOUND, 269
TARLETON, Sir Banastre 209 210 212 224 247-249 256 Defeated By Maryland Line At Cowpens 204 Planned Raid 211
TARRANT, Cesar-Runaway Slave In Virginia Navy 177
TAXATION, 41-42 Without Representation 13-14 36
TAXES, 4 Disputes Over 1 Tobacco-Replaced By Inspection Fees 29
TAXES AND REGULATIONS, Resistance To-Became Fight For Nationhood *xix*
TEA, Destroyed By Fire At Greenwich New Jersey 31 Dumped Into Chester River In Maryland 34 Illegal To Drink In Virginia 43 Not Allowed To Unload At Port Tobacco Maryland 39

TEA (cont.)
On Vessel *Mary And John* Not Allowed To Unload In Norfolk 34 Ships Could Dock But Not Unload In Boston 31 Ships Denied Permission To Dock In Philadelphia And Charleston 31 Spilled Into Harbor At New York 33 Vessel Burned In Annapolis 34
TEACKLE, Mrs Thomas 231
TEA PARTY, Annapolis 44
TENNESSEE, 21
TERNAY, Chevalier De 183
THACHER, Dr 226 252 254 260-261 Dr James 225
THOMPSON, Charles *xiv*
TICONDEROGA, Battle Of 57 Midnight Rider Captured At 52 Victory At 98 *See Also FORT TICONDEROGA*
TILGHMAN, 263-264 Col Tench 262 263 Matthew 9 25 128 148 176 William 38
TILLY, 197 Le Bardeur De 194
TILLYMONT, Baron Of (Lord Dunmore) 52
TOBACCO, *xix* Captured By British 202 Inspection Fees 29 Smuggling By Loyalists 173
TOBACCO WARS, 172
TOBAGO, John Paul Jones At 181
TOLERATION ACT, Of 1649 *xii*
TORIES, 59 67 93 99 104 215 219 269-271 And Raids 185 Eastern Shore-Allegiance To Lord Dunmore 127 Hanging Of 154 Maryland Eastern Shore 166 Of Norfolk Named As Ringleaders In Holt's Press Destruction 92 On The Eastern Shore 158
TORNQUIST, Lt Karl Gustaf-Account Of Atrocities Of British Raiders 230
TORY, Definition 42
TORY REBELLION, On Eastern Shore 153
TOWNSEND, Levin 101
TOWNSHEND, Charles 19

TOWNSHEND ACT, 19-20 Duties Rescinded 26
TREATY OF PARIS, 4 270
TRENTON, *x* 152 203
TUCHMAN, Barbara 111 267
TUCKER, Col St George 73 234 246 Fanny 234
TUPPER, Martin 163
TYLER, John 210
UNION, Never Suggested 28
UNITED STATES, Geography Defined 270
UPSHAW, John 36
URBANNA, 110
VALLEY FORGE, 167-168 172
VAUGIRARD, Chevalier De 237
VERGENNES, Count De 193
VERMONT, Constitution Granted Voting Rights To All Adult Males 151
VINCENNES, Indiana British Surrender At 159
VIRGINIA, 171 Acute Shortage Of Currency 3 And Tobacco Embargo 30 Capes British Blockade Of 175 Damage Done By Collier 175 Declaration Of Rights In Preamble To Constitution 123 John Paul Jones At 180 Most Populous American Colony At Time Of Revolution *xi* Poor Defense Of 192 Rivers To Be Fortified 120 The Peninsula *xi* Troops Supplied By *xxv* Western Territories 196 Would Have Been The Key To British Victory 109
VIRGINIA BEACH, 228
VIRGINIA CAPES, 153 157 165-166 178-179 182 194 197 227 229 Battle Of 233 264 British Fleet Arrives At 231
VIRGINIA CHARTER, Maryland, Carved Out Of *xii*
VIRGINIA CIRCULAR LETTER, 20

VIRGINIA COMPANY, *xii*
VIRGINIA CONSTITUTION, 123 140
VIRGINIA CONVENTION, 39 Second 49
VIRGINIA GAZETTE, 69 76 92 107 143 170 Alexander Purdie's 74 Holt's 76-77 Holt's-Destroyed By Dunmore 78 Purdie's 77 77 132-133 148 Williamsburg's 78-79 82 99
VIRGINIANS, One Third Of Washington's Army 159
VIRGINIA RESOLUTION, 131
VIRGINIA STATUTE OF RELIGIOUS FREEDOM, 125
VOLUNTEERS, *xxiv* Virginia 73
VON KNYPHAUSEN, Baron Wilhelm 141
VON STEUBEN, 202 209 213 218 Wilhelm Augustus 198
WARD, Sir Adolphu *xvii*
WAR DEPARTMENT, Forerunner Established 135
WAR OF 1812, And Star Spangled Banner 163
WAR STRATEGY, *xx*
WARWICK, 202
WASHINGTON, 28 47 80 85 88 93 96 98 103 115 118-119 147 159-161 165-166 168-172 174 183 186 189 193-195 197 199-201 204 207-208 212 214-221 223 227-228 232-234 240 243-244 246-247 249-251 254-257 260-265 271 275 Almost Shot At Brandywine Creek 167 Army Depended Upon Farm Commodities From MD And VA 153 At Brandywine Creek 167 Changes Plans To Invade New York 216-217 Crossed The Delaware 152 Decides To Turn Attention To The South 225 Declaration Of Independence Read In New York 141 Defensive War Tactics *xxiv* Designed His Own Uniform 60 Evacuates From New York City 152 Forces British Troops Out Of Boston 61 Gen 241 258 George 4 20 33 39 48-49 252 *ix xiv* George And Lafayette 164

WASHINGTON (cont.)
George Nominated General And Commander In Chief 60 George-Family Coat Of Arms And US Flag 163 His Deceit Of Clinton 226 His Personal Guard Executed 135 His Slaves Freed In His Will 140 Lund 201 Martha 61 Peak Strenth In The Field *xxv* Resigns Commission 274 Set On Winning The War In New York 224 Several Negroes Taken From Mount Vernon 205 Tory Plot To Assassinate 135
WATAUGA RIVER, 21
WATCHMAN, The-Essayist For *Maryland Gazette* 149
WAYNE, 213 218 228 230 Gen 208-209 Mad Anthony 218 Maj Gen Anthony 203
WEDDERBURN, Lord 85
WEEDON, Gen George 62 188 205 230
WEINERT, Richard P Jr 213
WERTENBAKER, Thomas J *xviii*
WEST INDIES, 116 171 179 214 216 259 264-265 268 Chesapeake Warriors In *ix* One Of Washington's Slaves Shipped To 140 Plea From Maryland To Send Salt From 191
WESTOVER, 190-191
WEST POINT, Virginia 264
WHALEY, 270 Commodore 269 Zedekiah 269
WHATELY, Thomas 14
WHELAN, Joseph Privateer And Tory 100
WHELAND, Joseph 185
WHETSTONE, Channel Blocked (Future Site Of Fort McHenry) 117
WHIGS, 148
WHIP, Washington 178

WHIPPLE, Commodore Abraham 186
WHITEHAVEN, John Paul Jones At 181
WHITE PLAINS, Battle At *ix* 203
WICKES, Capt Lambert 88 135 161
WICOMICO RIVER, 100 178
WILDERNESS ROAD, 159
WILKINSON, James 170-171
WILLIAM AND MARY COLLEGE, College Of 99 First Chair Of Law Established 176
WILLIAMS, Elisha 149 James 44 Joseph 44 Otho Holland 103 204
WILLIAMSBURG, *xi* 37 43 48 52-56 81 92-93 100 118 123 134 147 157 165 170 198 203 212-213 216 229-230 244 246 262 No Longer Capital Of Virginia 124
WILMINGTON, 206 264
WILMOT, Capt William-Last Man Killed In Revolution 264
WILSON, Samuel 176
WINCHESTER, Prison Camp 257
WIRT, William (Early Patrick Henry Biographer) 28 54-55 58 67 72 96 Reconstruction Of Patrick Henry's Famous Speech 50
WISCONSIN, 197
WOLFE, Gen James-Opinion Of Americans *xxii*
WOODFORD, Col William 81-83 93-96 Second In Command Of Virginia Forces 67
WORCESTER COUNTY, 158
WORMELEY CREEK, 247
WRIOTHESLEY, Henry-Earl Of Southampton *xv*
WYE HOUSE, Robbed By British Raiders 199
WYTHE, George 8 49 85 108 120 123 131 141 145 159 176 262 Replaced Washington At Second Continental Congress 61 Speaker Of The House Of Virginia 124
YORK, 182 203 214 216 244-245 257 263 Pennsylvania 168

INDEX

YORK RIVER, 53 60 110 169 213 220-221 223 229-230 234 246-247 252 255-256 258 264
YORKTOWN, 53 102 110 164 212-215 217 220-221 223-224 227-231 240-243 246-247 251-252 255-256 259-260 262

YORKTOWN (cont.)
264-265 267-268 American Victory At *xxiv* Battle Of 179 183 British Surrender At *x* Siege Of 246
YORKTOWN CREEK, 228 247
ZINN, Howard 151

www.ingramcontent.com/pod-product-compliance
Lightning Source LLC
Chambersburg PA
CBHW071955220426
43662CB00009B/1136